Acclaim for Bill Keeth's

Every Street in Manchester and M

'A fascinating read . . . First class writing,
Mancunian humour runs through all its page
truly sorry when I came to the end of the story. . .
warmth, acuity and wit' Billy Hopkins, best selling author of *Our Kid, High Hopes, Kate's Story, Going Places, Anything Goes* and *Whatever Next!*

'A tragicomic masterpiece . . . Rich in sustained manic humour and deeply moving and sincere emotion' Fr Brian Seale, Salford Diocese, author of *The Moston Story*

'Every sentence a tonic – bringing back many memories from my childhood . . . I savour every page. When I got to the end I went right back to the beginning and read it again. Superb! Excellent!' Martin McCawley, Bolton, Greater Manchester

'Bill Keeth has the observational qualities of Les Dawson, Bernard Manning and Peter Kay' Carl Spiers, author of *101+ Oldham Characters*

'A genuine, fascinating, uproarious and moving voice' Jack Connolly, Cheadle Hulme, Cheshire

'An excellent read . . . hard to put down . . . brought back so many memories of how life was as a teenager in the fifties and sixties. All the hopes [and] dreams . . . Places we used to go to, long since gone . . . I can recommend this book for its wit, humour, and down to earth honesty . . . It made me laugh, it made me cry, but most of all it made me happy' Mary Luke, Blackley, Manchester

'I had a really good laugh' George Krystek, Cheadle, Cheshire

'Colourful characters, often speaking in Mancunian vernacular . . . the action ranges between the 1950s and the present day' Anthony Skinner, *Lancashire Magazine*

'Liked the local history bits' Tony Coogan, Middleton, Greater Manchester

'Streets ahead of his rivals' Emma Mountford, *Middleton Guardian*

'Marvellous! A *real* seller. I was glued to it' Bob McClelland. Mawgan Porth, Cornwall

'Thanks for the book, reading it in bed at 5 am this morning . . . makes me laugh out loud . . . love it' Lynda Goodfellow, Unsworth, Greater Manchester

'Just wanted to let you know that . . . what you wrote . . . is perfect' Kim Caffrey, Shelby Township, Michigan, USA

'The story rips along furiously, dragging hundreds of precise details of Manchester life behind it . . . Open it at any page, and you'll be drawn in' David Gaffney, author of *Sawn-off Tales*, *Aromabingo*

'I love the dialog . . . It really puts me back there in my Manchester days. I can't wait to get back to it. It's like a trip home' Barbara Cunningham, Atlanta, Georgia, USA

'Acclaimed books about life in Manchester' Emma Unsworth, *Manchester Evening News*

'A great read . . . has an honesty and directness which drew me in immediately to a world of "times gone by" in good old Manchester . . . entertaining from the first page to the last' Janet Driver, Santa Monica, California, USA

'Exiled Mancunians will love this book . . . humour aplenty in a milieu the reader can almost touch and smell' Tony Bowers, author of *The Idle Hill of Summer*

'I'm reading [it] with a kind of eerie sense of being an invisible character in the book' Rob Spence, Dept. of English and History, Edge Hill University, Ormskirk

'Your book will have an honoured place in my bookcase' Edna Wright, Middleton, Greater Manchester

WRITE IT
SELF-PUBLISH IT
SELL IT

BILL KEETH

Halterburn

Halterburn
3 Naunton Road
Middleton
Manchester
M24 1FX

First published 2008

ISBN 978-0-9558863-0-0

by the same author:
Every Street in Manchester
Manchester Kiss

Set in TNR, Garamond, Baskerville Old Face

Published by Halterburn

For the 98% mentioned within and without

'Publish and be damned', tempting epigraph though it be,
is one of two quotations connected with the Duke of Wellington
that are invariably misunderstood. In reality this was the Iron Duke's
response to a former mistress who was threatening to blackmail him,
Wellington being nicknamed the 'Iron Duke' on account of
a set of iron shutters affixed to the windows
of his London residence.

And so, more appropriately:

I'll publish, right or wrong:
Fools are my theme, let satire be my song.

George Gordon, Lord Byron

Contents

AUTHOR'S NOTE

"Print-on-demand" (POD) is a generic term for an innovative form of publishing by means of digital imagery that has made self-publishing very affordable for the general public in addition to making the finished product available to the customer within a few weeks or even days of an order's being submitted. Accordingly, the author wishes to make it clear that, with just two exceptions, it is to the print-on-demand process and print-on-demand companies in general he wishes to be understood to refer throughout this work. The two exceptions to this rule are contained in Appendix 6 where 33 print-on-demand companies are listed, two of which operate under the name of the print-on-demand process itself. Only in this instance is the term "print-on-demand" intended to refer to a specific print-on-demand company (or, rather, companies). No comment is offered about these two companies other than that of drawing the reader's attention to the fact that, at the time of writing, they (and the other 31 print-on-demand companies so listed) are in the business of producing print-on-demand publications and may be contacted via their respective websites.

References to Bill Keeth's novels in the text relate to the 2nd Edition of *Every Street in Manchester* [ISBN 1859880657] and/or the 1st Edition of *Manchester Kiss* [ISBN 1859880672], respectively.

ACKNOWLEDGMENTS

Sincere thanks to librarians Sheila and Robert Harden for permission to refer readers to their UK libraries website and for additional advice in the matter. Thanks, too, to the *Middleton Guardian* for technical advice; to Limited Edition Press for helpful input on occasions too numerous to mention; and to the author of *Our Kid* on this same account, as well as for providing me with a copy of the very first press advertisement featuring his acclaimed debut novel together with his generous suggestion that I might reproduce it below.

FOREWORD

Every Street in Manchester and *Manchester Kiss* were self-published via Limited Edition Press, an imprint of The Small Print, under which same imprint Billy Hopkins' best-seller *Our Kid*, was originally self-published in 1996. And, looking to self-publish this, my third book title, *Write It Self-Publish It Sell It*, it is to Limited Edition Press that I turn once more since the self-publishing services they afford are precisely the services I require, the lack of an in-house distribution service being no detriment to my *modus operandi*. On this present occasion, however, I have opted instead to self-publish under my own imprint, Halterburn.

Other writers looking to self-publish may well decide to use a different publisher or print-on-demand company. So I have listed below contact details for no fewer than 33 POD companies, many of which (perhaps all) are also prepared to act as distributor for any book titles readers may commission them to publish. Access to local printers is facilitated too, for such may yet remain the reader's preferred vehicle of access to the world of self-publishing notwithstanding the higher start-up costs involved.

I mention these points prior to the commencement of proceedings lest readers imagine there perhaps exists between myself and Limited Edition Press a financial connection over and above that which a self-published author necessarily has with his publisher. Readers may rest assured, too, that any other commercial enterprise of which I express approval in the pages that follow has earned that approval by good business practice alone.

Something else I cannot emphasise too strongly is my sincere wish (and advice in the matter too) that, no matter what my personal enthusiasms, preferences and experience in respect of writing, self-publishing and selling my titles on, as revealed in the autobiographical sections of this book, readers should be on their guard at all times with a view to discerning the best way of proceeding on their own account.

Recently, I met a man who, having shifted upwards of thirty thousand copies of his four novels, must surely be accounted a self-published best-seller and an example to us all. And so he is.

Yet how many of us, I wonder, would welcome the workload attendant upon that man's success. A further point readers may care to ponder is that this same best-seller's bedroom at home, far from being the designer dormitory of most normal desires, is effectively a storehouse for boxes of books.

'I have a very understanding wife,' says he with candour surplus to requirements.

So, please consider at all times and throughout your personal reference points in time and space, remaining as you do so, quite selfishly (that is to say, very *sensibly*) alert to the fact that these are matters of considerable importance to you (and your family).

'Yes, that's all very well for you, Mr Keeth, sir,' you must remember to say to yourself, and keep right on saying. 'But, before I get too carried away with myself with regard to *my* self-publishing prospects, let me just ask myself exactly what there is in what you have to say here that suits *me* in respect of *my* personal interests and *my* enthusiasms and *my* capabilities – and not least in respect of the exigencies obtaining in *my* home life, at *my* time of life, at the stage I have reached in *my* career, in *my* life, and in *my* writing.'

Naturally, the comfort and opinions of your loved ones must constantly be borne in mind. But be wary, too, of the poltroon's alternative – of that perennially fearful refusal to act which would confuse inactivity with rectitude, and make of the word 'No!' the abiding Commandment of your personal Decalogue for good or ill. Say: 'No!' and . . . Okay, you will never be seen to make a mistake. Which is all very well provided you remain mindful, too, of the concomitant fact that: 'The man who never made a mistake never made anything.'

Accordingly, it occurs to me that the very best advice I may offer you at this stage in the proceedings is this: 'Whatever decision you may come to with regard to self-publishing your work, make it your golden rule ever to stay within a stone's throw of solvency.'

Bill Keeth
www.novelnovella.com

ONE: WHY WOULD ANYBODY WANT OR NEED TO SELF-PUBLISH?

In my mind's eye as I write these words I picture somebody reading them who is in exactly the same position as I was just twenty-four short months ago. *Short*, that is to say, in the sense that I have scarcely had a moment to myself ever since – since self-publishing my debut novel, *Every Street in Manchester*. Because *Every Street in Manchester*, self-published though it be, has sold approximately fifteen hundred copies at the time of writing, an achievement due solely to my own efforts in marketing the book, which culminated (the title's being spotted in Waterstone's, Deansgate, where I had previously contrived to place it) in *Every Street in Manchester* being shortlisted for the prestigious Portico Literary Prize, [see Appendix 1] whereupon I self-published a contemporaneous sequel, *Manchester Kiss*, in the same week in which the Portico Literary Prize Presentation Dinner was held at Manchester's Midland Hotel in November 2006.

This person I visualise (he or she – that is to say, *you*, dear reader; but let us say *he* wherever possible so as to save time, space and unnecessary reiteration), this person I visualise reading these words of mine, having picked up a copy of *Write It Self-Publish It Sell It* in Waterstone's or Borders, hope springing eternal in his literate breast despite a lifetime of experience to the contrary – this person (and/or prospective purchaser of *Write It Self-Publish It Sell It*) has perhaps completed a novel himself. Well, let's hope it's a novel, because it's about the self-publication of the Novel that I wish to speak, though what I have to say here is similarly applicable to the self-publication of a book of verse or short stories, of a memoir and/or a collection of personal reminiscences – and, in many respects, too, to any other work of non-fiction. Having said which, I would reiterate that it is the Novel which is my particular point of focus, and for the very simple reason that it is a novel (or, rather, novels) that I have been concerned to self-publish to date.

Of course, it may simply be the case that the person now reading these words of mine expects to complete his novel in the not-too-distant future, or perhaps anticipates finally getting around to putting pen to paper at long last in order to tell his tale – or (as is more probably the case nowadays) to placing Peter Pointer and Tommy Thumb to PC keypad and letting rip. And so it occurs to me, too, that it may even be the case that the Thing (N.B. it is not yet, a *damned* Thing, this typescript of yours), it occurs to me at this juncture that it may even be the case that the Thing has already been on its travels to London and back a good few times since you dotted or crossed that final *i* and/or *t* as appropriate.

This typescript of yours – your debut novel (whisper it: *your masterpiece* – well, okay, let's not get *too* carried away with ourselves just yet: your *major opus,* let's say) – yes, this novel of yours (your *debut* novel?) – if it has, in fact, been mailed to the metropolis a time or two, it has perhaps, too, stopped over on occasion – has sojourned there, so to speak. And, given said circumstance, it is possible (indeed, it is more than likely) that this typescript of yours did once upon a time absent itself from home for longer than you had been led to expect. For several months perhaps. Perhaps for as many as *seven* months, as did the typescript of my first novel on one spectacularly inconsiderate occasion.

Because, if this happened with your typescript (as, truly, it did with mine), then they were long months indeed, weren't they? *Very* long months. And they were made all the harder to bear (were they not?) since you/I/*we* had foolishly imagined that the recipient's advertised membership of the Association of Authors' Agents might represent some sort of guarantee of a particular standard of professional conduct in the matter – as, indeed, perhaps it *did*, though (sadly, in the instance to which I refer), this was *not* of the particular professional standard which you/I/*we* had expected and, again to speak truly, would in any case have very much preferred. [See Appendix 2.]

'Oh, and we would just point out to you, Mr Keeth, sir, if we may,' Tristram Klipspringer (let's call him) of Slushpyle & Trasher (let's call *them*) had made a point of warning me at the outset, 'that we would very much prefer it, we would, if this typescript of yours (*sniff*) were not submitted to any other commercial publisher and/or literary agent whilst Slushpyle & Trasher are giving it all due consideration in-house!'

Yea, thus spake Tristram Klipspringer, fiction reader and (so I'd like to imagine) direct male descendant of a more celebrated Klipspringer (the pianist and partygoer *manqué* on the morning after the night before *Chez* Gatsby back in 1925), this, his direct linear descendant, Tristram, being currently in the employ of Slushpyle & Trasher, fully accredited members of the Association of Authors' Agents – the very same Slushpyle & Trasher who (or, rather, *which*) cheerfully (or not at all cheerfully, as is more probably the case) advertises its professional services on an annual basis on the internet and also within the pages of the various writers' manuals, the most famous of which are . . . Cue: *ragman's trumpet – Dah-dah-dah-dah-dahhhhhhhh . . . The Writers' & Artists' Yearbook*, pub. A& C Black; and, *The Writer's Handbook*, pub. Macmillan. (More than one writer in the first instance, you'd imagine, apostrophically-speaking; and, presumably, a solitary importunate mortal in the second, according to similar punctuational logic.)

And then nowt, begob! No, nary a blinking word from Tristram Klipspringer and all his house for seven long months. Until, that is, I took my literary life in my hands and plucked up the courage to disturb his slumber via e-mail (on half a dozen separate occasions, as I now recall, Tristram disdaining to respond at first), until I finally succeeded in making contact with him . . . whereupon, at long last and eventually, somewhat time-worn (it's true), though otherwise minimally bestirred, the typescript of my debut novel, unread and unloved by all (save its creator), came home to daddy at long last – seven months older, yet thankfully betraying no further material evidence of its having been left to mature atop the cistern in the third toilet cubicle along adjacent to the post room in the offices of Messrs. Slushpyle & Trasher, from which agency there now emanated duplicated rejection slips in rapid succession. (Rejection slips, you'll find, function very much like the buses.)

And then, of course, subsequent to some necessary TLC that typescript of mine was sent off on its travels yet again – and repeatedly too, only to receive (*ad nauseam* and *infinitum*) similarly perfunctory treatment at the hands of umpteen literary agents and umpteener (if I may put it like that) commercial publishers of fiction – though this is not to say my typescript went out to *every* commercial publisher of fiction and/or literary agent listed in the writers' manuals. Because . . .

❍ In the first place, I got fed up after twelve months of it, realising I might be in my dotage before I got published.

❍ Secondly, it would have been quite inappropriate to submit the typescript of *Every Street in Manchester* to *every* commercial publisher listed in the writers' manuals, since many of the commercial publishers of fiction listed therein are concerned with other fields of literary endeavour, such as detective fiction, horror, mystery, romance, science fiction etc. Whereas *Every Street in Manchester* is general and/or, in my giddier flights of fancy without an oxygen mask, literary fiction. (If you don't believe me, check out *Manchester Kiss* with Van Stockum Boekverkopers www.vanstockum.nl on the internet. And if want to know what constitutes literary fiction, here's a handy yardstick, courtesy of electronic games designer, David Lubar: 'Look in the mirror immediately after reading the last sentence [in the book]. If your eyebrows are closer together than normal, the answer is yes.')

❍ Thirdly, many of the commercial publishers of fiction listed in the writers' manuals do clearly indicate their firm intention – nay, *determination* – that they will never stoop to dealing with ordinary mortals. (*Shudder!*) Accordingly, the entries of companies such as these clearly indicate that they are minded to accept "Submissions from literary agents only" and/or "No unsolicited manuscripts".

❍ And, finally, other some amongst the commercial publishers of fiction listed in the writers' manuals (the larger ones in the main) supply *no submission criteria whatsoever*, by means of which they do *not* so clearly indicate their firm intention – indeed, *determination of the dogged variety*, that they too will never stoop to dealing with ordinary mortals. (*Shudder supreme!*)

In other words, not a few of the commercial publishers of fiction listed in the writers' manuals will only deal with literary agents – which is to say they will only deal with others of their kind. Which is to say (to be absolutely clear on this point) that not a few of the commercial publishers of fiction listed in the writers' manuals will only deal with literary agents listed in the writers' manuals.

Yikes!

Still, it was in this way that I was very quickly brought face to face with what would appear to be TEN STARK TRUTHS CONCERNING THE EXISTING STATE OF AFFAIRS WITH REGARD TO COMMERCIAL PUBLISHERS/LITERARY AGENTS AND AUTHORS SEEKING COMMERCIAL PUBLICATION.

❑ STARK TRUTH No. 1 When a commercial publisher advertises submission criteria in the current writers' manuals to the effect that direct submissions (synopsis and sample chapters, for example) are invited subsequent to the exchange of a preliminary letter, the website of the publisher in question may well say the direct opposite to this – to wit, that direct submissions are *not* invited in such circumstances. In other words, no matter what a publisher may say in the writers' manuals with regard to his company's submission criteria, some publishers may be careless enough to supply misinformation to the writers' manuals. So you are best advised to double check with the website of the publisher in question, lest said publisher be supplying contradictory submission criteria, his entry in the current writers' manuals being thereby rendered out-of-date.

❑ STARK TRUTH No. 2 Be it also noted that due enclosure of a stamped, addressed envelope with a submitted typescript in compliance with said publisher's intimation that submissions must be accompanied by a stamped, addressed envelope, is no guarantee that the publisher in question will return to sender a subsequently rejected typescript, or respond via any other form of communication.

Because it was in circumstances such as these (that is to say, subsequent to a direct verbal invitation to submit my debut novel to a leading commercial publisher of fiction) that I "lost" two copies of *Every Street in Manchester* [see Appendix 3] to a leading publisher and Member of the Publishers' Association. (Let's call them Susquatch & Paraquat.) Therefore, readers will readily understand why I derive no small amount of smug satisfaction from the knowledge that this same leading publisher (Susquatch & Paraquat), which was unprofessional enough to "lose" two copies of *Every Street in Manchester* (plus two stamped, addressed envelopes, total cash value upwards of £20 approx.), is one of several leading publishers which famously (not to say pathetically and ignominiously) declined to publish J K Rowling's Harry Potter. (Cue: *bout of raucous laughter.*)

❑ STARK TRUTH No.3 When, upon your approach to her on the subject of personal representation, literary agent Agnetha Clambake (let's call her) tenders her sincere regret that she cannot represent you on the grounds that she has "retired from work", such may not necessarily be the case. True, Ms Clambake may well be unready, unwilling, and/or unable to represent you, but retirement from work will not necessarily be the reason.

Because as I write these words (and as you read them, I'm prepared to bet) Agnetha Clambake, who fully five years ago and more deflected my own tentative representational approach on precisely these grounds, continues to advertise her services in the current writers' manuals. Indeed, Ms Clambake has advertised her services in the writers' manuals in every year since her pretended retirement.

Of course, the writers' manuals necessarily rely on the honesty of purpose, intent and communication of those who apply to advertise their services within their pages – and I really and truly believe Ms Clambake operates a *bona fide* literary agency. But what I also believe is that Ms Clambake's declared "retirement" in the instance to which I refer was a simple ruse (unprofessional in the extreme) designed to get me out of her hair at a stroke. (As if I'd have thought to argue with a simple refusal.) Nevertheless, this is precisely the reason why I no longer feel it incumbent upon me to purchase the writers' manuals on an annual basis. Both books are, in any case, available from the reference section of the public library.

So, too, incidentally, is *Writer's Market UK* (pub. David & Charles, 2008), a completely new manual to the UK market. Although its contents are as yet untried, the good news is that the submission criteria as supplied therein by publishers and literary agents are accompanied in some cases by apposite additional information in three further categories which look very interesting indeed – specifically: *Insider Info; Recent Titles*; and *Tips*. Meanwhile, there is bad news, too, in that Agnetha Clambake, as I call her, is listed there, too.

❑ STARK TRUTH No. 4 A writer's manual may inadvertently provide you with something other than you bargained for. Witness one listing I came across under *IT and Internet Applications* (or some such category) which provided me with direct access (as unexpected as it was unwanted and uncalled for) to a photographic pornographer. Admittedly, the editor of the manual in question put a stop to the interloper's activities immediately I flagged the situation. (*Who said spoilsport?*) But to my mind it beggars belief that an advertisement of this sort should have succeeded in getting listed in the first place?

❑ STARK TRUTH No. 5 Before you can get a commercial publisher interested in handling your work you will need to get a literary agent interested in handling your work. But before you can get a literary agent interested in handling your work, you will need to get a publisher interested in handling your work. So Catch 22 assuredly applies. (Cue: *bout of giddy laughter*.)

❑ STARK TRUTH No. 6 Before you can get a publisher/literary agent to give your submission all due consideration amounting to more than a quick riffling of pages and several months confinement atop the cistern of the in-house water closet, you really would be best advised to prevail upon a publisher/literary agent acquaintance of the targeted publisher/literary agent to hand the aforementioned typescript across personally to the targeted party together with his positive recommendations in the matter.

Because the deeper one delves into the biographies of published authors, the more does it become apparent that the sheer physicality of the actual passing on and vociferous recommendation of acceptable typescripts between publishing acquaintances is an intrinsic, endemic and indispensable adjunct to the system. Indeed, it would appear to be the ground zero, rock bottom – perhaps *only* submission criterion that really counts. For example, Paul Scott on behalf of John Braine (so 'tis said); and – something that will be mentioned in much more detail below – the way in which the potential best-seller *Our Kid* was rescued from regional obscurity by *literati*-acquainted film producer, John Sherlock, who passed his copy of the book along to a literary acquaintance together with his enthusiastic recommendations in the matter, subsequent to which *Our Kid* was published to great acclaim by a commercial publisher. (Cue: *jackass laugh.*)

Well, whadder-ya know?
I know QED, for a start. That's what.
In addition to which, in support of my thesis, I quote:

❍ Michael Morpurgo, children's author: 'A colleague persuaded me to write [my story] up and gave it to a friend at Macmillan. Luckily he liked it, and it quickly led to my first book.' BK: *Luckier still was Michael Morpurgo, it occurs to me, to have a friend with a friend at Macmillan.*

❍ Geraldine McCaughrean, children's and teen author: 'I became friends with a children's publisher . . . I returned months later . . . with my finished novel . . . And the dear man published it.' BK: *Convenient, huh?*

❍ Bernard MacLaverty (author of *Lamb*, *Cal* etc.): "He published his first book of short stories . . . with . . . Blackstaff Press. His childhood friend, Micky Burns, ran the company for many years and Anne Tannahill, a university friend, [was] managing director." BK: *Sadly, no such figures loom large in my literary woodpile.*

❍ David Armstrong, author of thrillers, in his quite indispensable and eminently re-readable, *How NOT to Write a Novel*: "A literary agent, a friend of my brother-in-law, agreed to have a look at the book." BK: *Sadly, there was no luck for David Armstrong with his debut novel on this occasion, though I envy him having a brother-in-law with a literary agent for a friend, seeing as none of the blighters ever appears to be so readily accessible via the writers' manuals.*

❍ Martin Amis, author of *The Rachel Papers*, *Money*, son of Kingsley (*Lucky Jim*, *The Old Devils*), in the semi-autobiographical *Experience*: "My agent . . . and my publisher . . . also handled my father, and I had known both of them since youth. So, yes, the whole thing was tacitly nepotic. Any London house would have published my first novel out of vulgar curiosity." BK: *Nuff said, methinks.*

In fact, so much does it appear to be the case that the literary set is utterly dependent one upon the other in this and other respects that it sometimes seems as if no publisher, literary agent, or book reviewer ever knows if a book is any good until somebody of equal or higher standing has the nerve to stick his neck out and tell the rest of them that it is – or that it isn't, as the case may be. Witness the veritable shower of reviews, universally positive and/or negative, which duly materialise for a strictly limited number of titles immediately subsequent to some daredevil critic's having had the temerity to be the first amongst his peers to recommend it or condemn the title – whereupon the consensus of opinion will then unanimously recommend or condemn the same title to a man. On the last occasion I recall this happening (with Sebastian Faulks' *Birdsong*) it was necessary to trawl the net as far as distant Malaysia before I chanced across a solitary dissenting voice. To speak plainly, the fact of the matter would appear to be that, in the same way as an ordinary householder much prefers to employ a plasterer or a man to clear blocked drains on the recommendation of a trusted friend, say – publishers and literary agents, too, pay more attention to submissions arriving on their desktops accompanied by the support and/or recommendation of a trusted professional acquaintance than they are prepared to pay to submissions mailed to them, and therefore predestined for their respective slush piles and subsequent rejection slip rubberstamping.

❑ STARK TRUTH No. 7 If you are *unacquainted* with a literary acquaintance of the publisher/literary agent in question when duly submitting a typescript thereto: 'Then, tough! Forget it!'

❑ STARK TRUTH No. 8 Having duly succeeded in fulfilling all the required submission criteria, and/or avoiding all the pitfalls listed above, there is no way you are guaranteed commercial publication unless you also have: Prince Charles' mother; or Angelina Jolie's photogenic good looks; or Wayne Rooney's feet; or Jordan's wobbly bits; and, preferably, all six.

❑ STARK TRUTH No. 9 It would be similarly helpful, if you just happen to be a solvent neighbour, relation, family friend, and/ or an Oxbridge/Home Counties-based associate of the Oxbridge/ Home Counties-based publisher/literary agent to whom you are submitting said typescript. (Cue: *bout of maniacal laughter.*)

❑ STARK TRUTH No. 10 In addition to the aforementioned requirements you also need a bit of luck, because THE PLAIN FACTS OF THE MATTER WOULD APPEAR TO BE THESE . . .

❑ PLAIN FACT No. 1 It is more likely than not that you are an unknown quantity to any publisher/literary agent to whom you are submitting your typescript, and it is even less likely that any publisher/literary agent in his right mind is going to take the trouble to get to know a writer he has never heard of, least of all via a typescript said writer has duly submitted.

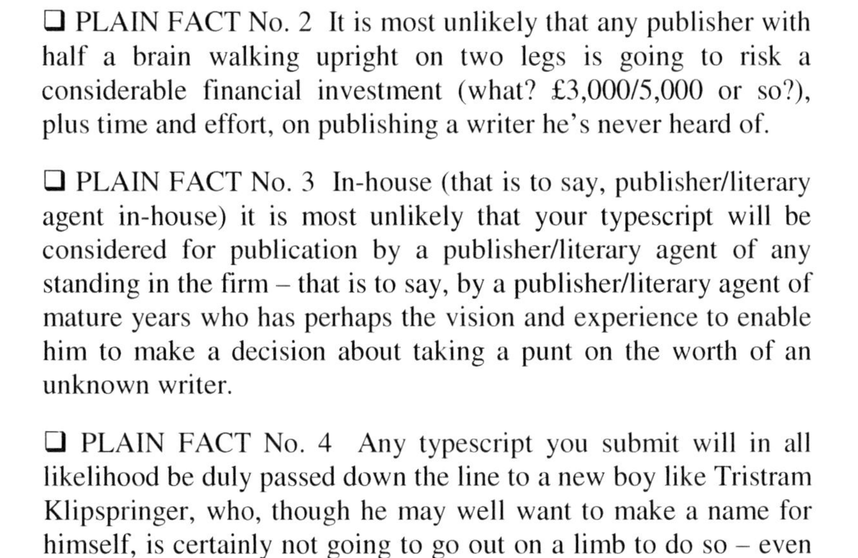
❑ PLAIN FACT No. 2 It is most unlikely that any publisher with half a brain walking upright on two legs is going to risk a considerable financial investment (what? £3,000/5,000 or so?), plus time and effort, on publishing a writer he's never heard of.

❑ PLAIN FACT No. 3 In-house (that is to say, publisher/literary agent in-house) it is most unlikely that your typescript will be considered for publication by a publisher/literary agent of any standing in the firm – that is to say, by a publisher/literary agent of mature years who has perhaps the vision and experience to enable him to make a decision about taking a punt on the worth of an unknown writer.

❑ PLAIN FACT No. 4 Any typescript you submit will in all likelihood be duly passed down the line to a new boy like Tristram Klipspringer, who, though he may well want to make a name for himself, is certainly not going to go out on a limb to do so – even if the quick riffle he gives the pages of your typescript endears the work to him. (Cue: *bout of laughter verging on the unhinged*.)

So hard cheese, you debut novelists! – and hard format too! But for all that, it exists, doesn't it? The novel – I mean, *your* novel! Yes, the little beauty now has shape, begob! And form, too – well, in time and space, it does, at any rate. Hey, and let's have it right. If your typescript has been on its travels to the publishers/literary agents of the metropolis a time or two, it is certainly in hard format. Because perish the thought that the self-same venerable (rather than dynamic) twenty-first century publishers/literary agents should purchase, either individually or collectively, a state-of-the-art PC, for the use of, so as to facilitate the transfer of documents via e-mail attachment.

No, not they.

Even so, it may be the case that this novel of yours exists only as a document on your PC hard drive. And, hopefully, in this instance, the document has been saved, too, to a floppy disk or a CD, or (preferably) to a digital back-up, portable hard drive or a pen flash drive/memory stick, lest it be accidentally lost to twenty-first century civilisation as we know it. And in this event too (in the event of its being saved rather than lost), your novel will most certainly have shape and form in time and space as soon as you get around to printing it off – slow-ly. *Far too slowly!* (Maybe you *should* have invested in that HP Laserjet 1200 after all.) Still, this debut novel of yours, which you (and the world) have been so long awaiting is now an entity in its own right at long last. Yep, this Thing that you personally have lived with for so long (years perhaps) is become something almost corporeal at last – a *living* Thing.

And nobody wants to know about it, do they? Nobody but you, that is. Well, certainly that's the way it would seem, judging by the almost total lack of interest any publisher or literary agent you've contacted has expressed in it so far. (At this stage a pencilled positive comment on a rejection slip is nothing short of wonderful, notwithstanding the eventual feeling of dejection that will surely be engendered by the realisation that it still means: 'Not on your nelly, chum!' And it's not as if you can boast to Slushpyle & Trasher that Susquatch & Paraquat are of the opinion that your typescript represents: "A promising attempt at the experimental tempered with an unusual admixture of Mills & Boon!")

Hey, lighten up! Do not by any means be downcast on this account. No, rather are congratulations in order. (Believe me, I jest not.) Because the rejection slips you have accumulated (over the past 5, 10, 20, 30 years) from those publishers and literary agents qualify you for membership of a very special band of brothers (and sisters) – by which I mean, of course, the regiment – nay, the *battalion* (maybe even an army) of FAMOUSLY REJECTED WRITERS who, before they became the famous writers they are today, accumulated between them (just as you/*we* have done) countless rejection slips (literally thousands of rejection slips in one instance: just look at William Saroyan's record) from the publishers/literary agents in their particular time and place, not all of them UK-based, by any means. And so . . . Cue: *triumphal fanfare of ragmen's trumpets – Dah-dah-dah, dah-dah-dah-dah-dah-ah* . . . FOR THREE DOZEN FAMOUSLY REJECTED WRITERS WHO COLLECTED REJECTION SLIPS IN THEIR TIME AND PLACE:

Richard Adams (with *Watership Down*), Jane Austen (with *Pride and Prejudice* and *Northanger Abbey*), Richard Bach (with *Jonathan Livingston Seagull*), Pierre Boule (with *The Bridge on the River Kwai*), John Le Carré (with *The Spy Who Came in From the Cold*), Agatha Christie (with *The Mysterious Affair at Styles*), Gustave Flaubert, Anne Frank's executors (with *The Diary of Ann Frank*), Frederick Forsyth (with *The Day of the Jackal*), James Joyce (with *Dubliners* and *Ulysses*), Thor Heyerdahl (with *The Kon Tiki Expedition*), Stephen King (with *Carrie*), Yann Martel, Margaret Mitchell (with *Gone With the Wind*), Vladimir Nabokov (with *Lolita*), George Orwell (with *Animal Farm*), Robert Pirsig (with *Zen and the Art of Motorcycle Maintenance*), Elmore Leonard (with *The Big Bounce*, his first thriller – and he already an established author with a posse of Westerns and film credits under his belt), Grace Metalious (with *Peyton Place*), Laurence J Peter (with *The Peter Principle*), Beatrix Potter (with *The Tale of Peter Rabbit*), Barbara Pym, J K Rowling with Harry Potter, William Saroyan (said to have collected as many as 7,000 rejection slips), Erich Segal (with *Love Story*), Dr Seuss, Zadie Smith (with *White Teeth*), Irving Stone (with *Lust for Life*), Jaqueline Susann (with *The Valley of the Dolls*), Anthony Trollope, HG Wells, Walt Whitman, Billy Hopkins (with *Our Kid*), Bill Keeth (with *Every Street in Manchester* and *Manchester Kiss*), YOU (with your magnum opus), and . . . THE VERY WORST SCENARIO OF ALL: John Kennedy Toole (with *A Confederacy of Dunces*).

John Kennedy Toole, an American novelist and academic, is best known for his New Orleans-based comic novel, *A Confederacy of Dunces*. Nowadays this book is widely-regarded as a work of rare comic genius – a masterpiece, no less. But during the author's lifetime no American publisher would touch it, with the dire result that John Kennedy Toole, brooding on the matter perhaps overmuch, ended up taking his own life.

Accordingly, it was left to the author's bereaved mother to hawk John Kennedy Toole's oft-rejected typescript around, finally prevailing upon Walker Percy, writer and faculty member at

Loyola University of New Orleans, to become interested enough to read it – and subsequently, in 1980, to publish the book to widespread acclaim.

(Incidentally, US publishers persisted even then in their studied indifference to the work – which is perhaps not altogether surprising when you consider that one Brahmin US publisher is said to have succeeded in losing author Stephen King to a rival publishing house by means of the simple expedient of snootily ignoring him when the house best-seller just happened to drop by one day on a chance visit to HQ.)

Nevertheless, *A Confederacy of Dunces* by John Kennedy Toole went on to win a Pulitzer Prize, becoming known as the sort of classic novel to which Anthony Burgess would be only too pleased to contribute one of his knowledgeable forewords in which the great man would rate the work of such consequence to humankind that he personally felt compelled to re-read it on an annual basis, if not more frequently.

Praise indeed.

And far too heavy a scenario by far – Toole and Burgess, both. Because – okay, we writers are going get the work done (Anthony Burgess, by way of example, wrote a thousand words every day of his writing life), but we're going to get down to the shops too. And we're going to get out in the fresh air as well – pick the kids up from school (if we really *must*); holiday when the fancy (and what's in our pockets) takes us there – and we'll maybe decorate the living-room when it doesn't. And we're going do all this:

❍ Secure in the knowledge that all work and no play makes Jack a dull boy.

❍ And knowing, too, that no less a person than Mario Puzo, author of *The Godfather*, recommends such a course of action to us. (See *The Godfather Papers* in which Mario Puzo, for many years dependent upon his family for handouts, claims to have got many of his best ideas whilst picking the kids up from school, or down the local supermarket as opposed to being chained to his typewriter all day long.)

❍ And hearing Mario Puzo's opinion in the matter endorsed by Katherine Way, a playwright who has written many episodes for prime time television shows such as *Casualty*, *Emmerdale* and *The Bill*: 'I do all my best work in Sainsbury's,' says she. 'It's valuable thinking time. No one cares if you walk around the aisles talking to yourself, so long as you don't break anything.'

❍ And perhaps we may even achieve a sense of perspective akin to that of author Bernard MacLaverty who, with as many as four novels and five volumes of short stories under his belt, asserts that: 'A novel is not a bowel movement – it's not a regular thing that happens. It's . . . a very now-and-again thing. I now devote all of my life to being a part-time writer.'

So let's get real about this. Because important though your novel is to you, there are other things that are just as important in your life – a happy family life for a start, personal security; a nest egg for a rainy day (ideally, just in case you're wondering, such a nest egg should be an amount equivalent to 25% of your total annual outgoings); pensionable employment and so on. And let's look at the other side of the same coin while we're about it too. Yes, let's look at what (to my mind at any rate) is surely . . . THE VERY BEST SCENARIO OF ALL: Tim Lally with *Our Kid*.

Who? you say. (Or, perhaps *whom*?)

Either way, I suggest you take time out at this juncture in order to consider the case of somebody, the aforementioned Tim Lally, as it happens, a man who is nowadays a best-selling author, despite his having once upon a time received repeated rejections from any and every publisher supposedly open to auctorial approach from writers such as ourselves – and an author who (hopefully, like ourselves in the near future) came up smiling in the end. But only because Tim Lally was so doggedly determined to be published, he took no notice of what the commercial publishers said, and initially *self-published*.

It is difficult to imagine now, but back in the mid-1990s, a dozen or so years ago as I write these words – the present-day publishing phenomenon that is Billy Hopkins, best-selling author of the widely-acclaimed Manchester-based family saga that now runs to half dozen books in all: *Our Kid*, *High Hopes*, *Kate's Story*, *Going Places*, *Anything Goes* and *Whatever Next!* – yes, nobbut a dozen years ago this was one writer who had failed utterly, despite all his efforts to the contrary (aka Tim Lally), to get any of the aforementioned commercial publishers to show even a flicker of interest in publishing his debut novel, *Our Kid*.

Yet, those same dozen years or so further on from that time *Our Kid* and the rest of that hilarious body of work have produced sales of around a million, assuring that same author of a packed house wherever he appears in public. And yet his debut novel *Our Kid*, a whimsical, quasi-autobiographical tale of a north Manchester childhood in the 1920s, '30s and early 1940s, originally struck not the faintest chord of recognition or appreciation with the UK literary establishment. Unbelievably, it seems to me, no UK film or television producer has dived into these books even this late in the day; and, though a Spanish language version of *Our Kid* has been available for some time (it's been translated into Finnish too: see www.billysbooks.info), American publishers have adjudged their own countrymen too dim to tackle *Our Kid et al.* Meanwhile, out in the Antipodes, where "there's no market for stuff like this", cargoes of this same "stuff" are having to be transhipped like the Botany Bay population of yesteryear due to a distinct lack of imagination amongst the Australian and Kiwi off-shoots of those same UK publishers which proved to be so slow on the uptake in the first place.

So I suggest you put your copy of *Write It Self-Publish It, Sell It* aside for a few minutes. (Are you still in Waterstone's or Borders, by the way?) Go on! Just do it! Put the book aside, switch on your PC (or the PC in your local library if you don't own a PC), and log on to: www.billysbooks.info. (Your librarian will show you how if you ask her nicely.) And take time out, please do, to read and enjoy (in particular those sections of the website sub-titled 'In His Own Words' and 'Life begins at 70') about the way it was for another unpublished writer of fiction just a few short years ago when he was himself collecting, not the accolades his work receives today, but rejection slips from all and sundry. Yes, that unpublished – nay, *unpublishable Our Kid* by Tim Lally was rejected by each and every publisher he approached – and more often than not for the daftest of reasons too. That is to say, until things began to move on apace subsequent to his self-publishing *Our Kid* under his pen name and selling on as many as a thousand copies of this self-published edition . . . whereupon consequent upon a rave review in the *Manchester Evening News* and *literati*-connected John Sherlock's personal recommendation to his literary acquaintance who had previously rejected the book, *Our Kid,* was then accepted for commercial publication. And the rest, as they say, is history, with *Our Kid* eventually becoming the best seller it always deserved to be in the first place.

'The more books you sell the better,' is the advice of the best-selling author of *Our Kid*, *High Hopes*, *Kate's Story*, *Going Places*, *Anything Goes*, and *Whatever Next!* 'Each book sold acts as a personal ambassador for you.'

And so, with you thoroughly refreshed on your return from www.billysbooks.info, let us agree to call your novel *MO* – for *magnum opus*, certainly, but also for *modus operandi* – which is something I intend to concentrate upon presently, by which I mean to say, specifically:

- how to get your book out, in the sense of its being "self-published"; and,
- even more particularly, perhaps (because there are positively oodles of books dealing with the self-publishing aspect) "out", too, in the sense of "on to the shelves in the book shops and public libraries".

And, just fleetingly, while we're marshalling our forces, so to speak, let us also consider the real reason why you must do these two things – that is to say, why you must self-publish your book in the first instance, in addition to selling it in quantity. And, incidentally, a thousand self-published books, sold, is most definitely "quantity". Because a thousand books is perhaps as many books as a commercial publisher would, in any case, consider publishing as the first hardback print-run of a book by an unknown author. I mention this because it is, in fact, as many copies as were published as a first print-run of *Our Kid*, only to find the book shops faced with a floodtide of potential purchasers for the book, which immediately required a second print-run, not to mention a third and so on. And therein lies the reason why you must self-publish your book and sell it. To wit:

SO THAT YOU WILL NO LONGER BE AN UNKNOWN AUTHOR
SO THAT YOU WILL NO LONGER BE AN UNKNOWN AUTHOR
SO THAT YOU WILL NO LONGER BE AN UNKNOWN AUTHOR
SO THAT YOU WILL NO LONGER BE AN UNKNOWN AUTHOR
SO THAT YOU WILL NO LONGER BE AN UNKNOWN AUTHOR
SO THAT YOU WILL NO LONGER BE AN UNKNOWN AUTHOR
SO THAT YOU WILL NO LONGER BE AN UNKNOWN AUTHOR
SO THAT YOU WILL NO LONGER BE AN UNKNOWN AUTHOR
SO THAT YOU WILL NO LONGER BE AN UNKNOWN AUTHOR
SO THAT YOU WILL NO LONGER BE AN UNKNOWN AUTHOR

(CHORUS)

LET THESE WORDS ECHO, PLAIN AS A SHOUT –
ONE FOR EACH HUNDRED BOOKS TO GET OUT!

Heck! What publisher in his right mind could reasonably argue with sales of a thousand books? None, I'd hope, having myself shifted close to 1,500 copies of my debut novel to date. Unfortunately, though, publishers as a breed do tend to be a bit slow on the up-take.

Witness the incredible fact, as I've already said, that, all these years on, and with one million books sold since Day One, the film, UK TV and American rights to *Our Kid* are, as far as I understand it as I write these words – *still up for grabs.*

And witness, too, a similarly incredible report that recently appeared in *The Author*, the quarterly magazine of the Society of Authors, to the effect that, by the time a commercial publisher came a-calling for Brian John's self-published *Angel Mountain* novels (*On Angel Mountain*, *House of Angels*, *Dark Angel*) this "unknown" Welsh author (it's Brian John to whom I refer in my Foreword, by the way), this "unknown" Welsh author had shifted as many as 30,000 self-published copies of his books, effectively flooding the Principality with them. So, pardon me, please do, whilst I indulge myself with a celebratory exclamation mark at this juncture in addition to Italic font and an expletive to boot: *30,000* [BLEEP – Ed.] *self-published copies sold before Corgi pricked up its ears!*

So why is it, do you think, that nobody wants to know? I mean, no commercial publisher wanted to know *Our Kid*, or Brian John's books, did they? And nobody wants to know that book of yours. *MO*, I mean. Go on, why is it, do you think, that nobody wants to know? And they really *don't* want to know, do they? I mean to say, here's a gushing memo from a metropolis-based literary agent – Trivia Bullworker, let's call her – who, for all her blather, genuinely did *not* want to know about *Every Street in Manchester*. I quote (the parentheses are mine):

"*I am really keen to discover new writing talent* [TICK MARK]. *So, if you are a first time novelist* [TICK MARK], *simply forward your typescript to me.* [TICK MARK – N.B. I sent the self-published book, no less, complete with Portico Literary Prize citation, plus SAE, if you please.] *Or e-mail me in the first instance* [TICK MARK]. *I am committed to discovering debut novelists* [TICK MARK] *and assisting them in developing their careers.* [TICK MARK] *Believe me, I will welcome with open arms any novelist with a genuine, fascinating and moving narrative voice.*" [TICK MARK]

Naturally, the answer that came to my door by return post was . . . er, well, NOPE, o*f course*. Ergo, the "welcome with open arms" so gushingly flagged by Trivia Bullworker rapidly (indeed, precipitately) translated into fingers, *two* – wagged vigorously at eye-level.

And it isn't only literary agents who positively don't want to know when they say they do. Because here, apart from another necessary name change, is a *soi-disant* commercial publisher's come-on as advertised elsewhere:

"Strabismus Books is something new to the world of fiction, a genuinely author-centred publishing house [TICK MARK] *whose ultimate aim is to nurture new talent prior to projecting their work*

worldwide. [TICK MARK] *Accordingly, we are keen to build-up an extensive list of good quality commercial and literary fiction* [TICK MARK?] *from first-time novelists of literary prize potential* [TICK MARK?] . . . *Therefore, we are particularly interested in receiving original typescripts* [TICK MARK] *from debut novelists* [TICK MARK] *who are as keen as we are to progress to a second novel without further delay* [TICK MARK]."

NOPE! *Of course*, NOPE. Indeed, NOPE, NOPE, *NOPE*! By which I mean to say that Strabismus Books – ignoramuses with knobs on that they evidently are (*ignorami* too, lest they come back at me on this point) – Strabismus Books didn't even have the common courtesy to *e-mail* a solitary dismissive word by way of reply. And the worst of it is that Strabismus Books really should know better. Because in the midst of a half-page of this unctuous twaddle bloomed a rare (perhaps unique) boast amongst commercial publishers to the effect that Strabismus Books (timewasters on stilts, more like!) is: "*The brainchild of a successful novelist and member of the Society of Authors.*" Ah, cruel indeed! Because a fellow writer really *should* know better, and a true member of the Society of Authors (were he to emulate the exemplary accessibility and helpfulness of that Society) really *would* know better.

So, that typescript of yours remains untouched, doesn't it? That is to say, it's untouched whenever it comes back to you . . . *If* it comes back to you. Well, okay, just occasionally it has been touched in the sense of its having been marginally riffled (the stray hair, assiduously positioned between folios 13 and 14 prior to its most recent metropolitan-bound despatch is missing, you'll quickly note) and, on occasion it has been damaged too – an indelible grease stain like a map of the Lesser Antilles alongside the epigraph caused by a rasher of Danish bacon impregnate with HP sauce as *MO* was being parked up atop the cistern in the in-house water closet for a good few months. Who *are* these people exactly – the commercial publishers and literary agents? They're supposed to be in the business of selling books, aren't they?

Well, yes, of course they *are* – and no, they're not.

I mean to say, it may very well be the case, as some commercial publishers, literary agents, certain self-satisfied published authors who've long since pulled up the rope ladder behind them, and the smugger type of literary critic profess to believe, that there really are no unpublished Hemingways out there. (By which, I mean to say, of course, out *here*). And, if this is in fact the case, then it is perfectly understandable if publishers and literary agents of the aforementioned ilk reckon it's not worth their while looking for any Hemingways or (if Hemingway be a commissioned officer, say) other ranks, so to speak. Therefore, it is similarly understandable if such types make a conscious decision to stick with what they know – hey, and let's have it right: *they don't know you*. Well, not till you've shifted a thousand copies of your book, they won't – and even then, as was previously indicated, they may very much prefer you to shift instead an italicised *30,000 copies* before realising something may be afoot.

Furthermore, it may well be the case (don't panic: we're celebrating, remember) that your work in particular is not good enough to be published. And, to be perfectly fair to the various commercial publishers and literary agents, who do seem to be doing nothing more with your typescript other than riffling through a few pages prior to parking it up in assorted water closets flanking the Central Line – to be fair to the them, it really is odds-on that your precious debut novel is *not* good enough to be published. [See Appendix 5.]

Nevertheless, let us just for a moment suppose that – wonder of wonders! – your novel *is* publishable, as was most certainly the case with the erstwhile *unpublishable* Frederick Forsyth, Stephen King and J K Rowling, to name but a phew. So, let us suppose for a moment that your book (your debut novel: your *MO*) really *is* good enough to be published. Well, what then?

Q. I mean, where *do* they get off, these people – these literary types?

A. Harrow-on-the-Hill and all points south, south-east, and south-west.

I jest, of course. But there really is a serious point at issue here. Because there are many different forces at work in UK public life, as you very well know – and not least in respect of the literary judgment of mainstream publishers and the like. And so, I put it to you in all seriousness that, in the UK, it is nowadays (as ever it was) very much a case of *who* you are, and who you are *not*, that carries the greatest weight with the London-based, Oxbridge-inclined *literati.* And from this it follows that middle to higher middle class writers who just happen to be domiciled in, or are in some way connected with London, Oxbridge and/or the Home Counties (as are the UK *literati* in the main) have a much easier time of it than writers from any other part of the UK.

What? You don't believe such tosh? You'd pooh-pooh what I say, here? Things surely can't be as bad as I suggest. Well, anyway, not in our outward-looking, independent, internetted, post-Thatcherite, post-Blairite, Euro-committed, racially-, religiously-, sexually- and socially-integrated, twenty-first century UK, they can't, can they? And certainly not with regard to literary taste, you would further aver? (Cue: *stamping of feet plus heartfelt harrumphing to some tune.*)

Well, I'll just have to take your word for it, though much of the evidence seems to point the other way. So, for what it's worth, here's my personal take on the situation currently obtaining in respect of literary matters in the UK, as I recently suggested to readers of – *whisper it!* – a Greater Manchester-based magazine with a readership 7,000 strong to which I contribute a monthly book review.

BOOKS BUT NO BOOKER

So, just books it is then – and, as my title puts it: *Books, But No Booker,* by which I mean to say you ain't never gonna hear this boy enthusing about the Booker prize – or the Whitbread.

Q. Why ever not?

A. Because they already get more press coverage than they deserve – and London, London, London, London, Oxbridge, London . . .

Q. Eh?

A. The respective home towns of every Whitbread prize winner from 1999 to 2004. So they don't seem to be sharing the prize money out fairly, do they?

Q. You reckon?

A. Flock of inbred carrier pigeons billing and cooing and reading each other's messages. In fact, Graham Greene was so disgusted with the Booker/Whitbread prizes, he refused to let his own books be submitted for consideration. John Fowles too.

Q. Who?

A. *French Lieutenant's Woman, The Collector.*

So what's the score, then? I mean to say, let's suppose for the sake of argument that the Booker/Whitbread prizes are a football tournament that's played on an annual basis. What do you reckon the full-time score has been over the past ten years? Well, here's my take on the state of play: Booker – *half* a good book: the first half of *Vernon God Little* by DBC Pierre; the second half is [BLEEP – *Ed.*]: Whitbread – *one* good book: *The Curious Incident of the Dog in the Night-Time* by Mark Haddon. The thing is, though, The *Curious Incident of the Dog in the Night-Time* is a very good book indeed. Briefly, a teenager with Asperges syndrome relates his story in the first person singular – which sounds pretty boring, I must admit. But it's very far from it, believe me. Let's put it this way – if you can get into this book, you won't want to put it down till you've finished it. And I can't say fairer than that! Okay, okay-y! I know I said you ain't never gonna hear this boy enthusing about the Booker/Whitbread prizes. But it's the exception that proves the rule.

Now don't take my word for it – or Grahame Greene's word, or that of John Fowles either. Because here's what Edna Healey, wife of former Anzio Beachmaster and Labour Chancellor of the Exchequer, Denis Healey, herself a published author, has to say about the situation currently obtaining with regard to UK literary matters: 'I was once a judge of the Booker prize . . . and frankly the experience rather put me off fiction.'

Personally, I'd go further. (You rather thought I would, didn't you?) Because it seems to me that in the UK at present novels dealing with any area of the UK other than the Home Counties/ Oxbridge corridor – e.g. *Our Kid*, the best-selling Manchester-based novel which has not yet been reviewed by a single London-based broadsheet (as was, of course: they're *all* tabloids now) – yes, novels from without the Home Counties/Oxbridge corridor, it seems to me, are in the main very sniffily regarded as "regional" by the *literati* amongst us, "regional" being a literary pejorative suggesting that novels set in the provinces:

- will not travel beyond the immediate locality within which their storyline is set; and

- will assuredly posit a theme which is necessarily less than universal.

And there is worse to come. Because the ultimate put-down beloved of the UK *literati* is the concomitant suggestion that regional works of fiction are also "primitive".

Thus, though the author of a regional novel (*Risen above his station in life, the pup!*) may well have struggled manfully with the intricacies of the English language, (*I say, fair play to the fella, too!*) eventually making landfall on the umpteen-1000th word of his saga (*Damned if I know how these red-brick university wallahs and the like do it, egad!*), dutifully dotting each *i* and crossing each *t*, whilst persevering stolidly to THE END – and that final (*Phew! Thank God for that!*) full-stop, nevertheless, said author, being *regional*, as is his theme and the location within which the action of his novel is set – said author is perforce *primitive*, having signally (indeed, predictably) failed to bring even a vestige of narrative art to the telling of his sorry little tale.

'Trouble-at-t'mill stuff', is the broadsheets' mind-set in this regard – the mind-set of the *Independents* (really?), the *Obverser* and the *Gruinard* (let's call them), the *Thameses* (*The Sunday* and *The*). Thus do the perennial spokespersons of the UK *literati* glibly dismiss regional fiction in much the same way as Dr Johnson once observed on seeing a dog walking on its hind legs, that: 'The wonder is, sir, not that it is done well, but that it is done at all.' (Incidentally, the good doctor then proceeds to make an overly contemptuous observation about womankind which his admirers prefer to forget.)

And the net result of this sort of restrictive thought pattern is, as former Whitbread winner William McIlvanney (otherwise a very talented writer: joke) points out is this: 'If literature is a testament to what it means to be alive, 98% of the witnesses haven't been called.'

Thought processes of similar silliness in the UK at large persist to this day in adjudging the Church of England, by way of example, "the Tory Party at prayer". By which I mean to say, of course, thought processes that are similarly many years out-of-date – the best (and/or worst) part of eighty-odd years out-of-date in the case of the Church of England. It is unfortunate, then, that ideas such as these, inert and uninformed as they are, should continue to prevail in UK literary circles, making it unlikely (I am minded to say *impossible*) that this novel of yours (*MO*, didn't we say?), that *MO* will ever be commercially published.

Let me remind you, too, of what Irvine Welsh, best-selling author of *Trainspotting* has to say on this score: 'I would never have been published if I started writing now. Publishing goes through cycles. It's never been so conservative.'

And similarly: 'Mainstream publishers aren't willing to take any kind of risk,' says an independent publisher who himself failed to respond to a message I left on his answerphone. (The boy's obviously a quick learner.) 'Literature is still one of the most expensive things to fund as a piece of art. It costs a minimum of £3,000 to publish a novel.'

If you can't trust mainstream publishers and you can't trust the independents, then it surely follows that if you *want* to be published, your novel must be *self-publish*ed.

WHO AM I TO SAY YOUR NOVEL MUST BE SELF-PUBLISHED?

Moi? Je m'appelle Bill Keeth. I employ the cod-French phraseology (as does Pub Landlord Al Murray to comic effect on occasion) because Bill Keeth is a pen name, my real name being Irish as the Bog of Allen and, therefore, not entirely appropriate to the Mancunian location within which my novels are set. An escaped teacher and lifelong bibliophile, I live in Middleton, Greater Manchester, and write fiction with a north Manchester-based storyline.

'Ooh, er, "regional", Dr Johnson! Perish the thought, "primitive" – and by a Bog Monster once removed!'

During the past two years I have self-published two novels – *Every Street in Manchester* and *Manchester Kiss*, and to date I've shifted close on 2,000 copies in Greater Manchester and beyond. (I'm including *Manchester Kiss* in the running total now.) That's nearly 4 books per day, or 27 books a week since I first self-published – and, please note, I number sales thus since they are ongoing.

Back in November, 2006, I was delighted to find my self-published debut novel, *Every Street in Manchester*, shortlisted for the prestigious Portico Literary Prize, the longlist for which had been fifty book titles deep, with just two other fiction titles being shortlisted, each of them by authors who are household names in the UK and beyond.

I've wanted to be a writer ever since I was in VIth form at the same school, coincidentally, as was Billy Hopkins twenty years or so before me, and Anthony Burgess, coincidently too, half a dozen years before him. ('I was in the sixth form in 1934': Anthony Burgess, *Flame into Being*, his biography of D H Lawrence. See also the autobiographical *Little Wilson and Big God* and *You've Had Your Time*.)

By this time (or, certainly, very shortly thereafter) I was very much into the great northern writers that emerged in the late-1950s – Yorkshire men John Braine, Keith Waterhouse, Stan Barstow and David Storey; Nottingham's Alan Sillitoe; and the late, great Bill Naughton from Bolton whose *June Evening* arguably paved the way for the long-running *Coronation Street* television series. And it was during this time too (or perhaps I'd just left school by then) that Burgess's *A Clockwork Orange* was first published, reading which adjacent to the coffee bar at Manchester Central Library's Library Theatre, was an eye-opening and keenly inspirational experience for me because, quite apart from the revolutionary quality of *A Clockwork Orange*, it was around this time, too, I first learned that Burgess was an old boy of the school I'd attended, and just as importantly perhaps (the favoured catchment area of the school in those days being Didsbury Village and adjoining districts) was the fact that Burgess was also a former resident of the north Manchester suburb of Harpurhey, which is contiguous to the suburb of Blackley where I lived for the first twenty-four years of my life and subsequently worked for twenty-two years more.

So, like my predecessors (N.B. the word is used in a chronological rather than a literary sense), I was born in north

Manchester, though unlike them, I have lived in and around north Manchester ever since, working in Manchester schools for more years than I care to remember.

Writing a long-binned first novel back in 1977, I subsequently (indeed, consequently) became a founder member of a writers' workshop at Manchester College of Building, where *Every Street in Manchester* was begun in 1982 as a short story entitled 'It Wasn't Consummation'. This was during a particularly dreary time in my professional life when my face didn't fit. I remember writing it in a towering rage at circumstances beyond my control that were affecting me and my family. (N.B. There are circumstances beyond the narrator's control in the short story, as it then was, though no way does rage have any part in it.) Then, much more recently – certainly since the turn of the new Millennium – I got a yen to develop the short story into a full-length novel, whereupon it took me about seven or eight months to do so, with *Manchester* Kiss, a contemporaneous sequel to it, following before the end of that same year.

And it was whilst trawling the writers' manuals with a view to placing *Every Street in Manchester* with a UK publisher/literary agent (Fat chance! To be blunt, *no chance*!), I learned that writer Billy Hopkins had nine years before that time been constrained to self-publish his debut novel, *Our Kid* with Limited Edition Press. (Check this out, if you will, on the back of the title page of any Headline paperback edition of *Our Kid* where you'll see Limited Edition Press gets a mention as the original publisher – and please refer also to www.amazon.co.uk and/or www.abebooks.co.uk for *Our Kid* by Tim Lally [ISBN 1859880134], the previously self-published edition of this book, nowadays a collector's item.)

And it was around that time too, with my forerunner's kind advice in the matter, he being one author who is warmly welcoming of his public, that I, in turn, after wasting a good twelve months submitting the Thing to UK publishers/literary agents, then dithering for a further twelve months, wondering whether I dare or could even afford to self-publish, that I, in turn, looked to Limited Edition Press to fulfil my own dream of foisting a work of fiction upon an unsuspecting public.

HAD I NOT SELF-PUBLISHED, I WOULD NEVER HAVE BEEN PUBLISHED

Take note of the foregoing statement and consider it in respect of your own work. Because at this juncture, I think it is perhaps advisable to issue a word of warning to prospective readers of this book, who will no doubt have realised by now (whether they are still in Waterstone's or Borders, or have made it back home again) that the theme of this book is, as I have said all along, concerned exclusively with the self-publication and sale of fiction. Therefore, to reiterate and amplify what has already been writ large: *WRITE IT SELF-PUBLISH IT SELL IT*, a personal guide to writing, self-publishing and marketing of fiction by the author of *Every Street in Manchester* and *Manchester Kiss*

Yes, the theme of the book you have to hand is concerned exclusively and quite unashamedly with the writing, self-publication and marketing of fiction. Indeed, this book is more specifically and particularly concerned with the writing, self-publication and marketing of the Novel, this having been my personal preoccupation for the past two years (for the past thirty years, in a sense), during which time (the last two years) I have, as I say, successfully self-published and marketed two novels, namely, *Every Street in Manchester* and *Manchester Kiss*, of which, to date, I have sold close on 2,000 copies either personally (to family, friends, acquaintances; and by means of book launches, book-signings, one-day sales, personal presentations – more about which anon), and via Amazon and the major book stores in the Greater Manchester conurbation and beyond, where both titles continue to sell at a steady rate of knots. (More about this, too, anon.)

There is, of course, as I have previously indicated, no good reason why readers of *Write It Self-Publish It Sell It* should not apply the principles and personal insights contained herein to the self-publication and marketing of short stories, verse or non-fiction. But this is the last time I intend to refer to these disciplines except for purposes of illustration. So, henceforward, be it noted, it is of the self-published Novel that I speak.

So, if you happen to be a short story writer, a versifier or a poet, or a non-fictionist perchance (as, indeed, am I for my present purpose, as you will not have failed to notice), this is your last chance to jump ship, should you so choose. If you are still in Borders or Waterstone's, simply close the copy of the book you have to hand, replace it on the shelf as you found it – and skedaddle (as we say, *regionally* – indeed, *primitively*). Yea, verily: *scoot*, should you so choose. For you short story writers, poets, versifiers and non-fictionists have been duly warned – albeit *warmed* too, I trust. And I thank you most sincerely for your interest.

If, on the other hand, literary sado-masochism lies not without your remit – that is to say, as a spectator sport, then all you short story writers, poets, versifiers and non-fictionists are most welcome to remain whilst I administer to *aficionados* of the self-published Novel (whose interests this book purports to serve – indeed, hopes and intends to serve) a very different course of treatment.

For they, poor benighted and perennial fictionists (novelists – *hah*!), they, fools that they be, need a "good sherracking" – as my late father-in-law (late, too, of the King's Own Borderers for the duration of WWII) was won't to observe with regard to slackers, spivs (as they were called back then: "wide-heads", as he termed them) and Tom-fools of every description. Though in the present instance, of course, it is the fictionists amongst us (Tom-fools of at least one description) who stand in need of the aforementioned "good sherracking" (it seems to me), indeed, a "good sherracking" that must be as wet blanket-like as it is thoroughgoing – a "good sherracking", be it noted, that will be as shocking to the system as are the Dettol and a wire brush administered to anally-accessed innards so beloved of barrack room persiflage.

To this end, then, what follows is the gist of what most self-publishing enthusiasts – N.B. self-publishing *enthusiasts*, I tell you! – what follows is what most self-publishing *enthusiasts* will tell you about the benefits consequent upon the self-publication of *fiction*:

'Self-publishing,' say They – for their name is Legion, self-publishing enthusiasts of this ilk – 'Self-publishing is most definitely *not* the way forward for your precious debut novel! No, notta tall.

'Okay, so you've probably heard somewhere or other on the grapevine that self-publishing is the means by which novelists such as Herman Melville, Ernest Hemingway and Margaret Atwood first foisted their wares upon an unsuspecting public – Herman Melville with *Moby Dick*, 'tis said, Papa with a volume of short stories, the future Booker prize winner amongst them (*hah!*) with a book of verse. But that was *then*, my friend, and this is *now* – and, whilst we're about it, let me just remind you too that this is Herman *Melville* and Ernest *Hemingway* and Margaret *Atwood* who self-published and then marketed their work – and *not* the likes of you!

'So I really would forget it if I were you, pal! Yeah, forget it! Put the idea right out of your head. Because only a raving lunatic would imagine you can self-publish fiction profitably nowadays – let alone market it successfully once you've self-published it.

'Because let's face it, chum: if that novel of yours (*MO*, didn't you say?), if that novel of yours were any good, a commercial publisher (or a good literary agent) would have snatched your hand off the minute you submitted it, leaving you (literary genius that you are – *hah*!) to get on with writing your next best-selling novel.

'But that hasn't happened, has it? Well, *has it*? No, it hasn't! Far from it, in fact! Nobody snatched your hand off, did they? Well, *did they*? Nope! Took them all their time to send the damned thing back to you, as I recall. SAE enclosed, though it was. Seven long months, didn't you say it took them? And how many reminders was it you had to send 'em before they finally got around to unearthing the thing from under the Air Wick in the second cubicle along? . . . Okay, the *third* cubicle. Have it your own way. But correct me if I'm wrong, please do. It *was* the cubicle with the zany graffiti scrawled on the right-hand partition at head-height, wasn't it? Well, head-height for someone writing said zany graffiti in capitalised Times New Roman from a sitting position with a black, wedge-shaped felt tip marker:

PRAY, TELL ME, FELLOW BOOKMAN, WHAT *IS* THAT AWFUL PONG? ESS-AITCH-ONE-BLOOMIN'-TEE, PERCHANCE? OR WRITING GONE AWRONG?

'A good half dozen, wasn't it?' *Reminders*. Reminders you had to send 'em about it. Phone calls, e-mails, that official-looking letter from your kid, the solicitor's clerk.

'Hey, and let's have it right, pal, if that book of yours (okay, *novel*, since you insist), if that *novel* of yours (*hah*!) wasn't good enough to interest a commercial publisher or a literary agent, how in God's name will you get Joe Public to go for it? Buy it, I mean. Because the major bookshops won't take it, will they? What? The likes of Waterstone's and Borders? Carry a self-published book by a complete unknown? I don't really think so, pal. Do you? Fat chance of that. They'd most likely laugh you out of town.

'Still, as luck would have it, my self-publishing friend, all is not lost. Because what you should do – yeah, what you should do, if you really *must* self-publish, is self-publish *non-fiction* . . . Yeah, *non*-fiction. You know the sort of thing – self-help manuals . . . *How I Earned a Fortune and Never Once Got Out of Bed Till the Crack of Noon . . . How I Ended Up Ten Bob Behind Bill Gates Without Taking My Feet Off the Mantelpiece . . .*

'Because self-publishing *non*-fiction – yeah, self-publishing *non*-fiction . . . Now, that's a whole different ball-game, I tell you. Because self-publishing non-fiction can be a real money-spinner. I'm talking multi-million pound turnover if you do it right.

'So that's what I'd do if I were you, pal – concentrate on self-publishing and marketing non-fiction! Self-help manuals, for the use of. Yeah, that's the way to do it. Forget fiction. Stick that unpublishable debut novel of yours back in your bottom drawer – or, better still, put it to good use like that outfit – oozit? Shyster and Bluster was of a mind to do. Yeah, append it to the wall alongside the cistern in the smallest room, for the use of!'

You know the sort of self-help manuals the aforementioned self-publishing enthusiast has in mind, don't you? And I must admit to being a bit of a sucker for self-help manuals myself over the years, beginning with the daddy of them all:

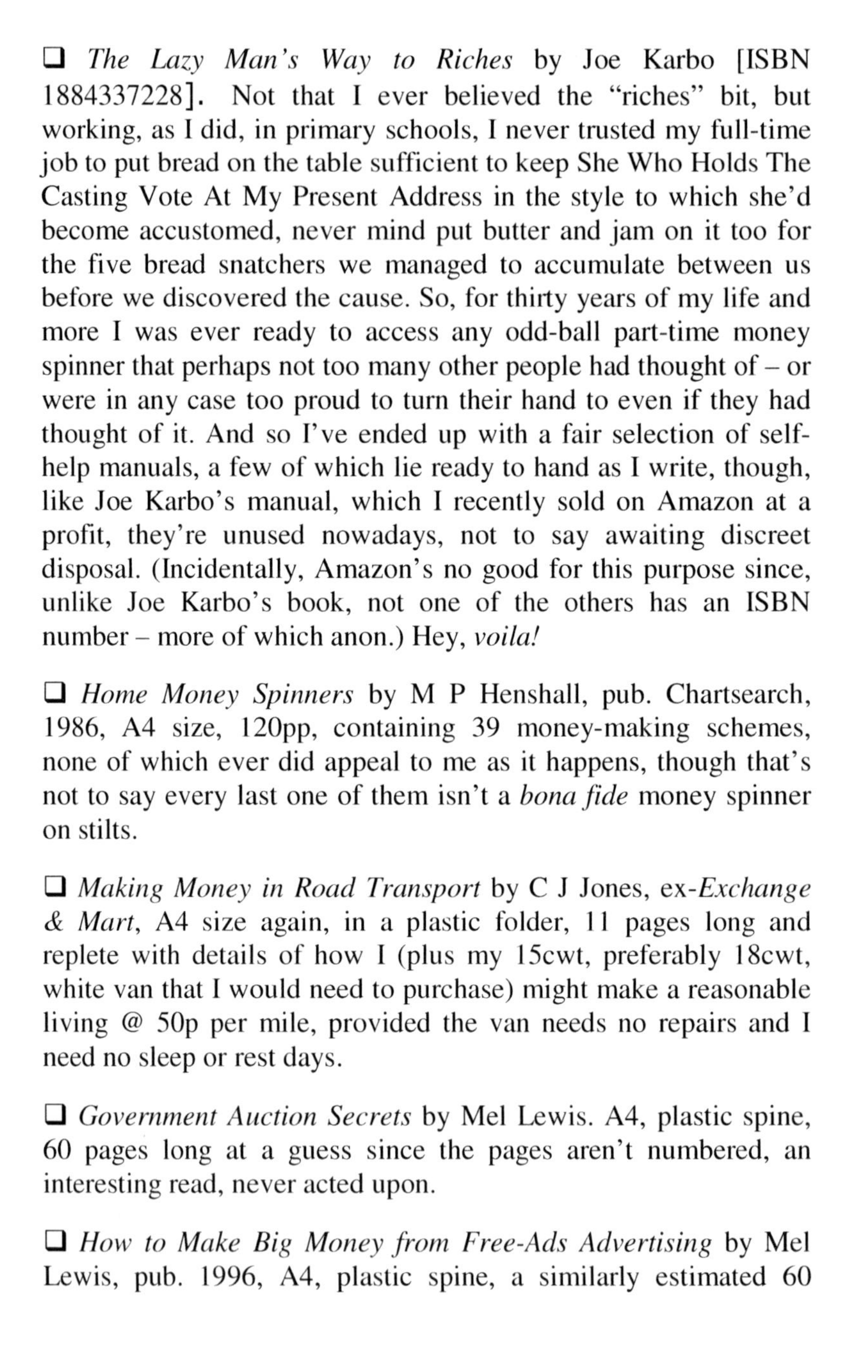

❑ *The Lazy Man's Way to Riches* by Joe Karbo [ISBN 1884337228]. Not that I ever believed the "riches" bit, but working, as I did, in primary schools, I never trusted my full-time job to put bread on the table sufficient to keep She Who Holds The Casting Vote At My Present Address in the style to which she'd become accustomed, never mind put butter and jam on it too for the five bread snatchers we managed to accumulate between us before we discovered the cause. So, for thirty years of my life and more I was ever ready to access any odd-ball part-time money spinner that perhaps not too many other people had thought of – or were in any case too proud to turn their hand to even if they had thought of it. And so I've ended up with a fair selection of self-help manuals, a few of which lie ready to hand as I write, though, like Joe Karbo's manual, which I recently sold on Amazon at a profit, they're unused nowadays, not to say awaiting discreet disposal. (Incidentally, Amazon's no good for this purpose since, unlike Joe Karbo's book, not one of the others has an ISBN number – more of which anon.) Hey, *voila!*

❑ *Home Money Spinners* by M P Henshall, pub. Chartsearch, 1986, A4 size, 120pp, containing 39 money-making schemes, none of which ever did appeal to me as it happens, though that's not to say every last one of them isn't a *bona fide* money spinner on stilts.

❑ *Making Money in Road Transport* by C J Jones, ex-*Exchange & Mart*, A4 size again, in a plastic folder, 11 pages long and replete with details of how I (plus my 15cwt, preferably 18cwt, white van that I would need to purchase) might make a reasonable living @ 50p per mile, provided the van needs no repairs and I need no sleep or rest days.

❑ *Government Auction Secrets* by Mel Lewis. A4, plastic spine, 60 pages long at a guess since the pages aren't numbered, an interesting read, never acted upon.

❑ *How to Make Big Money from Free-Ads Advertising* by Mel Lewis, pub. 1996, A4, plastic spine, a similarly estimated 60 pages, a really good, informative read with loads of worthwhile advice, utilised only to pick Mr Lewis's brain as a fellow advertiser of anything and everything once upon a time in free-ads papers such as *Loot*.

❑ *Frame It: Sell It* by R. Van de Calseyde. A4, 120+ pages (the latter 50% of them inadvertently affixed upside down) detailing how I might set myself up as an art dealer specialising in the sale of oil paintings and frames – which in my experience (its stock in trade duly extended to include framed art prints) was WORTH ITS WEIGHT IN GOLD. Truly! (Upside-down pages notwithstanding.) Oh, yes, indeed. And not least because, together with this inspired money-spinning manual the author very kindly enclosed as a bonus, free-of-charge, a quality 8 inch X 10 inch oil painting to be sold on at my, or, rather, our (my fire service pal being roped in as a partner) very first commercial art sale (with Kevin Townson's Lancastrian Fairs at Gargrave Village Hall in North Yorkshire, as I quite clearly recall, the Pennine Way running past the front door thereof), where said quality 8 inch X 10 inch oil painting was sold on at a price sufficient to recoup the *full cost* of Mr Van de Calseyde's self-help manual. And last, but by no means least:

❑ *Switch On to Profits* by A Duncan, pub. Chartsearch again, 1986, A4-size, 60+ unnumbered pages dealing with the intricacies of selling ex-rental television sets (ex-Granada in the main). And another self-help manual that was, to my way of thinking: WORTH ITS WEIGHT IN GOLD. Truly, I say again! Yes, indeed! Mr Duncan's self-help manual proved to be a veritable treasure trove of information and worthwhile advice, somewhat dated now perhaps, but by means of which, Once upon a time, A Thousand and One Greater Manchester Nights would see the sale from home of A Thousand and One Ex-Granada Rental Television Sets to A Thousand and One Square-Eyed Television-Viewers who had returned from their place of work only to find themselves, however temporarily, regrettably bereft of the Object of their Square-Eyed Affection.

BUT – and this is a very big BUT, indeed: 'Man doth not live by bread alone.' Matt. 4;16. Or as author Jeanette Winterson more recently put it: 'Money is part of the picture; it is not the point of being alive.' By means of which I intend, *not* to bring any unduly solemn and/or quasi-religious note to bear upon the consideration of commercial proceedings, but rather to point out that, lucrative though the self-publication of self-help manuals may be (as, given my present purpose, I'd rather hope it would be), it remains, barring my present commitment to *Write It Self-Publish It Sell It*, an activity that is *not* in accordance with our present purpose (yours *and* mine, that is) – which is, to reiterate, concerned with the writing, self-publishing, and sale of fiction (indeed, of the Novel), pure and simple. Notwithstanding which, this is *not* to say that self-publishing self-help manuals is in any way:

❍ an intrinsically wrongful activity; or,
❍ an inferior and/or undesirable activity; or,
❍ an activity to be shunned, if such be your purpose (as, indeed, it is mine for the immediate present, as I must needs remind you yet again).

But neither, by the same token, may it reasonably be supposed by human beings walking upright on two legs and possessed of a smidgeon of non-Thatcherite intelligence (for "Thatcherite" in this present instance, please read, "knowing the price of everything and the value of nothing, always provided that somebody else will be called upon to pay the price") that self-publishing fiction is wrong; and/or, folly – simply because it is an activity that is unlikely to prove profitable. Because if writing as a paying concern were the only point at issue, here, then, by way of example:

❍ *Our Kid* is tripe compared with the zillion-selling *Dr Atkins' Low Carbohydrate Diet*;
❍ Henry Fielding's *Joseph Andrews* is trash alongside the more popular Argos Catalogue;
❍ Thomas More's *Utopia* is dross when set against the profit-yielding Yellow Pages.

So let us leave all such silly arguments behind us now, confident in our new-found assurance that:
1. If fiction is what we truly *want* to write, we should *not* be asked, or expected, or misdirected to write anything other than fiction; and that;

2. if we choose, or are constrained to self publish due to circumstances beyond our control, then we are *not* alone. No, rather are we just one in a long line of at least . . . Cue: *ragmen's trumpets revisited – Dah-dah-dah-dah-dahhhhh* . . . FIFTY-TWO FAMOUS AUTHORS WHO CHOSE TO SELF-PUBLISH BEFORE US.

Margaret Atwood, Honoré de Balzac, L. Frank Baum, Willam Blake, Elizabeth Barret Browning, Robbie Burns, Lord Byron, Willa Cather, Tom Clancy, Stephen Crane, e e cummings, Alexander Dumas, T S Eliot, Howard Fast (with *Spartacus*), Edward Fitzgerald (with *The Rubaiyat of Omar Khayam*), Benjamin Franklin (with *Poor Richard's Almanack*), John Galsworthy, Zane Grey, John Grisham (rumoured to have self-published, though certainly he self-marketed his debut novel, *A Time to Kill*), Thomas Hardy, Nathaniel Hawthorne, Ernest Hemingway, James Joyce, Stephen King: on the internet (N.B. Do NOT on any account be tempted to follow suit since it doesn't work), Rudyard Kipling, Louis L'Amour, D H Lawrence, Herman Melville (with *Moby Dick*), A. A. Milne, Timothy Mo, Anais Nin, Tom Paine, Edgar Allen Poe, Alexander Pope, Beatrix Potter, Ezra Pound, Marcel Proust, Robert Service, George Bernard Shaw, Percy Bysshe Shelley, Upton Sinclair, Gertrude Stein, Laurence Sterne, Alfred Lord Tennyson, Henry David Thoreau, Leo Tolstoy, Mark Twain, Horace Walpole, Walt Whitman, William Carlos Williams, Virginia Woolf, Alfred Wainright (Okay, so AW's Lakeland Guides are non-fiction. But come *on* — they were originally self-published, and they sold in their millions!

And then, of course, there are too: A GOOD NUMBER OF SELF-PUBLISHED AUTHORS WHOM I JUST HAPPEN TO KNOW PERSONALLY. I make a specific point of listing these authors [see Appendix 7], tainting them perhaps with mention of my personal acquaintanceship with most of them for no other reason than that I know it for a fact, in a way that I cannot possibly know it about A. A. Milne, say, that there was a time in the not too distant past when each of the people listed in Appendix 7 was asking himself, as you are at present perhaps asking yourself, whether it might be possible to self-publish and, if so, how to go about self-publishing – hey, and wondering, too, exactly what self-publishing would entail for themselves and their families both in monetary terms and on a human level too.

So, perhaps you, dear reader, as I myself determined to do just two short years ago, and as so many famous writers have done before us (though not necessarily in the same easy way in which you and I may nowadays access digital imagery), would care to try your own hand at self-publishing, its having finally dawned on you (as it eventually dawned on me) that:

- mainstream commercial publication is no longer the only game in town, and,
- it is only by self-publishing your work that you will be enabled to present your literary credentials to the world.

As I say, this is exactly what I decided to do just two short years ago: to self-publish my debut novel, *Every Street in Manchester*, and then, seeing how well the original experiment turned out (umpteen hundred copies to the good at that time – by which I mean, *sold*, in addition to the novel's being included on the Portico Literary Prize shortlist), I repeated the exercise with a second self-published novel, *Manchester Kiss*.

And so, provided you proceed with caution, adhering to a minimum number of rules which should afford you a good margin of financial safety plus a satisfactorily published product, self-publishing is what I would unhesitatingly recommend to anyone like yourself who is convinced the story he has to tell is worth the telling and is doggedly determined to tell it. True, commercial profit may *not* result from the exercise. (Nobody is *entitled* to be a best-seller, you know – and, in any case, receipts from the sale of my own books are promptly reinvested in the next print-run.) But much more importantly, at least for the time being, is the distinct

possibility that, by adhering to the aforementioned minimum number of rules:
1. Monetary expenditure may be kept to an acceptable minimum – which, to my way of thinking, is a particularly important consideration for any author who has a family, each member of which (e.g. a wife who needs a new spring outfit, say; a toddler that's ready for its first bike; a teenager who's of an age to go to college, a daughter who plans to be married) has a claim, equal or otherwise, to whatever shekels remain in the familial coffers after the thieving taxman has had his way with them; and

2. it should also be possible to self-publish your book exactly as you would want to self-publish it, dealing only with properly professional publishing personnel (and ancillary tradesmen) who are not out to "rip you off", and with whom it is nothing less than a pleasure to deal.

So what's keeping us? Let's go to it – let us self-publish without further ado.

TWO: THE FAST-TRACK ROUTE TO SELF-PUBLISHING

Long experience, not only of self-publishing, has taught me two things if nothing else. In the first place:

1. There is absolutely no point in reinventing the wheel; rather are you best advised to invest your money in a well-proven make of motor car and have done with it. And, secondly that:

2. there comes a point in any self-help manual when the brighter, more widely experienced reader, chafing at the bit (so to speak), suspects the author is perhaps padding things out a bit, or that he is, at best, catering for dimmer, less experienced wits than said reader may lay claim to, in addition to which said brighter, more widely experienced reader just cannot wait to get on with it

without further ado – 'it', in the present instance, being the self-publication of his book (*MO*, so to speak).

In making these observations, I intend no disrespect to anyone, impatience being (as She Who Holds the Casting Vote At My Present Address is not slow to assure me when she's on my case) a marked character trait of my own. And in any event, the plain fact of the matter is that the true capabilities of individual readers in respect of self-publishing are quite unknown to me. So it may well be the case that there are readers amongst you who will gladly permit me to direct them forthwith to the handful of excellent titles listed below, each one of which is eminently suited to either one, or both, of the aforementioned exigencies listed above.

How to Publish Your Own Book: Everything You Need to Know About the Self-Publishing Process by Anne Crosbie ISBN 1845281063

The Easy Step by Step Guide to Publishing and Promoting Your Book by Pauline Rowson ISBN 0954804538

What Do I Have to Do to Get a Book Published by Jo Anthony ISBN 1905203586

Self-Publish: How to Launch Your Book into the World by David Arscott ISBN 0954258738

How to Publish Yourself by Peter Finch ISBN 0749003014

Each one of these books deals, too, with various intricacies attached to self-publishing which this book does not care (or dare) to tackle, this book of mine being – as it set out to be from the start – a "*personal* guide to writing, self-publishing and selling". So I'll be telling it as it happened to me, and/or as it *didn't* happen to me, as the case may be. And all I shall claim about what happened to me and what didn't happen to me with regard to self-publishing is that:

- I have twice self-published to my personal satisfaction – indeed, I have self-published three times in all, counting the 2nd edition of *Every Street in Manchester* when readers' comments were inserted in the text and a change to the front cover image was effected (see www.novelnovella.com);

- I have at the time of writing shifted close on 2,000 copies of the books I self-published;
- I did not unduly inconvenience my family with regard to funds expended and household space commandeered;
- I did not go broke.

So please do not hesitate to buy any or all the five titles listed above. To speak plainly, I recommend them to you unreservedly. I'll be advising readers to buy (or, at least, access) upwards of a *dozen* books before we're through. I mean to say, what kind of writer is it who imagines he can get away with buying no books whatsoever? More to the point, what kind of writer is it who *wants* to get away with buying no books whatsoever?

Incidentally, the impecunious amongst you may *not* resort to pleading poverty, but to the public library system instead. If the books I recommend to you herein are not on the library shelves, then they should be – and readers of this book will be performing a service, not only to themselves, but to their fellow citizens in placing a reserve order for them.

It will save time and effort, too, if whilst you're about it (either buying the aforementioned books or reserving them), you also get hold of (or at least make sure you have sight of) some or all of the self-published titles mentioned in Appendix 7, most of which were self-published by authors I know of.

Oh, and by the way, please do not imagine that I am recommending the books in Appendix 7 to you, hopeful of enriching myself and my acquaintances, although this would obviously be the net result of readers' rushing pell-mell, Christmas crush-like (not to say Northern Rock investor-like, albeit somewhat less cheerfully in the latter instance), to the nearest Waterstone's/Borders' pay point to snap up the aforementioned books, as opposed to ensuring they merely have sight of them, as I alternatively suggest. (Though I do offer my sincere thanks to all such prospective pell-mell pay point rushers in anticipation of such a potentially happy result.) No, what I really want to do here is to give you ample prior notice that very soon I am looking to list all the things that, speaking as a self-published writer, I personally feel are either right and/or wrong, desirable and/or undesirable with regard to the format of the self-published books mentioned in Appendix 7, including my own – and then setting readers to discover for themselves precise instances of such shortcomings (and/or benefits) amongst the aforementioned titles so that such may be avoided (or, indeed, emulated) when they themselves eventually set their caps at becoming self-publishers on their own account. In this latter case, of course, readers who hang back with their orders (and/or library reservations) just won't be acquainted with the book titles I'll be itemising, and may end up merely hazarding a guess as to the hard-won information I fully intend to bestow on them.

Which brings us face-to-face with THE MOST IMPORTANT RULE OF ALL WITH REGARD TO SELF-PUBLISHING – AND IT IS IN THREE PARTS.

❑ Part 1 Never, ever self-publish without first *having had sight of* at least one example (preferably, several examples) of a book (or books) which your chosen printer/publisher has produced in the past – and recently. (Why recently? Well, by way of example, the printer/publisher who produced such a wonderful example of his craft back in 1982 may since have turned to drink, as a consequence of which he does a lousy job nowadays.)

❑ Part 2 Never, ever self-publish without first *having physically handled* a book your chosen printer/publisher has produced in the past – and recently.

❑ Part 3 Never, ever self-publish without *personally possessing for detailed study* at least one book your chosen printer/publisher has produced in the past – and, recently.

❑ NOTE This rule (in its three parts) is a *sine qua non* absolute, should you be looking (as I sincerely hope you will be looking) to combining:

❍ eminently reasonable self-publishing expenditure with
❍ complete personal satisfaction with the finished product.

Self-publishing can be expensive, as well you know. But it is never so expensive as when an author ends up, due to insufficient caution, preparation – call it what you will – with an inferior product differing in so many respects from his personal expectations in the matter. To be a self-published author you must never take anything on trust. You will need to specify, specify, specify – much as Amundsen is said to have specified 'dogs, dogs, dogs' for his trip to the South Pole. Only by so doing, will you succeed in protecting yourself against the printer's/publisher's possible incompetence in the matter and/or (very occasionally) villainy. Also, by gaining *physical access* to a copy of a book which your chosen publisher has produced you will have ready to hand:

❍ a prime example of the quality of book your prospective publisher is capable of producing; and,

❍ a hard copy which will serve as a useful template upon which you may base, build, and/or re-arrange the necessary requirements of your own work. (e.g. the type and size of font to choose, the width of margins, how many lines to the page etc. etc. etc.)

In other words, the book (or *books*) which you acquire from your prospective publisher will provide you with an entire array of clues, both visual and to a lesser extent tactile, about the best way in which *your* book may be prepared for presentation according to *your* personal specifications.

You'll find it well worth the cover price, should you need to pay for it, though some printers/publishers will volunteer samples of their work, free-of-charge. I know Limited Edition Press does so when books become available, though I can't pretend I ever thought of applying for a freebie elsewhere. But, even before I approached Limited Edition Press I had already imported a copy of Tim Lally's *Our Kid* from the USA, courtesy of Amazon. Total cost? Best part of £30. Ouch! Yes, it hurt. But Tim Lally's *Our Kid* is a collector's item nowadays, and remember too that I was looking to spend around £650 on a first print-run of my debut novel at the time – and that £30 or so didn't hurt me (or my family) as much as a potentially misspent £650 would have done.

Enough said. Get the recommended titles ordered, reserved, or at least located (or some of them, preferably most) so that you will have unrestricted direct access to them as and when you need it.

THREE: THE DOZY DITHERER'S ROUTE TO SELF-PUBLISHING

The Players:

DD: Dozy Ditherer (that is to say, an interested party who is, quite naturally, cautious)
BK: Bill Keeth (that is to say, an erstwhile dozy ditherer)

DD: Exactly what do you mean when you talk about "self-publishing"?

BK: I mean any publication (handout, pamphlet, report, journal or book) that is published, *not* by a commercial publisher and at the expense of that commercial publisher, but by the author himself, or by a third party acting on the author's instructions in the matter – for which service, of course, the author will be called upon to pay an agreed fee as and when the finished article (that is to say, a print-run of a debut novel in the present instance) is produced and delivered in accordance with whatever prior agreement exists in the matter. So, there are just two factors that come into play with my personal definition, and I'm re-iterating to some extent when I specify that when it comes to self-publishing it is the author who publishes and/or commissions the publication of his work; and, it is he who picks up the tab, foots the bill, pays the piper – or however else you care to express the concept of the author's being called upon to pay for the privilege of being self-published.

DD: Well, that's a mouthful, it certainly is.

BK: I just needed to make sure you understand what it's all about before we kick off.

DD: Kick off?

BK: An association football analogy.

DD: Oh, I see. Well, bully for you.

BK: Bully off?

DD: No. Just tell me about self-publishing, please.

BK: It's self-explanatory in a way.

DD: Well, okay. But is it self-publishing if I just run off a few pages on my HP 1200 LaserJet printer and staple them together?

BK: LaserJet printer, eh? Get you!

DD: Well, is it or isn't it?

BK: Indubitably.

DD: Par-ding?

BK: Of course it is. In fact, it's probably the cheapest possible method of self-publishing, though it bears about as much resemblance to the sort of self-publishing of fiction, such as I am at present advocating for your precious debut novel as does a dog's dinner to *cordon bleu* cuisine.

DD: As a matter of fact, I don't particularly care for *cordon bleu* cuisine.

BK: And much prefer to tuck into a dog's dinner?

DD: Well, no. I don't mean that exactly.

BK: I'll just bet you don't. But you like nice scran, don't you? A good nosebag? A blow-out with all the trimmings when occasion presents itself.

DD: I have been know to succumb to that temptation.

BK: *Moi aussi*, if I may put it in *cordon bleu* terms, so to speak. And, believe me, running off a few print-offs on your HP 1200 LaserJet printer and stapling them together is nowhere near the same calibre of self-publishing at all. And it's certainly not the sort of thing I'm suggesting for one minute that you do with your debut novel.

DD: Well, suppose I up the ante a bit and go in for a bit of desk-top publishing. Is that self-publishing of a good enough standard for you?

BK: For *you*, you mean, don't you? Good enough standard for *you*, meaning for your debut novel.

DD: Yeah, of course.

BK: Well, yes, it may be, though I'd very much doubt it. Besides, there's absolutely no need for you to go to all the trouble and expense of setting yourself up for desk-top publishing in order to self-publish your debut novel. Mind you, if you already have access to a desk-top publishing facility (at work, say) and you're already adept at using it, it certainly can't hurt to play about with it a bit. May give you a better idea about how you want your book to look when it's in print. And if you're just looking to publish a few personal reminiscences, rather than a novel, you may well decide that desk top publishing is sufficient unto your needs.

DD: Seems to me you're a bit of a dab hand at telling me what sort of self-publishing *isn't* of the right standard for this debut novel of mine. But how about telling me what sort of self-publishing *is* of a sufficient standard for it?

BK: No problem at all. We just needed to get those bottom-endish methods of self-publishing out from under our feet, so to speak. However, to self-publish to a standard sufficient for your debut novel you'll need to commission a local printer or a publisher to do so on your behalf – and, of course, subsequent to his having produced the book to your personal satisfaction and, in accordance with whatever agreement you previously came to with the man, you'll have to pay the bill when he presents you with his invoice.

DD: Hang about. How can it be self-publishing if you get somebody else to do it for you?

BK: The same way you can talk about a self-build despite the fact that you get contractors in to build a house for you.

DD: Eh?

BK: Well, you've got to write the book for a start, haven't you? And then you simply commission someone else, a printer or a publisher, a professional in his own field, to publish the book for you.

DD: So that's it, is it? I write the book, then someone else does the publishing. And it's still self-publishing?

BK: Of course it is.

DD: So it's as simple as that, is it?

BK: Well, no. I mean to say, it's as *straightforward* as that, but it's not that simple.

DD: Eh?

BK: Now, you weren't born yesterday, were you? I mean, you know how things go in this man's world. There are rip-off merchants on every street corner – and in every profession, sad to say. And publishing is no exception. Why on earth should it be? Just because a publisher wears a suit and tie? Well, that's the best giveaway of all, as you'd be quick enough to tell me if it were solicitors or accountants or MPs we were talking about, rather than printers and publishers.

DD: True.

BK: I mean, you wouldn't dream of taking that car of yours into a main dealer, would you? Not unless somebody else was offering to pay the bill. And you certainly wouldn't trust the guy in that back street garage to do your MOT unless . . .

DD: A very good friend of mine recommended him to me. I'll have you know they do a perfectly good MOT – parts are cheap too.

BK: Precisely.

DD: So you reckon I need a personal recommendation, do you?

BK: Well, not necessarily. No. But it just so happens I came across a very promising looking advertisement in *The Gruinard* the other day . . .

DD: Don't you mean *The Guardian*?

BK: Nope, I mean *The Gruinard*. Mind you, maybe it was in *The Thames*, now I come to think of it. Nope, *The Obverser* maybe.

DD: And?

BK: Well, like I say, I spotted this advertisement for a publisher who seems really keen to publish books the other publishers have rejected. Anyway, to cut a long story short, I cut it out to show you.

DD: Gee, thanks.

BK: Anything for a pal.

DD: So what's it say, then? You got it with you?

BK: Yeah. Gimme a minute and I'll . . . I've put it in a safe place and – well, you know how it is if you put something in a safe place . . .

DD: You end up forgetting where the safe place is, I know the feeling, don't I just?

BK: I'm sure I'd stuck it in the back of my . . . Nope here it is, with my library card, not my Visa. Knew I had it somewhere. Right, here you go . . .

DD: Ta.

BK: So what d'you think?

DD: Gimme a minute, will you?

BK: (*Reads aloud.*)

WRITERS
YOU COULD BE THE NEXT J K ROWLING
IF YOU PUBLISH YOUR DEBUT NOVEL
WITH
MYXAMATOSIS PRESS
GOOD FICTION ALWAYS WANTED
Adventure, Thrillers, Crime, Mystery, Suspense,
Gay/Lesbian, General, Historical, Literary
Romance, Science Fiction, Teen, Ethnic,
Erotic, Graphic, Horror, Humour,
Experimental
MAIL YOUR TYPESCRIPT TODAY

DD: Wow!

BK: Impressive, isn't it? Thought you'd like it. And, what with the shaft of sunlight, there, illuminating the text and that writer-type with a quill pen in his hand, a dreamy look in his eyes and a stack of library books at his elbow . . . Well, it really looks the biz, doesn't it? Look, they've got a

London address too, N22, and an e-mail facility. Know what? Bet they'd even let you send your debut novel off as an attachment unlike the other publishers.

DD: Wow!

BK: I take it you're interested then?

DD: Too right I am!

BK: Forget it!

DD: Eh?

BK: I said: Forget it!

DD: Forget it? It's just what I'm looking for.

BK: On the contrary, it's the very last thing on earth you're looking for. It's what they call "vanity publishing".

DD: What's that when it's owt?

BK: It's a well-known scam. Vanity publishing is where you get a firm like Myxamatosis Press advertising for submissions – you'll find advertisements like this in all the so-called quality press and the literary magazines. They promise you the earth, whereupon –

- somebody like yourself will promptly send off his typescript to Myxamatosis Press, whereupon –

- Myxamatosis Press will express sheer amazement that no other publisher has snatched your hand off for the opportunity to publish such an imaginative, well-written, not to say, utterly compelling example of the novel form, whereupon –

- you are absolutely delighted at having had the good fortune to come across a publisher who apparently shares your own deeply-felt commitment to your debut novel, whereupon –

- you are most definitely inclined to let Myxamatosis Press have the privilege of publishing your debut novel, and prove it by indicating your gracious, albeit temporarily tentative, assent to their proposal, whereupon –

- Myxamatosis Press, in receipt of your typescript and your positive response, now requests a personal financial contribution from you, upfront, toot-sweet and via banker's draft, if you wouldn't mind, please, whereupon –

- you are somewhat nonplussed, not to say seriously put out, to discover that the requested financial contribution from yourself amounts to some (wait for it) £10,000 – or certainly a minimum of four very large smackeroonies.

DD: *Gulp!*

BK: On the positive side it should be said that Myxamatosis Press does promise that, once your debut novel is published, it will undertake to distribute it widely throughout the UK. Nevertheless it will very likely transpire that, once Myxamatosis Press has deposited your umpteen thousand pounds in its account and has published your debut novel (probably, to a very acceptable standard indeed) Myxamatosis Press will then discover various reasons appertaining to time, place, content and/or other temporal, locational or qualitative exigency which necessarily precludes its being able to distribute your book widely, if at all.

DD: Oh, dear! So that's vanity publishing, is it?

BK: That's vanity publishing, I'm afraid.

DD: But isn't *all* self-publishing vanity publishing in a manner of speaking? I mean, in the sense that the urge to self-publish, the determination to self-publish – the final decision to self-publish – all these things originate with nobody other than the author. In other words, it's a completely subjective, very personal point of view ("vanity", if you like) that informs the entire process from start to finish.

BK: Good point. You've hit on a very contentious issue with that one, I'll have you know. Because the UK Advertising Standards Authority has come up with a pretty long-winded definition of what a vanity publisher is, which may be summed up more succinctly by Johnathon Clifford thus: "Any company that wants to charge you to publish your book is, by definition, a vanity publisher, whatever they may try to tell you to the contrary." [See Appendix 9: www.vanitypublishing.info]

DD: So I was right, wasn't I?

BK: Well, no, you weren't. Well, not in my opinion anyway.

Because, in my opinion, Johnathon Clifford (not to mention the UK Advertising Standards Authority) is guilty of an error of logic which, does an injustice to the vast majority of self-publishing companies.

DD: Eh?

BK: In addition to which Johnathon Clifford's "definition" of vanity publishing is, also in my opinion, a self-centred definition of vanity publishing.

DD: How d'you make that out?

BL: Well, inasmuch as it is Johnathon Clifford who claims to have invented the term "vanity publishing" back in 1959/60.

DD: Oh, I see.

BK: So, do you also see that he's presuming to use that self-coined definition, whatever its original weight and worth (for example, I'd certainly agree it applies to Myxamatosis Press) as a means of pillorying every self-publishing company whether it be good, bad or indifferent?

DD: No, I don't really see that.

BK: Well, let me put it to you like this . . . Suppose we take the case of John Profumo, the MP, who lied to Parliament back in the 1960s and John Stonehouse, say, another MP, who once upon a time did a disappearing act from some remote littoral – and then suppose, too, I get so angry about this that I describe these two MPs as "mendacious members of parliament" . . .

DD: Which they were, weren't they?.

BK: Liars, yes. But would it then be reasonable of me subsequently to pillory – let's see – William Wilberforce, Robert Peel and John Bright as "mendacious members of parliament" because they had the letters MP after their names for the simple reason that this just so happened to run foul of the pejorative definitive term that I had personally invented?

DD: I see what you mean. You're saying you can't define something by using a definition – least of all if it just so happens to be a definition of your own invention.

BK: Good lad. In any case, though it might just be possible to argue Johnathon Clifford's entirely dismissive point of view about *all s*elf-publishing companies, many of which, as a matter of fact, do sterling work of an exemplary standard . . . Well, it strikes me, it's just the same sort of stuff you might expect to hear being put out by a particularly stand-offish publisher scratching his unmentionables at Henley Regatta when he really ought to be dealing with business back at the office . . .

DD: And it plays right into said publisher's hands, of course.

BK: Precisely. It's a point of view which deliberately chooses to ignore the impressive number of self-published authors who have consistently contrived to prove their personal literary worth, in addition to their eminent marketability by means of the self-publishing process – and by means of which, too, they have thereby convinced some other publisher or literary agent who is perhaps – well, let's say somewhat more attuned to the demands of the marketplace that he really ought to take one or all of these originally self-published authors into the mainstream, so to speak, that is to say those 52 FAMOUS AUTHORS WHO SELF-PUBLISHED to whom I previously referred you.

DD: Right.

BK: And let's look at it another way. Just because every lad who wants to play football isn't playing for a Premiership team like Man United, doesn't mean to say that, when those same lads turn out for Gary Appleton's Old David's (Middleton, Manchester) AFC on a Sunday morning, say, *they aren't playing football*! They're playing football all right. Okay, maybe they're not (indeed, they're most definitely *not*) playing football of the standard that's played at Old Trafford on occasion by players earning a trillion pounds a fortnight. But there's no way some football pundit like Sir Alex Ferguson, let's say, would dream of pretending the Old Trafford game is the only game in town.

DD: Whoa, whoa, whoa, *whoa* . . .

BK: Sorry. It just makes me see red.

DD: Red and *white*, you ask me.

BK: That's only by way of example. I don't follow football. But what I mean to say is, gimme one good reason why the mainstream boys should be allowed to have it both ways? The majority of them are less than helpful to first time authors, to begin with – then some of them have the nerve to pretend it's vanity publishing if those same first time authors they've declined to help (this literary *salon des refusés*, so to speak) subsequently discover that mainstream commercial publishing is no longer the only game in town, and subsequently decide to self-publish.

DD: Well, that advert for Myxamatosis Press wasn't much use to me, was it?

BK: No, it wasn't. But it would have been even less use to you if you'd fallen for it. In any case, what you really need to publish your book for you is a local printer – or one of the new POD facilities.

DD: What?

BK: What *what*?

DD: What's a POD facility when it's owt?

BK: Print-on-Demand? It's where a firm of publishers sets itself up to receive typescripts for publication, say, and you come to an agreement with them to publish a certain number of copies of your book for an agreed fee. Thereafter, you can order more copies of your book from them as and when you require them, usually at a fairly economical rate – and, certainly, with a very short delivery time.

DD: That's for me, then.

BK: Well, *is* it, do you think? I mean, there may be some local printer who's perfectly capable of doing the same job for cheaper money.

DD: Like the guy who did the invitations for our kid's wedding?

BK: Well, no. It's a different kind of printing we're talking about, here. Never mind the technicalities. They're not important. But the sort of printer you'll need to look out for will be somebody in your neighbourhood who's set up to print company reports and that sort of thing. Like the guy who printed *The Moston Story* for Fr Brian Seale.

DD: One of the books on the list of local authors you mentioned.

BK: See Appendix 7, as the man said. Well, most of them are authors local to me, which is how I happen to know them, of course. So Fr Seale must have decided to go to his local printer to get his book published.

DD: Which one?

BK: *The Moston Story*.

DD: No. Which printer did he go to?

BK: Oh, I see? I don't know, as it happens. Because *The Moston Story* doesn't supply me with that information. Not that it matters, of course. Because you won't be using the same printer as Fr. Seale. Well, not unless you happen to live in the same neighbourhood, in which case you'd better address your enquiry to Fr Seale because I can't see the identity of the printer is mentioned in the book.

DD: Gotcha.

BK: *Doing Our* Bit, on the other hand, was printed by Cox and Wyman, it says on the bibliographical details page.

DD: The WWI reminiscence?

BK: Yes.

DD: The printer's Moonraker Publishing, isn't it?

BK: Nope.

DD: That's what is says on the title page.

BK: Yes, but that's not the printer; that's the publishers' imprint.

DD: Par-ding?

BK: Martin Purdy and Ian Dawson wrote *Doing Our Bit*, right? Then they self-published it under the imprint Moonraker Publishing. A Moonraker's a Middletonian, you see – it's slang for a Middletonian; and the book's about the people of Middleton in WWI.

DD: Thought you said it was published by a local printer.

BK: No, I said was it was *printed* by Cox and Wyman – and not too locally at that. But by using their personal imprint, Martin Purdy and Ian Dawson show they're the *publishers*.

DD: Publisher/*shublisher*! What's it matter.

BK: Well, it matters quite a lot as a matter of fact. Because it's only by using an imprint of his own that a self-published author may protect his copyright unconditionally.

DD: Eh?

BK: Well, take Moonraker Publishing, for instance. As I say, it's what you call an imprint – and, in the case of *Doing Our Bit*, as I also say, it's the means by which Martin Purdy and Ian Dawson contrived to protect their copyright in the matter.

DD: Hang on. Don't go all lawyer-speak with me, please. Let's just get this straight. If I write a book and get somebody to publish it for me, my copyright is not protected unless I use a personal imprint.

BK: Well, not unless your publisher agrees it is as part of the deal.

DD: That's bonkers.

BK: Yes, it *is*. But, if you use a personal imprint on the book, your printer has, in fact, *printed* the book, so your copyright is unconditionally protected. But, if you don't use a personal imprint on the book, your copyright may be at risk.

DD: That's a bit below the belt, isn't it?

BK: Where your brains are, eh? No, listen. Pin back your lug-holes, in fact. Because if your personal imprint *isn't* on the book, then your printer/publisher could claim to have published the book, not just printed it . . .

DD: So my copyright is *not* protected unless I use an imprint.

BK: Well, not necessarily.

DD: What d'you mean: 'not necessarily'? Is it, or isn't it?

BK: Well, yes and no. It depends how trustworthy your printer/publisher is.

DD: But, legally, he could get away with publishing the book under his own name instead of mine?

BK: No, your name would probably have to be on it. But unless you previously agree with him that the copyright is yours, your printer/publisher might get away with publishing another edition of the book without your express permission.

DD: Why on earth would he want to do that?

BK: Well, if your book proves to be popular. In fact, I know somebody this happened to.

DD: Really?

BK: Yeah, this guy's publisher brought out a new edition of a book he'd written with a completely different cover picture, and the author only found out about it when the new edition was spotted by a friend in a local shop.

DD: Bit under the arm, that, isn't it?

BK: You just bet it is. But quite legal, apparently. The thing is, though, if it's at all possible for a publisher to get away with something as blatantly obvious as that, how much easier would it be for him to get away with a bit of creative accountancy by failing to pass on royalties that are due to the author.

DD: You've got me dithering now all right.

BK: All I'm saying is you really do need to be on your guard – which is not to say you should shelve your plans to self-publish. In any case, you won't be the only person grasping this same nettle. Look at it this way: if your self-published book has only a few limited sales, nobody's going to want to invade your copyright by printing extra copies off at his own expense. It's only when a book appeals to a lot of people you might encounter problems. For example, an autobiography by a speedway rider might be an unexpected best seller because there are speedway fans all over the world. Still, forewarned is forearmed, as they say, and the Society of Authors, 84 Drayton Gardens, London SW10 9SB publishes a *Quick Guide to Self-Publishing and Print-On-Demand* at a cost of £7.50, post free (which is free to members, incidentally). And relevant to the question of copyright, you'll find the important things to consider are . . . ❍ Point 3 (first bullet point); ❍ Point 6 (b); and ❍ Point 7 (i).

DD: So what would you advise me to do then?

BK: Apart from studying the Society of Authors' publication, you mean?

DD: Yeah.

BK: It's not for me to say.

DD: Wait a minute. You've got me umpteen pages deep into a

book entitled *Write It Self-Publish It Sell It* and now you're saying it's not for you to advise me in the matter!

BK: You've got me wrong, pal I don't mean it like that. What I really mean to say is it's not for me to *specify* what you should do, in much the same way that it's not for me to tell you what to eat for your breakfast, what kind of car to buy, where to go for your annual holiday. What I mean to say is, I really do believe it would be beneficial for you to eat a cooked breakfast, but perhaps you'd much prefer to do without for reasons of your own. Similarly, I honestly and truly believe that everybody should drive a car that is sufficient unto his needs, whereas you may very much prefer to have a gas-guzzling Hummer H3 Luxury 3.7 Auto parked up on the path so as to impress the neighbours. And I really do reckon you should have a good annual holiday after working all the hours God sends, whereas you may be happy as Larry, pigging out under canvas. So you pays your money and you takes your choice – and what you pay for your book to be self-published, plus who you choose to self-publish it should in any event be decided according to your personal preferences in the matter, not mine.

DD: So that's it, is it? You're just gonna clam up and leave me to it, are you?

BK: Notta tall, old bean. What I intend to do is tell you exactly how it seemed to me when I first started thinking about self-publishing my debut novel, namely:

- all the things that worried me when it came to approaching a local printer, or
- using a Print-On-Demand company; and, last but certainly not least:
- my personal inadequacy when it came to using a PC.

DD: Oh, I can use a PC all right.

BK: Of course, you can. Most people can operate a PC nowadays, and much better than I can too. And this is one reason why I think it would be quite wrong of me to refer readers to a particular printer or Print-On-Demand company. Let me make myself perfectly clear: I am nobbut a PC plonker, as I term my aforementioned PC inadequacy. Oh, I'd used a typewriter for thirty years or more, so I had keyboard skills – at least of the two-fingered variety . . .

DD: And the same to you too, pal.

BK: Oh, very droll. But let's not get too frivolous about it. Because self-publishing's a serious business.

DD: You're telling me it is.

BK: Indeed, I am. And I will continue to tell you, if I may now proceed, that, immediately prior to the new Millennium, She Who Holds the Casting Vote At My Present Address suggested I should not dream of entering into it inky-fingered, and lacking computer skills. So, I applied for a place on a very basic PC course ("Computers Don't Byte" – *hah, hah*), attendance at which has at least permitted me to: access the facilities afforded by Microsoft Word in order to write correspondence and (says he) literature: two published novels so far; this book plus a further non-fiction title that is nearing completion; send and receive e-mails; browse the internet; buy and sell on Amazon and elsewhere; buy, but not sell on eBay; (What's a digital camera when it's owt?) listen to music on YouTube. End of story.

DD: Not exactly pre-eminent PC accomplishments, are they?

BK: I'd be the first to agree. Therefore, you will readily understand that, when it came to self-publishing, I needed (and will *continue* to need) the ministrations of my publisher, Limited Edition Press (www.limited-edition-press.co.uk), the full (indeed, fulsome) benefits of using which will be listed presently. [See Appendix 12.] Please note, though – and to reiterate the Foreword, that apart from my own *need* (and intention) to employ Limited Edition Press as my publisher on this and every future occasion where self-publishing is concerned (in part, for reasons of my PC inadequacy, as mentioned above), there is, no financial connection between myself and Limited Edition Press other than that of author/publisher. In other words, do please rest assured that Limited Edition Press has not paid me or offered to pay me, an advertising fee to receive favourable mention within these pages. And I should perhaps say that the same applies to anyone, anything, everyone and everything within these pages about whom or which I make favourable mention. Accordingly, such advice as I do offer is disinterested advice, my only duty of care being to the reader, who has presumably paid for such disinterested advice via the cover price of this book, or whose library service has paid for it on his behalf.

DD: *Ahem.*

BK: Dither ye not: I haven't forgotten you. But I really do need to make a few things clear before I begin.

DD: *Begin?* You're already rattling on to some tune. Or hadn't you noticed?

BK: I mean *begin* with regard to putting you on to a list of local printers and Print-On-Demand companies too – and, via their FAQs, on to the sort of services they'll be able to offer you. (And, incidentally, do not deal with any company which offers you no assurance about your copyright in the matter.) Local printers first, then. So it's over to you.

DD: Eh?

BK: Local printers. They're in your locality, so it's up to you to find them.

DD: Oh, I see.

BK: Right. No problem then?

DD: Nope – Yellow Pages, the internet?

BK: Fine. Be loads of them there.

DD: Probably.

BK: And the closer to home, the better, remember.

DD: Yeah, right.

BK: Meanwhile, cop for this lot . . . Turn to Appendix 6 for 33 POD Companies & Easy Access to Local Printers.

DD: Ooh, er . . .

BK: Now, don't forget. You're in the chair. Tell 'em exactly what you want and ask 'em how much they'll charge you for doing it.

DD: You *know* what I want. I want them to publish . . . I mean, I want them to *print* my debut novel, that's what.

BK: If that's all you're going to tell 'em, I'm afraid it's not enough.

DD: Ooh, er . . .

BK: And you'll be lucky if you get a Print-On-Demand company to *print* your book, as opposed to *publishing* it.

DD: *Ooh, er . . .*

BK: Now, dither ye not. These are some of the same things that worried me when I decided I wanted to self-publish. That is to say, I didn't know exactly what to specify with regard to presentation, format and the rest of it.

DD: Hay-ulp!

BK: Dither ye not, because since that time – thanks, in part, to studying umpteen self-published books and to the advice I received in the matter from Limited Edition Press and elsewhere – I've devised a list of requirements I would unhesitatingly put to a printer and/or a Print-On-Demand company when it's self-published fiction I'm looking to commission.

DD: Thank goodness for that.

BK: So don't contact anybody just yet, local printer or Print-On-Demand publisher – at least not until you've studied, noted, and assimilated the suggestions below, these being based on my personal experience with my own two self-published books. Once you've studied these suggestions you should then be in a position to relate the specified requirements to your own specific requirements in the matter which should also become more evident as you immerse yourself in the format details and the book titles listed below and in Appendix 7.

DD: Ooh, er . . .

BK: Just look upon it as a job of work, rather than as some mystic practice steeped in the *Thames Literary Supplement* blather of high art. For you at this point in the proceedings self-publishing is a trade like any other. And the plain fact of the matter is that you must become a self-publishing expert for a month or so in very much the same way as you become a tiling expert when the bathroom needs doing, or a carpetfitter when the hall, stairs and landing need attention, or my kind of Alan Titchmarsh (a 20mm. gravel-cum-tree bark expert) when, like me, you never ever want to dig and delve in your garden again.

DD: Ooh, er . . .

BK: Dither ye not! The next chapter, you'll find, contains 25 suggestions for you to be going on with; and I'll be bunging you another 100 suggestions before we're finished.

DD: Ooh, er . . .

FOUR: 25 SPECIFICATIONS FOR SELF-PUBLISHED FICTION

The twenty-five suggested specifications for self-published fiction which ensue and which you should bear in mind when you eventually get around to discussing your requirements with POD companies and local printers may be referenced via detailed individual study of the format of my own two novels, *Every Street in Manchester* and *Manchester Kiss*, and of the other self-published books mentioned above and below, every one of which may be found in the complete list contained in Appendix 7. Hopefully, by utilising these twenty-five questions and their accompanying commentaries, you will then begin to recognise, by direct comparison, the potential strengths and/or foibles, if any, of the printer and/or POD company which has produced any particular book or books listed in that appendix, and, by the same token, be alerted to the potential strengths and/or foibles of any other printer or POD company you may subsequently care to approach in respect of self-publishing your own debut novel [see Appendix 6] – and eventually, of course, to feel quite confident that your decision to commission your chosen printer or POD publisher is the right one for you.

Remember, too, that, as also previously stated, not one of the books listed in Appendix 7 is to be studied for its content (unless at some point in the future you subsequently care to do so), but quite simply (and very strictly at this stage) with regard to its format, texture, feel and overall visual and tactile presentability.

Something else about which I should perhaps reassure you as we veer within the orbit of critical appraisal is that I have honestly and truly enjoyed the majority of the self-published books featured in Appendix 7. One of them, in fact – namely, *Jackie Brown – the Man, the Myth, the Legend* by Brian Hughes MBE – I have described elsewhere as "my favourite non-fiction title of all time", thereby leaving Alan Moorehead's *The White Nile* and *The Blue Nile*, and *Hitler and Stalin – Parallel Lives* by Alan Bullock to compete for the second, third and fourth positions in this category. Even so, the *content* of the books in Appendix 7, I would remind you, is not the point at issue; for rather is our concern at the moment quite exclusively with format. Here's why . . .

Okay, a book is a book is a book. (Unless it's a "*Booky-Wook*", God help us!) But we self-publishers (ergo, self-*publicists*) really are up against it all round – and not least with regard to the book-buying public. And so, in much the same way as a bespectacled blue-rinsed matron in a run-of-the-mill Astra saloon has an infinitely better chance of escaping the unwelcome attention of the traffic police than does a tattooed punk in a Starsky and Hutch-striped Maserati, so will our self-published books, provided they look exactly the same as every other paperback on the bookshop shelves, fail to set off any unwelcome alerts (short of the check-out) amongst the book-buying public.

Bearing this proviso in mind then, pick up and open the first book on your list, looking to the front cover, the spine and to the back, skimming the title and blurb, then perusing the book you have to hand from start to finish, asking yourself each of the questions that follow, whilst submitting each book on the list, individually and in turn, to similar scrutiny.

❑ 1. ARE THE PAGES OF THIS BOOK 90 GSM OR BETTER?
The pages of my novels are 80 or 90 gsm white bond paper – that is to say, 80 or 90 grams per square metre, a reference to the weight, hence the thickness of the paper used. Affordability may well dictate that you need to make do with 80 gsm paper for your

own self-published book. But *do not*, whatever you do, settle for 70 gsm paper. Because even 80 gsm paper may require you to arrange to store your books indoors, whereas you may have planned to use an exterior storage facility, such as your garden shed and/or garage.

❑ 2. IS THE COVER OF THIS BOOK 270 GSM OR BETTER? The covers of my books, *Every Street in Manchester* and *Manchester Kiss*, are 270 gsm card. Under no circumstances should you try to make do with less than 250gsm card for the covers of your self-published book – and go for a thicker card if at all possible. Because even 270gsm card likes to curl up in the foetal position, given half a chance and outdoor temperatures. Some of Brian Hughes' books are hardbacks, so discount these, except for *Starmaker – the Jimmy Murphy Story*, the format of which is eminently suitable for fiction. Because it's paperbacks we're interested in, there being absolutely no need to go to the trouble and expense of publishing a hardback copy of your book. To speak truly, it never ceases to amaze me that so much commercial fiction is still published in hardback, since paperback first editions are not unknown. (See, for example, *Salt is Leaving* by J B Priestley, pub. 1966.)

❑ 3. HAS THIS BOOK GOT THE "DEAD FISH" FEELING OF A MAGAZINE, GLOSSY OR OTHERWISE? This is self-explanatory, I think, and certainly does not apply to 90 gsm white bond paper. A book, with its projected longer life span, really should feel a bit more substantial than a monthly magazine.

❑ 4. DOES THIS BOOK HAVE MORE (OR LESS) THAN 37 LINES PER PAGE? To my mind, 37 lines of 11pt. text per page (give or take a line or two) is pretty well near perfect for an A5-sized book. Any fewer, and you will be incurring unnecessary expense; any more and the book becomes more difficult to read and may even look cheap.

❑ 5. ARE THE PAGES OF THIS BOOK WHITE, OR DO THEY HAVE A GREYISH/YELLOWISH TINGE? Not my books, if you don't mind, *please*!. But check out the rest of the list in Appendix 7. Is there anything there that has greyish or yellowish pages? I mean it. And, if so, say: 'No, thank *you*! Under no circumstances; this is definitely *not* for me.'

❑ 6. IS THE FONT IN THIS BOOK TIMES NEW ROMAN? Under no circumstances should any font be used for your self-published book other than Times New Roman (or perhaps Garamond). This is because readers in general are so accustomed to seeing TNR (with its distinctive serifs*) used in books, that they will most definitely find any font lacking a serif (e.g. Arial, Verdana) visually jarring. Which was presumably the intention of Mark Haddon when he selected a serif-less font for *The Curious Incident of the Dog in the Night-Time*. A wonderful book! But, of course, the author must have wanted it to look a bit odd (given the "oddness" of his subject matter), whereas you certainly don't want readers to think your book is odd – at least not by accident, you don't. (Incidentally, my publisher tells me that Arial is the preferred font for autistic readers, which may suggest another reason why it was chosen for Mark Haddon's story of a child suffering with the autism-related Asperges Syndrome.) Repeat: *insist* on Times New Roman for your debut novel. On the other hand, Garamond is a very clean-looking text-cum-serifs, though I personally think Garamond needs to be 14pt. Even so, you may care to consider it as a fresh alternative to TNR.

* Serifs are the printed representation of those marks on letters sculpted in stone in Ancient Rome that enabled the stonemason to access the stone in order to chisel the letters and, of course, to exit his work, come the end of the working-day.

❑ 7. IS THE NAME OF THE PUBLISHER MENTIONED REPEATEDLY IN THIS BOOK? What should catch the reader's attention are the title, the author's name and the image on the cover. (That is to say, *your* title, *your* name and *your i*mage on the cover.) Any printer (though, more likely than not, it will be a POD publisher who will do this), any publisher who repeats his company's name umpteen times on the cover or inside the book has performed a singular disservice to his customer. Limited

Edition Press is mentioned just three times in my books. Its initials can be seen on the spine; and its name is listed on the title page, and (by legal requirement together with a business address) amongst the bibliographic details.

❑ 8. IS THE PUBLISHER'S NAME TOO OBVIOUSLY A PRINT ON DEMAND NAME? We don't want this, do we? The imprint "Moonraker Publishing" on the title page of *Doing Our Bit*, by way of example, passes muster in a way that print@the-drop-of-a-hat.com can never do.

❑ 9. IS PAGE 1 OF THE NARRATIVE A RIGHT-HAND PAGE (OR "RECTO", IN PUBLISHER-SPEAK)? It is never acceptable for page 1 of the narrative to appear on a left-hand page (verso). In fact, some ultra-fussy authors won't even begin a chapter on a left-hand page. So, how can you avoid this? This "page 1" Philistinism, I mean. Well, you'll just have to get physical with your typescript. At some point prior to submitting your document to the printer/publisher you will need to number a series of A4 pages from No. 1 to No. 15, say (that is to say, by way of example, if No. 15 is the first page of the narrative), and then ensure, by laying each A4 sheet out on the floor that everything is in its proper position (as a right hand page or a left-hand page, as the case may be), accommodating this arrangement by using blank A4 sheets as spacers wherever appropriate.

Ah, dither ye not, dear reader. Refer instead to No. 23 below and also to Appendix 11: The Component Parts of Your Novel.

❑ 10. ARE THERE INCONSISTENCIES IN THE TEXT IN THIS BOOK? 'Mistakes,' says John Braine, 'can creep into any text.' But this is an explanation rather than an excuse for misuse of language or spelling mistakes or errors of punctuation. And, though a word like "s*ou*briquet", by way of example, may be spelled thus, or alternatively: "s*o*briquet", once you've opted for the way you prefer to spell the word, you must stick with that decision throughout your book. By the same token, for further example, "Jacqui", a perfectly correct abbreviation of the name "Jacqueline", must never, once used in your book, be subsequently rendered (albeit similarly correctly), as "Jackie" – and quite specifically for reasons of consistency, rather than orthography Again, dither ye not! Refer instead to the next chapter and to Appendix 9.

❑ 11. DOES THIS BOOK HAVE AN ISBN NUMBER? Every book requires a 10 or, of late, a 13 figure identification number (the ISBN number – that is to say, the International Standard Book Number). Without this you will never be able to sell your book on Amazon or in a book shop since it is by the ISBN that booksellers identify a specific book title and a specific edition of that book title.

Hopefully, your publisher will provide you with an ISBN number, as did mine, at a very reasonable inclusive price. The ISBN number of *Every Street in Manchester* being ISBN 1859880657, for instance; that of *Manchester Kiss* – ISBN 1859880673. Alternatively, you can easily make your own arrangements, something that I personally very much prefer *not* to have to bother with since ISBN numbers are bought in batches of ten and only one is required per book title. But if you really do want to be independent, contact the ISBN agency via e-mail: isbn @nielsenbookdata.co.uk or see www.isbn.nielsenbookdata.co.uk – or write to the ISBN Agency at: ISBN Agency, 3rd Floor, Midas House, 62 Goldsworth Road, Woking, Surrey GU21 6LQ.

❑ 12. IS THE COVER OF THIS BOOK (PARTICULARLY THE FRONT COVER) AS DULL AS DISHWATER AND ABOUT AS UNINSPIRING AS A COMPANY REPORT FOR THE LOCAL WIREWORKS? Since the storyline of my novels spans the second half of the twentieth-century from the 1950s on, I specifically wanted monochrome covers as a means of looking back to the days before colour television. Until the late 1960s, remember, The Beatles were monochrome, and colour photographs were not widely available. (My 1967 wedding photographs are monochrome and I don't recall we ever felt hard-done-to on this account.) But the problem of the dull-as-dishwater cover really is something to watch out for with local printers where you will need to take very firm control of the process if they don't appear to have had much experience with presentable artwork. Even POD companies are occasionally guilty of producing an inferior cover finish reminiscent of that on plates destined for discreet disposal on the Aunt Sally stall at the Summer Fayre. Whatever you do, dither ye not! Instead, refer to No. 20 below.

❑ 13. DOES THIS BOOK SHOW THE PUBLISHER'S IMPRINT OR THE AUTHOR'S? With books produced by POD companies it will invariably be the company's imprint on the title page. So make quite sure your copyright is protected. That is to say, refer to the advice of the Society of Authors in the matter and to the various websites listed in Appendix 9. Also, look to your chosen publisher, as and when you commission one, to provide you with a satisfactory written warranty concerning your copyright.

❑ 14. IS THE PROOF-READING POOR? Proof-reading is one of the most difficult jobs you will have to undertake when preparing a document to be published in book form. Why? Well, if you, the author, are the person responsible for doing the proof-reading, you'll be checking far too many aspects of the narrative (flow, pace, spellings, punctuation etc. etc. etc.) to be of much use in the matter. Having said this, there are more mistakes in some books than there are in others. Neither is poor proof-reading confined to books that are self-published. But, in the case of the books listed in Appendix 7, do umpteen items require correction or amendment? If so, beware ye of a printer/publisher who let's umpteen mistakes get past his less than Hawkeye-like oversight. Still, dither ye not. Instead, please refer to Chapter Eight: Proof-Reading.

❑ 15. IS THERE NO INDEX IN THIS BOOK WHEN AN INDEX IS PERHAPS WARRANTED? This only applies to non-fiction titles and, even then an index may not be required in some instances. You'll note no index is provided here, though certainly, the inclusion of an index was considered. It was the realisation that I have never once thought to peruse the index in David

Armstrong's *How NOT to Write a Novel* during as many as three re-readings that decided me against including one.

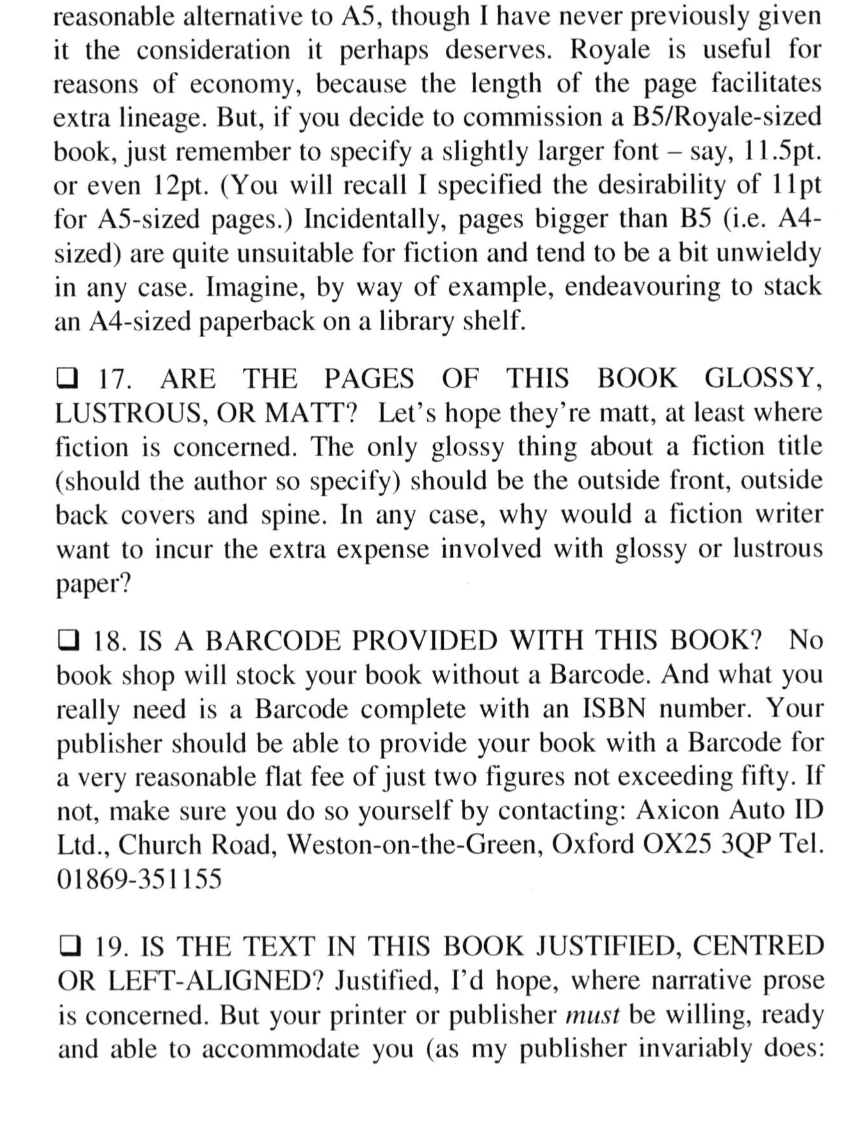

❑ 16. IS THIS BOOK BIGGER/SMALLER THAN A5-SIZE? Some novels are published in Royale (B5) size, which is slightly taller, though perhaps not as wide as A5. This is a perfectly reasonable alternative to A5, though I have never previously given it the consideration it perhaps deserves. Royale is useful for reasons of economy, because the length of the page facilitates extra lineage. But, if you decide to commission a B5/Royale-sized book, just remember to specify a slightly larger font – say, 11.5pt. or even 12pt. (You will recall I specified the desirability of 11pt for A5-sized pages.) Incidentally, pages bigger than B5 (i.e. A4-sized) are quite unsuitable for fiction and tend to be a bit unwieldy in any case. Imagine, by way of example, endeavouring to stack an A4-sized paperback on a library shelf.

❑ 17. ARE THE PAGES OF THIS BOOK GLOSSY, LUSTROUS, OR MATT? Let's hope they're matt, at least where fiction is concerned. The only glossy thing about a fiction title (should the author so specify) should be the outside front, outside back covers and spine. In any case, why would a fiction writer want to incur the extra expense involved with glossy or lustrous paper?

❑ 18. IS A BARCODE PROVIDED WITH THIS BOOK? No book shop will stock your book without a Barcode. And what you really need is a Barcode complete with an ISBN number. Your publisher should be able to provide your book with a Barcode for a very reasonable flat fee of just two figures not exceeding fifty. If not, make sure you do so yourself by contacting: Axicon Auto ID Ltd., Church Road, Weston-on-the-Green, Oxford OX25 3QP Tel. 01869-351155

❑ 19. IS THE TEXT IN THIS BOOK JUSTIFIED, CENTRED OR LEFT-ALIGNED? Justified, I'd hope, where narrative prose is concerned. But your printer or publisher *must* be willing, ready and able to accommodate you (as my publisher invariably does:

just see what he did for me with Chapter 22 of *Every Street in Manchester*) should you occasionally require centred or left-aligned text within the same prose work. For instance, suppose you need a line or two of verse in the text and your printer/publisher refuses to accommodate you with this. Such an attitude is no use to you whatsoever except as an indication that this is the sort of printer/publisher you do not want to be having to deal with. Make no mistake about it, this is the sort of printer/publisher who will do you down any way he can (e.g. poor proof-reading, misalignment of text etc.) in his pursuit of the be-all and end-all of his "professional" career – namely, the speedy, no-holds-barred, devil-take-the-hindmost making of a big fat profit for himself. In other words, this is the sort of "professional" who is not *truly* professional. Because a true professional (be he a lawyer, an accountant, a doctor – or a publisher) will ensure he extends to his clientele a proper duty of care in addition to collecting a professional fee for services that are adequate and/or appropriate to the job in hand. (N.B. This is not to say a true professional should *not* collect a professional fee for a job done to the best of his ability. In fact, an essential part of the definition of a professional has it that, unlike an amateur, a professional is paid to do what he does.)

You may well counter, of course, that there is no verse in your story, so this point is superfluous. But think very carefully about your requirements in this respect. Because even a simple inscription on a headstone (should there be need for one in your story) or a two-liner on a birthday card would need to be centred in print. And, for your printer/publisher to say he can do justified text and no other within the same book is tantamount to saying: 'There's no way in the world I'll be scrutinising whatever rubbish you send in to me. I'll just bung it on the machine, crank up the gubbins – and (hey presto!) your rubbish comes out the other end in book form. Money in the bank! Talking of which, hand it over – quick! This is a stick-up!'

❑ 20. ARE THE ILLUSTRATIONS IN THIS BOOK OF A REASONABLE STANDARD? This is the age of the digital camera, remember. There should be no illustrations that look like they were unearthed by Schliemann at the excavation of Ancient Troy, unless, of course, they were indeed unearthed by Schliemann at the excavation of Ancient Troy. And don't settle for some cheap, in-house provided front cover either. Because there should be some way, without extortionate charges being applied to the facility, by means of which your own photographs may be utilised for the front cover (or alongside the text), should you care to use your own photographs. Certainly, Limited Edition Press willingly accommodated me in this matter, the cover photographs for the 2nd Edition of *Every Street in Manchester* and for *Manchester Kiss* being taken by the most amateur cameraman in the UK (i.e. yours truly) with a Kodak single-use camera. Then Limited Edition Press arranged by means of whatever form of jiggory-pokery it could muster (I'll spare you the technicalities since they are completely beyond my ken) for my chosen photographs to fit the respective front covers.

❑ 21. ARE THERE TOO MANY PAGES IN THIS BOOK TO FACILITATE ECONOMIC POSTAL COSTS? This is not an artistic argument, I know. But, as the man said – said man being Foster J Dickson in his article, 'The Tricky Art of Self-Publishing': 'Writing is about art and publication is about money.' So, with the Royal Mail contriving to ensure it cashes in to some tune on the current e-Bay marketing boom, postal costs have risen enormously of late. This is bad news for booksellers* because paper weighs heavy, and at 358pp, *Every Street in Manchester* (at 500 gms weight) only just squeezes into a Jiffy bag – and *only just* qualifies to be mailed for less than £1. (Don't forget you are going to have to mail your book to reviewers, customers, book shops and book wholesalers.) Meanwhile, mailing multiple copies is a financial nightmare. Five copies of *Every Street in Manchester* are not, as you might reasonably expect, discounted for bulk. Far from it! Nope, the Royal Mail bills me an extortionate £8.24 for the privilege of my giving them the extra business. It is only the fact that arranging five separate, more economic mailings for the five books is a considerable chore that makes me bite the bullet.

What I'm saying is that my debut novel, *Every Street in Manchester*, weighs in at 132,000 words, so you may care to get your business head in gear and write a shorter novel. Remember John Braine's advice in the matter to the effect that the modern novel is between "40,000 words and 150,000" words. Act ye, therefore, accordingly. No reader can possibly turn his nose up at a novel of 40,000 words when the MAN Booker committee so frequently endorses them, the 2007 shortlist underlining the fact that no change of heart is in evidence at the time of writing.

In all seriousness, though, I suggest you aim at 60,000 words minimum on the grounds that, no matter what anyone says, anything less still feels like a novella.

* The problem of the swingeing postal charges at present decreed by the Royal Mail insofar as they apply to books is an abuse Parliament really must turn its attention to soon. Consider, if you will, the fact that successive UK governments of every complexion have hitherto applied neither purchase tax nor VAT to books since this would have been tantamount to levying a tax on the dissemination of knowledge and culture. So, it would be no more than just if, according to similar logic, the Royal Mail were to be legally compelled to operate a much more considerate postal rate with regard to books.

❑ 22. IS THE MAIN BACKGROUND COLOUR ON THE FRONT COVER OF THIS BOOK CONTINUED THROUGH TO THE SPINE AND BACK COVER? One of two possible reservations I have with regard to the format of my own two fiction titles (as freely decided off my own bat, by the way) is that . . . Well, okay, the front cover is monochrome with white lettering and a black background. But it now occurs to me that perhaps I should have wrapped this black background (instead of a white background) around the spine and on to the back cover, necessitating white script instead of black on the spine and the back cover too. Even now, I just don't know. As I say it's a "possible reservation".

The other reservation I have is with regard to printing information on the respective inside front covers and inside back covers of my books – as I noticed Tim Lally had done with the self-published *Our Kid*. I decided to do this when I was an absolute beginner in order to save paper, and expense. But we're talking about four pages maximum over two book titles, which doesn't really save much paper or money.

There again, had I moved the information on the respective inside front covers into the body of the books by one page, say (where there is other information, it just so happens), then the information I was so keen to display would have ended up being obscured by ticketing materials on those copies of my books which are available via various public library services in Greater Manchester and beyond.

I have pondered this matter at length, as you. in turn, must ponder such matters at length. Because very soon, I trust, your debut novel – *MO*, didn't we say? – yes, in the foreseeable future, you will need to visualise *MO* as a physical entity rather than as an A4-sized document, saved to your PC hard drive (and floppy disk, flash drive etc.) . . . even if you do not need or intend to print the document off as an A4-sized typescript in order to transmit it to your chosen printer/publisher. Heck! *Especially* if you do not need or intend to print it off as an A4-sized typescript to your chosen printer/publisher!

DD: Ooh, er . . . Why's that?

BK: Because the end product of this exercise is going to be a book, don't forget. We're talking about something that will be a three-dimensional object in the real world, in which incarnation, so to speak, the book will be: A5-SIZED, in addition to being, numbered sequentially ON BOTH SIDES OF THE PAPER from page 1 to whatever page number the book finishes at, PLUS the book will have a front cover, and an inside front cover, a spine, an inside back cover and a back cover and, unlike your present A4-SIZED DOCUMENT, saved to your PC hard drive, where it is numbered sequentially ON ONE SIDE OF THE PAPER ONLY from page 1 to whatever page number the document finishes at, INCLUDING a front cover and an inside front cover and an inside back cover and a back cover.

All of which means, of course, that, at some point in the very near future you are going to have to accommodate (or at least visualise) a necessary transition from the A4-sized document on your PC hard drive to the A5-sized document that will be your self-published book. See No. 23 below, particularly where a series of blank pages are necessarily inserted to accommodate the aforementioned transition from one-side of the paper number sequence to both-sides of the paper number sequence.

❑ 23. ARE THE VARIOUS COMPONENT PARTS OF THIS BOOK IN THE CORRECT ORDER? These should be in the order set out below, as per the *MHRA Style Book* [See Appendix 9 – and Appendix 11 below] . . .

- ❍ the front cover of the book, where the book begins, through to
- ❍ the page on which the narrative begins (N.B. We'll only be using the first page of the narrative for the purposes of this illustration),
- ❍ and then through to last page of the narrative, and the inside back/back covers where the book ends. (N.B. Remember right-hand pages are "recto"; left-hand pages are "verso".)

❑ NOTE The different component parts of a book must be annotated on your practice sheets as left-hand or right-hand pages according to the specific information (if any) each is supposed to convey.

- ❍ The front cover, *right-hand page*
- ❍ The inside front cover, *left-hand page*
- ❍ page 1, BLANK FLYLEAF, *right-hand page*
- ❍ page 2, BLANK FLYLEAF, *left-hand page*
- ❍ page 3, TITLE PAGE, *right-hand page* – inc. book title, author, publisher
- ❍ page 4, BIBLIOGRAPHICAL DETAILS, *left-hand page* – publisher's address; copyright statement; ISBN number (page may be left blank for the publisher to complete, though do not chance it)
- ❍ page 5, DEDICATION, *right-hand page*

❍ page 6, BLANK, *left-hand page*
❍ page 7, EPIGRAPH, *right-hand page*
❍ page 8, BLANK, *left-hand page*
❍ page 9, THE NARRATIVE BEGINS, *right-hand page*
❍ page (whatever the number is), THE NARRATIVE CONCLUDES
❍ page (whatever the number is) plus one or two BLANK FLYLEAVES
❍ page (whatever the number is), INSIDE BACK COVER, *right-hand page*
❍ page (whatever the number is) BACK COVER, *left-hand page*

Other bits of information have their particular designated position (e.g. readers' comments; contents list etc.) but you won't need these with your debut novel. But please refer to the *MHRA Style Book*, and also study the further example of the order of the component parts of your book in Appendix 11. However, as it at present stands, your novel, *MO* by D. DITHERER needs only the 15 page references that are supplied here. So what you will need to do at this point (or just before you commission your printer/ publisher) is to lay them all out (A4-sized) on the floor as indicated in Appendix 11, using a spoof *MO* by D. DITHERER as your exemplar.

Dither ye not on this score. You really do need to lay out A4 sheets on the floor to understand the full implications of what I'm saying here about the necessary transition from document to self-published book.

❑ 24. ARE BREAKS IN THE TEXT AND OTHER MATTERS DEALT WITH IN AN APPROPRIATE MANNER IN THIS BOOK? For example, the ellipsis, the dash, spacing of text (at the beginning of a chapter; for a new paragraph; after a break in the narrative; after a break in the narrative at the bottom of a page. Are such things dealt with as they need to be dealt with? That is to say, are these things dealt with in the manner that they are dealt with in the generality of books on the bookshop shelves?

Pray dither ye not. You've encountered all these things in your reading over the years, so all you really need is for me to underscore them for you. The really important thing is that you want your book (apart from its content) to look just like every other book on the bookshop shelves in order that potential customers won't shy away from buying your book or feel uncomfortable with it once they've bought it. So, please see the next chapter where everything will be made clear, the real point at issue being, as I say, that your self-published book must not raise eyebrows in any way other than the way in which you might want it to do.

❑ 25. IS THE PAPER USED IN THIS BOOK BOOKWOVE, OR IS IT WHITE BOND? To pinpoint exactly what I mean by this, please turn to *Doing Our Bit* by Martin Purdy and Ian Dawson, the pages of which are a good quality bookwove; and then turn to *Every Street in Manchester* or *Manchester Kiss*, the pages of which are 90 gsm white bond.

Vive la différence!

Or, more appropriately and specifically, can you spot the difference?

Bookwove is the kind of paper that's used in the majority of the paperback fiction titles you'll find in your local book shop. And, in respect of this, together with its overall size and cover art, *Doing Our Bit* is of all the books in Appendix 7 the most indistinguishable from any other book in the commercial marketplace, and, therefore, in my opinion, it is surely the best presented.

Boo-hoo?

Well, yes, but only up to a point. Because, to my mind, *Doing Our Bit* would be a better book if it had an index and perhaps a bit of additional proof-reading. Also, bookwove tends to be more expensive than the 90 gsm white bond on which my books are printed. And bookwove paper is expensive because printers must buy it in greater quantity than white bond, its being more suitable to the litho publishing process which, due to factors connected with the preparation of print-runs at an economic cost, more usually applies to print-runs in excess of 300 copies. So if your print-run doesn't use up that greater quantity of bookwove the publisher would need to buy in (that is, unless your print-run will be upwards of 1,000 copies or so, depending on the length of your book), then there will be extra costs involved, which makes a print-run in bookwove an expense I personally would not care to run to. To speak bluntly, the first print-run of *Doing Our Bit* must have been in excess of 1,000 copies – and I feel sure that it was. (More of which later.) But the first print-run of *Every Street in Manchester*, by way of contrast, weighed in at just 50 copies. And there is a very good reason why it made sense to order in excess of 1,000 copies of *Doing Our Bit* in its first edition – just as there is another good reason (or rather two very good reasons) why only 50 copies were commissioned for the first print-run of *Every Street in Manchester*. Ah, dither ye not. All will presently be revealed to your satisfaction, believe me.

DD: Ooh, er . . .

BK: Steady on now. We've got stacks to do before you approach a printer or publisher. For instance [see Chapter Seven], I've got a further 100 questions for you to put to him yet. So, just check out his FAQs for the time being, amongst which you may find you are offered an incredibly cheap price PLUS royalty payments. So, if you really do fancy an undignified dither, pray ask yourself this . . .

❑ IF A PUBLISHER OFFERS YOU A CHEAP PRICE PLUS ROYALTY PAYMENTS, HOW WILL YOU "POLICE" THE ROYALTY PAYMENTS? To expand on this just a little, some POD publishers will in all likelihood quote you a price for publishing your book to your agreed requirements:

❍ complete with an ISBN number and Barcode
❍ with perhaps a minimum of as few as 25 copies in the first-print run
❍ listing on Amazon
❍ at a very affordable price
❍ plus royalty payments if and when any books are sold via Amazon or the book shops.

To reiterate, then, how will you police your royalty payments, not to mention the relevant paperwork? Make quite sure you obtain some assurances on this point.

DD: Ooh . . .
BK: *Er?*

FIVE: THE QUEEN'S ENGLISH & SIMILAR CONCERNS

A good friend of mine whose advice I invariably find invaluable, though not as a rule in any literary sense, his most recent fictional outing having occurred as long ago as the early to mid-fifties in the company of William Brown and Richmal Crompton, his creator – a good friend of mine, as I say, has issued me with a stern warning not to write this present chapter, the words "your grandmother", "to suck eggs" and "teaching" ringing loud and clear throughout, though not necessarily in that order – and certainly not as loudly or as clearly as other words from the same oracle, namely, "an unwarranted auctorial intrusion", not to say "a studied insult to the reader's intelligence".

And so, dear reader, I must apologise in advance, lest offence be unwittingly caused, on the one hand, and/or your boredom threshold crossed on the other. For it is not my intention, believe me, to give rise to upset or *ennui*; neither is it my intention to deal with matters of a presentational kind concerning which I have not personally needed to exercise especial care. Because the real points at issue are these:

- If we don't get the spacing of the text and breaks in the text right, we're going to end up with a self-published book that looks a bit odd, at best, and, at worst, amateur; and,

- if we don't express ourselves in the Queen's English, we're going to look like self-publishing clodhoppers.

So this chapter is dedicated to getting a few things straight before we proceed – punctuation, for example, and the correct spacing and separation of sections of text; and we are going to consider, too, how best we might express ourselves within the text in accordance with our true intentions in the matter. [See also Appendix 9.]

You see, something that occurs to me at this point is that there must be many people who come to self-publishing late in life when they are perhaps retired from work with an interesting tale to tell. And for once in their lives (Oh, happy day!) they have a bit of spare time on their hands plus a modicum of wherewithal, both of which are undoubtedly necessary to the telling and self-publication of their tale.

Now, many people, given their age at this juncture, will be somewhat set in their ways – perhaps set in their regional vernacular too, particularly if their personal field of professional expertise over the years has involved them in a preponderance of verbal exchange at the expense of (let us say) the decidedly literary. This is not to say, of course, that such folk won't have tons of life-experience behind them which will positively enthral their prospective readership when they finally get around to setting it all down on paper. But many of them, as I say, having worked over the years in industries where no great store ever was set by the finer points of English grammar, punctuation, syntax and the rest, may now discover to their chagrin that they must needs "temper" their language, so to speak, or they run the risk of being scorned as foul-mouthed (invective must be the first thing to go: swear words lose all power to stun if used without restraint) or even illiterate by the scoffers in our midst – that is to say, by the sort of reader who is looking to hide his own inadequacy and insecurity by taking a specious delight in catching out the autodidact or self-taught.

'So you're self-educated, are you?' say I to the contrary. 'Well, fair play to you for that!' Indeed, how dare I say otherwise, knowing that Sean O'Casey was self-educated (as was Winston Churchill in many respects) – and knowing, too, that no less a personage than Matthew Arnold, the poet and schools inspector, exulted in the knowledge that William Shakespeare was himself "self-schooled, self-scanned".

Therefore, all I ask of any reader who may care to consider the few words to the wise this chapter purports to convey is that he bear with me with patience for the present, conscious of no affront's being intended, and assured of my sincere respect for autodidactic achievement in whomsoever it may reveal itself.

Meanwhile, to readers needful of assistance none (though perhaps of the chapters that follow), I offer advice of an internet trawling kind when I say: *'Four syllables speed your flight wither thrice their number stand proud with auctorial weight profound . . . Horseman, pass by.'*

❑ THE ELLIPSIS is the three little dots which are sometimes used to indicate that a character has perhaps stopped short of what he intended to say due to interruption . . . or because he has had second thoughts in the matter . . . or is hesitating to continue for some other reason, or, sometimes too . . . in order to indicate that a superfluous part of the text has been omitted from a quotation. Hence, to indicate hesitation, for example, the use of ellipsis on page 56, line 6 of *Manchester Kiss*:

> 'Yes . . . yes, of course I did,' said McClintock quickly.

The important point to notice here from the writer's point of view is how the three little dots of the ellipsis are properly rendered, as follows, via your PC key pad:

SPACE, DOT, SPACE, DOT, SPACE, DOT, SPACE

Thus:

> 'Yes SPACE, DOT, SPACE, DOT, SPACE, DOT, SPACE yes, of course I did,' said McClintock quickly.

Which will, of course, give you an ellipsis that is eminently serviceable:

> 'Yes . . . yes, of course I did,' said McClintock quickly.

I don't care to illustrate the amateur (that is to say, the *incorrect*) way of rendering the three little dots which make up the ellipsis. But, if you'd care to use a practice sheet and do it this (*incorrect*) DOT, DOT, DOT way, I feel sure you'll notice immediately the (pathetically amateur) difference . . . and, thereafter, will determine to eschew this (amateurish) DOT, DOT, DOT practice for evermore.

❑ THE DASH (or M SPACE) is a really useful punctuation mark that should be rendered as follows: see page 245, line 11 of *Manchester Kiss*:

> His suit – the trousers retaining a crease where there should be a crease . . .

The dash (in this instance) is rendered thus:
SPACE, DASH, DASH, the, then insert a SPACE between the 2nd DASH and "the".
Thus:

> His suit SPACE, DASH, DASH, the (then insert a SPACE between the 2nd DASH and "the") trousers retaining a crease where there should be a crease . . .

Which (*yawn*: boringly, I know – but, reader, it's just got to be done) gives you:

> His suit – the trousers retaining a crease where there should be a crease . . .

QED – and, hopefully, *goodbye* to the shorter N SPACE, as opposed to the longer DASH or M SPACE, again, for evermore.

❑ THE APOSTROPHE is a perfectly legitimate linguistic device denoting ownership or kinship – e.g. *the dog's dinner*: the dinner that belongs to the dog; or, *the dogs' dinners*: the dinners that belong to the dogs). And the apostrophe is perfectly simple to use. Thus, one dog? Then the apostrophe comes *before* the "s". More than one dog? the apostrophe goes *after* the "s". Do not be tempted to use the apostrophe the way your local greengrocer does: e.g. cauli's 80p . . . potatoe's £1 a bag . . . strawberry's £1 a punnet.

Wrong . . . wrong . . . *wrong*! Your local greengrocer uses apostrophes for no good reason other than that he hasn't used one for some time – which is a perfectly stupid reason for using an apostrophe, and tantamount to using a car jack when you haven't got a puncture or a comb if you're as bald as a coot. [See Appendix 9: *Eats Shoots and Leaves* by Lynne Truss.]

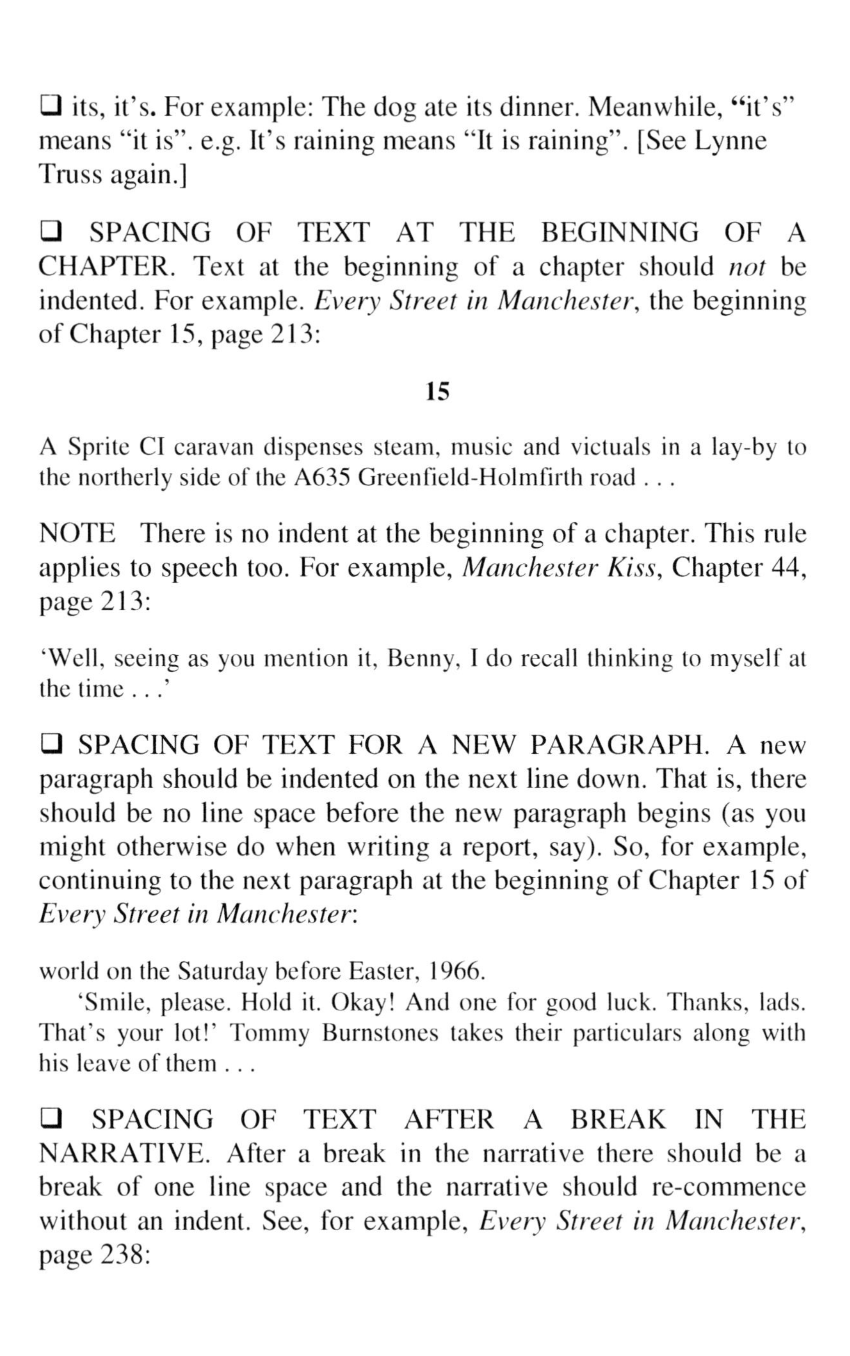

❑ its, it's. For example: The dog ate its dinner. Meanwhile, "it's" means "it is". e.g. It's raining means "It is raining". [See Lynne Truss again.]

❑ SPACING OF TEXT AT THE BEGINNING OF A CHAPTER. Text at the beginning of a chapter should *not* be indented. For example. *Every Street in Manchester*, the beginning of Chapter 15, page 213:

15

A Sprite CI caravan dispenses steam, music and victuals in a lay-by to the northerly side of the A635 Greenfield-Holmfirth road . . .

NOTE There is no indent at the beginning of a chapter. This rule applies to speech too. For example, *Manchester Kiss*, Chapter 44, page 213:

'Well, seeing as you mention it, Benny, I do recall thinking to myself at the time . . .'

❑ SPACING OF TEXT FOR A NEW PARAGRAPH. A new paragraph should be indented on the next line down. That is, there should be no line space before the new paragraph begins (as you might otherwise do when writing a report, say). So, for example, continuing to the next paragraph at the beginning of Chapter 15 of *Every Street in Manchester*:

world on the Saturday before Easter, 1966.
    'Smile, please. Hold it. Okay! And one for good luck. Thanks, lads. That's your lot!' Tommy Burnstones takes their particulars along with his leave of them . . .

❑ SPACING OF TEXT AFTER A BREAK IN THE NARRATIVE. After a break in the narrative there should be a break of one line space and the narrative should re-commence without an indent. See, for example, *Every Street in Manchester*, page 238:

I had to find out the hard way.

It's this Sunday in July, see – hot and sunny and balmy and happy and free – and we're on the boating lake in Boggart Hole Clough, me and Huge, in this clinker-built rowing boat . . .

❑ SPACING OF TEXT AFTER A BREAK IN THE NARRATIVE AT THE FOOT OF A PAGE is dealt with as follows:

❍ If there is *sufficient* line space at the foot of the page:
a) leave one line space;
b) insert an asterisk, centre-aligned, on the next (remaining) line;
c) re-commence the narrative with no indent on the following page. For example, see *Every Street in Manchester*, pp. 219-220:

'ZZZzzzzzZZZ . . . ZZZzzzzzZZZ . . . ZZZzzzzzZZZ . . .'

*

Friday, 12.04 pm

❍ If there is *insufficient* line space at the foot of the page:
a) insert an asterisk, centre-aligned, on the first line of the next page;
b) leave a space of one line;
c) re-commence the narrative with no indent. For example, see *Every Street in Manchester*, pp.227-8, the asterisk being centred-aligned on the next page:

Victor saloon, one Ford Transit van, and the girls.

FOOT OF PAGE [NO LINE SPACE AVAILABLE]
NEXT PAGE [ASTERISK]
LINE SPACE

Verdict on the main course at The Great Western: fine, fine, fine . . .

NOTE With an asterisk being such an indistinct mark, I would nowadays (that is to say, post-*Manchester Kiss*) prefer to render the above passage thus – that is to say, employing a bolder symbol:

Victor saloon, one Ford Transit van, and the girls.

Verdict on the main course at The Great Western: fine, fine, fine . . .

That is to say, by using a Webdings capitalised Bold B (as it so happens) which is twice the narrative font size. So, where the narrative font size is 11 pt, say, the Webding capitalised B is 22pt. Now, let's see that again, using the lower case version of the initial D (for Dozy Ditherer) in Bold, 22pt. Wingdings 2 font:

Victor saloon, one Ford Transit van, and the girls.

Verdict on the main course at The Great Western: fine, fine, fine . . .

Incidentally, I first came across this utilisation of Wingding/ Webding symbolism in *Slab Rat,* a novel by Ted Heller, son of James Heller of *Catch-22* fame, a novel deserving of a wider public than it has had to date – though perhaps not as wide a public as Ted Heller's all-time classic, *Funnymen* deserves. *Funnymen* is an absolute gem of a great American novel which is arguably *sans pareil.*

❑ "I was laying on the bed" Please note that only carpets, eggs and bricks are laid, people only ever being said to be "laid" in American slang of the coarser variety. Because in any sentence featuring the verb "to lay" an object is required or the word just doesn't work. (That is to say, " to lay" is a verb transitive.) Thus, if another (necessarily stronger) person (perhaps a parent) picks up a sleeping child, say, in order to do the laying down on the aforementioned bed – said child on waking might truthfully assert (as ought you, the novelist, should occasion arise}: 'I was *lying* on the bed'. However, it can safely be depended upon that no human being (other than in this Cockney aberration) was ever guilty of *laying on the bed* of his own account.

❑ "I was stood at the corner" Never write (or say) in your north of England way, 'I was *stood* at the corner'. This should, in fact, be: 'I was *standing* at the corner.' The mind boggles. Because, if I really *were* '*stood* at the corner', I might conceivably be either:

- a Subbuteo figure in a child's game of association football, said child having *stood* me at the corner in order to take a corner kick; or alternatively,

- an unfortunate mobster with feet cast in cement whom Dutch Schultz has *stood* temporarily at the corner of South Street adjacent to Battery Park whilst debating whether to ditch me in the East River or the Hudson.

Remember: 'I was *standing* at the corner.'

❑ "I was sat on the desk." Similarly, 'I was *sat* on the desk' conjures up a vision of my northern self as a manikin – Tom Thumb, say, being *sat* on the desk by a person or persons unknown for purpose or purposes unknown. 'I was *sat* on the desk' should correctly be written thus: 'I was *sitting* on the desk'.

❑ You and I . . . you and me. The rule here is pretty simple: "you and I" do any doing that is done, whereas "you and me" have it done to us. For example:

- You and I got the horse into the pasture.
- The horse chased you and me around the pasture.

And so – onwards and upwards we go . . .

SIX: SETTING YOUR STALL OUT AS A WRITER

Okay, you may well have completed your debut novel by now, or be pretty close to completing it – and, to be perfectly honest, not one of the following items and/or facilities is absolutely necessary for a writer of fiction. (John O'Hara, by way of example, wrote his debut novel, *Appointment in Samarra*, sitting on a bentwood chair with his typewriter resting on his bed.) But you will certainly make life a whole lot easier for yourself if you will only treat yourself to:

❑ A SPACE OF YOUR OWN "The will to work," says John Brainc, "builds all the seclusion one needs." But you really should contrive to create a space of your own in which you may do your writing undisturbed – even if it's only your garden shed, the family car parked up in some quiet spot, or your place of employ when everybody else has gone off home for the day.

For instance, I have a room, small in itself, which is invariably commandeered as and when a guest stays overnight or household items no longer enjoying the approval or regard of She Who Holds the Casting Vote At My Present Address are temporarily side-lined en route to the charity shop or the council tip. The room contains my PC, printer, hi-fi, bookshelves, and a small filing cabinet (aka a bedside cabinet with a deep drawer). It is not a perfect location, partly for reasons already stated; and certainly, an upstairs room would be marginally better in order to distance myself from household noises and to afford me a more expansive outside view. (From the upstairs window on a good day I can see the Pennine Way above the M62 footbridge at Windy Hill.) But the room I have serves its purpose well enough, affording me shelter, privacy, reasonable quietude, and the triple benefits via an opening window on the wall beyond my PC of daylight, ventilation and an exterior vista consisting of a couple of hardy perennials, the door of an outbuilding and a beech tree which, luckily for me, is a neighbour's responsibility.

❑ A PC Technophobe though you may be (as am I), if you have not already succumbed to the blandishments of PC World or its competitors in the marketplace, I do strongly urge you to get hold of a Broadband compatible PC forthwith. And, while you're about it, do yourself a very great favour and sort yourself out with a basic computer course that will enable you to:

- use Microsoft Word, by means of which you may write your debut novel and, thereafter, transmit it as an attachment to your chosen printer and/or publisher;

- browse the internet in order to glean factual information for your book, not least about printers and/or publishers included in the list I provide below;

- e-mail your printer and/or publisher when you acquire one (and he you, of course); plus

- create the possibility of eventually having a personal website for reader access (see below), and access, too, to the Nielsen Teleordering facility (to be explained anon), which you will presently find is an excellent tool enabling bookshops to access stocks of your book once it is published.

❑ A VIEW FROM A WINDOW Once upon a time, when typewriters* were in vogue, a writer was best advised, I've heard it said, to face a blank wall, enabling him to look inwardly for his ideas. But the advent of the PC has made a window with a view preferable so that you, the writer, may rest your eyes away from your PC screen from time to time, thereby postponing the need to visit an optician and/or purchase a guide dog.

*Take absolutely no notice of professional writers who say they use a typewriter still. I strongly suspect that writers who say this do so in order to deter people like ourselves from endeavouring to make contact with them via e-mail. *Pshaw!* As if we would! (I've long nurtured the desire to employ a Dickensian *pshaw* in my work – and I'll *warrant* I won't find a better occasion than in commenting upon the continuing *putative* use of typewriters, *egad*!)

❑ A PC OPERATOR'S CHAIR Make no mistake about it, a PC operator's chair is an absolute must for a writer. Spend as much or as little as you choose, though £35-£55 will usually suffice to secure a swivel chair with castors, two arms and adjustable back. (Recently Netto had one priced at just £20.) Do *not* contemplate saving money by continuing to use an ordinary dining or office chair. This is false economy. Writing a book involves long hours spent at your PC screen. So a proper operator's chair is just as necessary for your physical well-being as is a window with an exterior view, seven or eight hours sleep, and an intake of calories sufficient to keep the wolf from the door.

❑ A REST BREAK AWAY FROM YOUR PC AND FRESHLY BREWED TEA/COFFEE EVERY HOUR ON THE HOUR Make no mistake about this either – if you intend to ignore my advice in the matter and insist on writing your debut novel in a windowless room, sitting astride a bentwood chair, then remember you really must:

- ❍ take a rest break away from your PC and freshly-brewed tea/coffee every hour on the hour; or,
- ❍ find an optician you can trust and an orthopaedist, both, before ever you contemplate finding a publisher.

❑ DIGITAL BACK-UP/PORTABLE HARD DRIVE AND/OR PEN FLASH DRIVE/FLASH MEMORY STICK There are any number of ways of backing your work up. But whatever you write on your PC *must* be saved daily, twice daily, and/or on the half-hour. Please yourself about the frequency, just as long as the frequency of backing up your work does not exceed your last work secession at your PC. Back it up, back it up – *back your work up, or there will be tea*rs. Please note, I do not say there *may* be tears; I say: 'There *will* be tears.' Never was I so serious: back your work up or there *will* be tears.

❑ A PC PRINTER Okay, I pushed the boat out when it came to it and got myself a Hewlett Packard 1200 series LaserJet printer. There are cheaper LaserJet printers on the market, and there must be dearer ones too. But the important point is that, as a writer, you're not likely to have much need for colour. However, what you *do* need is printer speed, a facility that is certainly not available with an Inkjet printer. Even so, a LaserJet printer is not an essential, merely a preference.

❑ A BOOKCASE My counsel of perfection (please feel free to differ or to add to it as you choose) is a bookcase for all the books you should have ready to hand, namely:

- ❍ all the self-published titles recommended in Appendix 7;
- ❍ all the self-help books about writing fiction recommended in Appendix 8;
- ❍ all the reference books recommended in Appendix 9;
- ❍ all the self-help, reference and books you enjoy which you personally find indispensable.

❑ A FILE OF SOME DESCRIPTION This may be a box file, or a small filing cabinet, containing – well, let's have a look at the files I think fit to keep on hand: contact details (e-mail, telephone, postal addresses); a personal telephone directory; a personal appointments book in diary form; PC info; Public Lending Right info; photo paper; Society of Authors info; correspondence with publishers and literary agents; unfinished short stories etc. etc. etc.

SEVEN: FINDING THE RIGHT PUBLISHER FOR YOU

By this stage, hopefully, having reviewed and considered the 25 suggested specifications with regard to the self-published books in Appendix 7, you will no longer be a mere beginner when it comes to discussing the format of self-published fiction. True, different levels of personal confidence, *savoir-faire* and PC proficiency will continue to have a bearing on the situation. So, though it is now time to begin thinking about choosing the printer/publisher you think best suited to your personal needs, no commitment is to be made for the present. Never hurry, never worry are, as ever, the operative words with regard to your self-publishing aspirations. Time is only of the essence in the sense that it must be seen as being on your side as opposed to hurrying you onward towards a premature decision. You must not, whatever you do, go off (as the saying goes) half-cocked. Nobody (least of all myself) must be allowed to hurry you into your self-publishing project ill-equipped and ill-prepared. No consideration is to be permitted to supercede the limitations necessarily dictated by your personal capability, preparedness and readiness in the matter. Nobody (least of all yourself) is going to delight in a sub-standard self-published book. Therefore, nobody must be permitted to push you headlong where you would, as yet, rather not go. This is not to say you must not bite the bullet and self-publish. Far from it. Rather is it to say that, when you *do* bite the bullet and self-publish, you must feel confident enough to know that you will not be shooting yourself in the foot by so doing. So I really do think it's time to back off just a bit (as, in part, was the idea behind the two chapters preceding this one) and try to learn a little bit more about the business of self-publishing before finally getting around to making a definite decision in the matter.

How should you proceed, then?

Well, I certainly wouldn't approach a local printer at this stage in the proceedings, even if you think it's a local printer you'd prefer to deal with in the end. Every one of the POD companies listed in Appendix 6 is interested in your business and most of them, as far as I can see, feature a list of Frequently Asked Questions (FAQs). So avail yourself of this facility to begin with, contacting the company in question for any further information you may require. Certainly, I don't think you'll need to go through the entire list of 33 POD companies before a general picture of what's on offer starts to emerge together with comparative costing – and *this* will be the right time to initiate discussions with a local printer, should you care to do so.

If you log on to Spire Publishing, for instance (though this is not to say I am recommending Spire Publishing to you, merely using their website as an exemplar), you'll notice Spire provides a three-tier list of self-publishing facilities. So, it really is up to you to decide which of the services on offer you are capable of taking on personally and which of them you simply *must* buy in due to personal incapacity in respect of any of the required processes and/or, indeed, your personal preference with regard to procedure.

Speaking personally, by way of example, I really would not want to have to supply the typescript of my novel to a publisher as anything other than a Word document, whereas this may present no problem whatsoever for you. Also, something else I am personally very keen on is potential access to the person in overall charge of publishing my novel, either by telephone, e-mail or by personal visit. (Why ever not? Even Amazon will give you a call back if you request it.) You, on the other hand, may be perfectly content being restricted to e-mail contact.

Of course, one thing you will have to bear in mind, is that the more facilities you need to avail yourself of, the more it's going to cost you. Even so, according to at least one POD company I researched recently, it is perfectly feasible to publish your debut novel for as little as £30 set-up charge plus £10 per book. And so the crazy thought occurs to me that it might even be a good idea to tip up your £40 and get hold of a self-published pilot copy of *MO for personal use only* (that is to say, minus ISBN number and Barcode and any other associated expenses) so as to utilise this self-published book as a working model by means of which you will then be able to construct a much better looking book – *the* book, in fact, which you will eventually want to self-publish as your debut novel. Because, believe you me, every last little thing that is wrong with the original copy is going to stick out like a sore thumb immediately your book gets into print.

So, cheapness in the sense of genuine economy is the real strength of self-publishing via a POD company, the potential downside being that such economy is only achieved courtesy of quite intensive input on the part of the writer (e.g. supplying the typescript as a pdf document, something which a local printer or another publisher would probably consider to be part and parcel of the printer/publisher's job). But there is nothing wrong or untoward as such in commissioning a POD company to publish your self-published book, provided that:

❍ the process suits your personal requirements;
❍ you are up for and capable of undertaking any tasks that may be involved;

❍ you need somebody to market your book once it's been published.

Even so, the sad fact seems to be that, though there must be hundreds of POD companies which are tried, tested and perfectly business-like, this industry (like the car sales industry) has the potential of attracting the rogue, the chancer, the flash, the disreputable, the slick, the liar and the cheat. What do they care about your book? (The question is rhetorical, of course: because all they care about is what's in your pocket.)

So study the FAQs on the POD companies' websites very carefully indeed, utilising the 100 questions that follow. And ask yourself other questions too, such as: Are the FAQs the POD company suggests comprehensive enough for me? Do any of the answers serve only to raise other questions in my mind? Do any of the answers seem to obfuscate any issue as opposed to making matters as clear as day? Do any other questions occur to me that are not featured amongst the FAQs? If so, contact the POD company direct – by e-mail initially. Does the POD company respond? Is the response satisfactory? If you're tempted by what's on offer from any POD company or by the tenor of their response, try a telephone call to them as well. How do they respond via telephone?

I repeat, you are not quite ready to commission anybody to publish your book as yet, though, hopefully, you will be so as and when you've asked the following 100 questions a few times. And by that time you'll be ready to deal with your local printer too. For the present, though, you are fishing, trawling (if you like) through the various POD websites. You are cruising, picking and choosing, suiting yourself, *crossing off* the list any company you don't like the sound of.

DD: Don't like the *sound of*? In what way?

BK: Oh, come on, you've lived in the world. By their works shalt ye know them. Have absolutely nothing to do with the "hurry-up merchant", the snapper, the impatient, the man who's grabbing his lunch while he's talking to you on the phone, the man who sucks his teeth when you ask for a quotation, the publisher who is a lot more expensive than his competitors. Even more particularly, tie your correspondent down with the 100 questions that follow . . .

DD: 50, you mean.

BK: What?

DD: You said 100 questions, there're only 50.

BK: 50 *written* questions, you mean,

DD: Well, yeah.

BK: The other 50 questions are the same question repeated over and over and over again.

DD: Oh? What's that when it's owt, then?

BK: 'Do you charge extra for that?'

DD: Do you *what*?

BK: Do you charge *extra* for that?

DD: Ooh, er . . .

BK: Dither ye not. Never hurry, never worry. Somewhere out there, believe me, there is a consummately professional POD company or local printer who's your baby bear's porridge . . .

DD: *Eh?*

BK: A POD company or local printer who's just right for you – is not out to rip you off; and will be only too pleased to do the job you want him to do.

DD: Oh, right.

BK: Now, all you've got to do is find him by means of . . . Cue: *ragmen's trumpets a go-go – Dah-dah-dah-dhhhhhhh . . .*

50 QUESTIONS TO ASK POD COMPANIES
(AND YOUR LOCAL PRINTER)

❍ Remember to keep on asking: 'Do you charge extra for that?'

❍ 'If you see a good idea, look for a better one. Good thinking is a matter of making comparisons' Bruce Pandolfino, chess master.

1. May I submit my book to you as an A4 Word document via e-mail attachment to be typeset by yourselves? BK: *To my way of thinking, if your publisher requires you to submit your book as a*

pdf document or in Quark, he's asking you to do an integral part of the publisher's job. So it could be argued that what he's actually advertising is a printing service as opposed to a publishing service. So, don't deal with such a publisher unless, of course: a) this presents you with no problems whatsoever; and, b) it means the self-publishing process itself is going to be a whole lot cheaper than anything comparable on offer from his competitors.

2. I still use a typewriter, I'm afraid. May I submit my book to you, typewritten in A4 hard format, leaving the typesetting to you? BK: *If you still use a typewriter, your options are going to be pretty limited, so make sure you get this query out of the way early on. Also, see Appendix 12 where Limited Edition Press responds to these same questions – positively, as it happens, in this particular instance.*

3. Or, do you specify that my book must be submitted to you as a typeset pdf document? BK: *See Question 1 above. Personally, I consider typesetting to be the printer/publisher's job, I want my publisher to be willing to afford me this professional service and, as is the way with professional service, I am, of course, prepared to pay for the privilege.*

4. What is the minimum number of copies I must order from you as a first print run? BK: *This is where POD companies may win out. On the other hand, there is no way 25-50 copies (if quoted as a minimum number) is going to entail your storing them under the bed. In my experience they'll take up space equivalent to three or four shoeboxes.*

5. Should I decide to place an order with you, how long will it be before the books are delivered to my door? *BK: You'll find most POD companies have very competitive delivery dates – that is to say, a few weeks, if not days.*

6. Are you willing to publish the size of book I prefer – e.g. A5-sized; A6; Royale (B5), A4? BK: *Check this carefully if it happens to be a particular requirement, though see, too, my suggested specifications for self-published fiction.*

7. May I choose the paper I prefer – white bond or bookwove? BK: *Fair comment. But remember bookwove: a) may be more expensive than white bond; and, b) is more suitable to print-runs in excess of 250-300 copies. That is to say, to litho rather than digital printing.*

8. If I were to opt for bookwove, what quality would it be? BK: *If you require bookwove, don't settle for any old rubbish. Some bookwove is unsightly, with a greyish and/or yellowish cast; some is more like card. Try to arrange for you and your publisher to have sight of the precise quality (and, incidentally, the size of book) you prefer by presenting him (if you must) with a paperback copy of* Doing Our Bit *by Martin Purdy and Ian Dawson, say, or (off the top of my head) any paperback written by Michael Connelly.*

9. I know the text of the book will be justified. But, should the narrative occasionally require the text to be centred – or perhaps aligned differently to right or left, would you be able to accommodate these variations? BK: *Make sure the answer to this question is an unequivocal 'Yes!' There are loads of good publishers who want your business, so why would you want to deal with an awkward cuss?*

10. Do you have a selection of cover artwork from which I may make a selection? BK: *I hope so: hope, too, that it's not too bland.*

11. Would you be prepared to accept a photograph of my own for cover artwork? BK: *Watch out for the publishers who crank the costs up quite unreasonably at this point — and those who don't.*

12. Do extra charges apply if I opt for a full colour book cover? BK: *This is certainly, a reasonable expectation.*

13. May I use an imprint of my own? BK: *Your local printer will naturally permit this; certain POD companies will too.*

14. If I use your company imprint, do I still retain my copyright and international rights in every respect? BK: *Again there should*

be no problem with your local printer, and some POD companies go out of their way to specify they concur. If not, make a specific enquiry regarding copyright, and make quite sure you understand the answer.

15. What written assurance, warranty or guarantee will I have with regard to copyright? BK: *An eminently reasonable question, it seems to me.*

16. How much will it cost me for the first print run? BK: *See* Appendix 12 *where you'll find my publisher supplies his personal responses to these 50 questions – and further suggests 10 further details (see below) which it will be necessary to supply to a prospective publisher when enquiring about costs* . . . Here's what Limited Edition Press says: 'I thought it might be helpful for you to provide your readers with some of the details a publisher needs to know before a quotation may be supplied. By way of example, when an author requiring details of my publishing services approaches me, I always ask him to provide answers to the following questions . . .'

- 🕮 In which format will you be submitting the book?
- 🕮 How many words are there in your book?
- 🕮 How many illustrations/photos are there in your book, if any?
- 🕮 What size would you like your book to be? (A4, A5 or some other size)
- 🕮 What colour cover would you like?
- 🕮 Would you prefer hardback or paperback?
- 🕮 Would you like a laminated cover (gloss or matt)?
- 🕮 Do you have an illustration or a photo you'd like to appear on the cover?
- 🕮 How many copies would you like to order?
- 🕮 Finally, where do you want the finished books delivered?

Then further discussion via telephone is usually necessary.'

NOTE The "open book" is a Wingding symbol used as a trademark by Limited Edition Press.

17. How long will it be before the books will be delivered to my door? BK: *Never hurry, never worry, A few days, a few weeks are the norm.*

18. If I were to order a few thousand copies, say, would the cost per copy be more advantageous to me? BK: *I would certainly expect the item cost to decrease in line with an increasing number of books ordered. So the real question is: 'What are the magic numbers relating to decreasing item cost?*

19. Do the quoted costs include the cost of delivery? BK: *Make sure you ask this question since it has a direct bearing upon the item cost.*

20. Do you then retain the digital file of my book in the event of my requiring further print runs? BK: *Whether they do or they don't, your real concern is copyright and unauthorised print runs.*

21. Will I be committed to a long-term tie-in of some kind? BK: *Hopefully not, because you may not like the finished product.*

22. Should I be dissatisfied for any reason, may I go elsewhere for future print-runs? BK: *Hopefully yes, because you may find a better deal elsewhere.*

23. Will the cost of a second print run be any cheaper? BK: *Again, hopefully yes, though this may not be the case with a POD company where the first print run was done at a rock-bottom price. But by this time you'll surely be getting a better idea about costing.*

24. If I order a second (third, fourth) print run, how long will it be before it is delivered to my door? BK: *Never hurry, never worry. See previous comments.*

25. Will you let me have a recent sample of your work free-of-charge? BK: *I don't see why not if the cost of the job warrants it.* (N.B. *Pay for a book or get it free, but never ever deal with any printer or publisher who refuses to supply you (free, or for a stated fee) with a recent sample of his work).*

26. May I arrange to purchase a recent sample of your work? BK: *See above.*

27. May I telephone you to discuss things from time to time? BK: *You may be happy as Larry conversing exclusively via e-mail, I personally feel much happier given telephone contact – and personal access too, should this be required. This is not to specify a right way or a wrong way of doing things, just a right way and a wrong way for me.*

28. May I pop into the office or meet up with you to iron out any problems that may arise? BK: *I would much prefer this facility, – and I am quite prepared to meet up by appointment.*

29. Will my requirements be attended to throughout by a named member of staff? BK: *It is certainly preferable to deal, as I do, one on one. A personal choice only.*

30. Will I at any time see a proof copy of the book you propose to publish so that I may proof-read it, amending or correcting it where required? BK: *I see A5 proof copies on two occasions – first of all, when they are being prepared for the printer; secondly, before the finished article goes off to the printer. In the first instance, I proof-read the copy carefully, amending where necessary; in the second, no amendments should be necessary, though a few marginal amendments are still possible.*

31. On how many occasions will I be sent a proof copy for inspection? BK: *Make sure you know how many times your publisher will provide you with proof copies – and the extent to which you may amend the text free-of-charge.*

32. Will you be prepared to advise me about a suitable retail price for the book? BK: *This is not absolutely necessary, though it may prove helpful to receive some input. Check out the paperback novels in the bookshops, though you may need to ask a bit more due to costs.*

33. Do you provide the necessary ISBN number? BK: *Yes or no? This is a job that is quite easily effected by you personally, should*

need arise. However: a) the provision of an ISBN number for every book published for re-sale is a legal requirement in the UK, and, b) unless your book has an ISBN number, you will not be able to sell it via Amazon or the other bookshops.

34. May I provide my own ISBN number? BK: *A sure-fire way of protecting your copyright.*

35. Do you provide a Barcode with the book? BK: *Yes or no? This, again, is a job that is quite easily effected personally. It's not a legal requirement, but book shop sales points prefer a Barcode.*

36. Do you attend to all requirements under the Legal Deposit Scheme? BK: *Yes or no? Again, this is a job that is quite easily effected by you personally, should need arise. N.B. It is a legal requirement in the UK. (See below.)*

37. Will you provide me with a certain number of author copies of the book? BK: *If the answer is in the affirmative, you may depend upon it that you are dealing with: a) a vanity publisher; or, b) a POD company or printer who intends to charge you more than the job is worth. Shysters like this will easily be able to afford to provide you with author copies of your book whilst their competitors are struggling to fulfil your order at an honest price.*

38. Will you register the book with Nielsen BookData? BK: *Yes or no? This is another job that is easily effected personally.* [See Chapter 11.] *N.B. Books not registered with Nielsen BookData will never be picked up by Amazon or the other book shops.*

39. Will you list a) the book; b) details about the content of the book; and an image of the front cover of the book on Amazon? BK: *Amazon gets details of books via Nielsen Bookdata, though your publisher may provide Amazon with further details about the book (e.g. reviews, readers' comments) and with an image of the cover illustration. But you may do these things on your own behalf immediately Amazon picks up the book title from Nielsen BookData.*

40. Once the book is published, will you then distribute it on my behalf? BK: *Some publishers distribute your book once they've published it; others (e.g. Limited Edition Press) do not. So, if your publisher also acts as your distributor it must have answered: 'Yes' to Questions 33, 35, 36, 38, 39 and to those aspects of Question 40 which apply. By contrast, Limited Edition Press makes its own response in Appendix 12.*

41. Do you distribute the book via Gardners, Bertrams and Askews? BK: *Given that the publisher is also your distributor and has fulfilled all the requirements mentioned in Question 40, the answer will be 'Yes'. In reality all this means is that the wholesalers Gardners, Bertrams and Askews may choose to access your book via the wholesaler; it does not mean your distributor will distribute the book to them in any proactive sense of the word. Meanwhile, in the case of a publisher who does not also act as your distributor (e.g. Limited Edition Press), the answer will be 'No'.*

42. Do you make the book available to all the major bookshops and the independents? BK: *See Question 41. The same answer applies.*

43. So, is it the case that you will sell the book on and pay me royalties? BK: *When your book sells (that is to say, as and when somebody applies to your distributor to order a copy) royalties will be payable.*

44. How much will the royalties amount to per book? BK: *Make sure you get a precise figure.*

45. How and when will royalties be paid to me? BK: *Make sure you tie your distributor down in this respect.*

46. Does the fact that you distribute the book prevent my contacting the various bookshops and public libraries and asking them to stock my book? BK: *No, but they won't be able to order from you; they'll go direct to the publisher.*

47. Will the various bookshops and public libraries then send their book orders to you, the distributor, directly? BK: *Yes.*

48. Does the fact that you distribute the book prevent my selling the book at a book launch, presentations and to friends and acquaintances? BK: *No. You'll just need to buy the books in first – at a discount rate, of course.*

49. How and when may I pay you once I commission the first print run? BK: *They won't be too shy to tell you.*

50. How much will it cost me to commission a print run of 5,000 copies, say? BK: *There are only two possible answers to this question, the right answer and a wrong one – and the right answer will be in the form of another question. Because THE RIGHT ANSWER, as that good man and true, my publisher at Limited Edition Press (and, hopefully, others like him), would have it is this:*

'Are you quite sure you can sell 5,000 books?'

Meanwhile, THE WRONG ANSWER is quick mention of a sum of money running into several thousands of pounds, which must NOT (I do sincerely hope) bring 5,000 copies of your book to your front door a few weeks hence, but Bombardier Billy Wells instead – and immediately, hammering a resounding warning note on J Arthur Rank's gong.

Let me be perfectly frank (though I hasten to add that this is just my personal gut feeling in the matter), POD companies make me feel uneasy – and the more FAQs POD companies throw at me, the more uneasy do I feel. And this despite the fact that I know loads of people who have been perfectly happy in their dealings with POD companies. Still the feeling persists, and I just can't help it – and I really do think it's very much tied up with the fact that, apart from e-mail access, there is usually (though there may well be POD company exceptions to this rule) . . . there is usually no way the customer may contact a specific individual at a POD company for explanation of specific points.

Why hide, I wonder. Why distance oneself from the customer? I know umpteen man-hours can be wasted on the telephone, but come *on*! Inaccessibility, to my way of thinking, is redolent of dishonesty and/or fast-dealing tricky-dickery. I mean to say, there is only so much readers are able to understand from reading a FAQ and its answer. And there must surely come a point when, as a customer with limited experience of self-publishing, you will need someone to talk to. And in the absence of any facility whereby I may communicate by telephone and/or in person, the more I become confused – and, worse still, *wary* of any company, POD or otherwise, which seeks to do business this way.

Permit me to explain myself thus.

Yesterday, in servicing my car, I needed to know the engine oil capacity. Now, the manufacturer's handbook supplies no less than 26 pages, headed "Capacities and specifications", and the Index to the handbook indicates that the details I required relating to "Engine Oil" were to be found on pages 171-172, and 193. Sadly, this was not, in fact, the case: the information I required (a capacity of 5.6 litres, including oil filter, as it happens) was located on page 95 – 11 pages into the 26 pages dealing with "Capacities and specifications" and *nowhere* listed in the Index.

Puzzlement naturally ensued, accompanied by cynical wonderment. Why would a major car manufacturer be so imprecise with such an important matter? Could it really be accidental? Could it really be sheer carelessness at national level? Or was it deliberate? Why deliberate? Well, without oil (to speak crudely) engine break, and when engine break, work is created for the manufacturer's agent. That is to say, the manufacturer's original mistake (deliberate or not) tends to create a situation where more money than expected will need to be expended by the unwary customer.

Similarly, I just cannot help being suspicious of POD companies' stock answers to FAQs. Is what the company tells me *really* the case? (For example, is what they boast of doing out of the kindness of their hearts, actually a legal requirement incumbent upon them as the publisher?) Is what the company tells me in the FAQs the full story? Or will extra costs ensue without my prior knowledge? And so on. All I'm saying is this: the more a POD company seeks to distance itself from the customer, the more do I require reassurance about fair dealing and best practice.

Now, I am not for one moment seeking to imply that books ordered from a non-communicative POD company will not turn up, or will not turn up when expected. However, I am worried that, when they do turn up, such books may (due to this policy of non-communication) turn out to be somehow different from what you, the customer, expected.

By way of further example, let us consider an example from one of my earliest (read, *gormless*) attempts at DIY. "Sand down between coats when dry", said the instruction on the gloss paint tin. Now, given access to somebody with whom I might have conferred, I might not have made the mistake of sanding down to such an extent between coats that I cut back to untreated wood.

So what's the alternative? Well, though I would sincerely hope you find a POD company that suits you (because it certainly seems to be the cheapest route to self-publishing), I cannot in all honesty say it's the route I would personally choose from preference. But that's me – and, as I've said all along, when it comes to self-publishing, *you* must please *yourself* from first to last. I, personally, would want to use a local printer, I think – or, use, as I did, someone like Limited Edition Press: a sort of halfway house, as it were, in that Limited Edition Press will iron out all the problems associated with self-publishing your book, from typesetting it to commissioning a publisher to do the job according to agreed specifications. [See Appendix 12.] Of course, the problem with my solution to the problem is the very different start-up cost. So, you now have three additional problems to consider prior to commissioning the first print run of your book:

- ❑ How would you raise the money to pay for the much higher start-up costs, should you want to commission a local printer or somebody like Limited Edition Press to self-publish your book?
- ❑ What retail price should you ask for your book?
- ❑ How many copies should you commission for a first print-run?

Something I will never be able to understand if I live to be a hundred is how some people don't mind blowing a shed load of money on beefburgers, pizzas, candy floss and fairground rides, then complain bitterly about the undertaker's bill when Grandma passes away – as though this is not money well-spent on a professional service, and use of the family estate car instead of a hearse and perhaps diving into the local chip shop for the funeral breakfast might represent a feasible – or, indeed, a civilised alternative.

Similarly, when it comes to self-publishing, why on earth (despite a lifetime of experience to the contrary) would anyone expect the cheapest to be the best – or even of acceptable quality. You get what you pay for, as you very well know, and though you must always be on your guard against the out-and-out rip-off merchants, it surely stands to reason that your local printer is probably going to bill you at least as much as your local painter and decorator will bill you for painting the house.

So permit me, if you will, to give you some indication of what a local printer is going to charge you by referring you to my own experience in respect of the first print-run of *Every Street in Manchester*, which (to use a ball park figure, as opposed to resurrecting the actual invoice from my files) was quoted at approximately (very approximately) £650 for 50 copies of the book, delivered to my home address.

Okay, this was a quotation substantially in excess of that quoted by the cheapest POD company I'd quizzed to date. (£40, remember, though, admittedly, with only one copy of your book in the equation.) Nevertheless, it was a quotation infinitely preferable from my personal perspective (remember, too) in that Limited Edition Press was going to assist me in so many ways in which the POD company in question perceived no need or advantage. In other words, I supplied Limited Edition Press with a Word document and ended up with 50 published copies of my book in my hand. Besides, if you can't please yourself, whom can you please?

Even so, how was I going to meet this bill? Because, I could not in all conscience dip willy-nilly into what remained in the family coffers after the thieving taxman had had his way with them. And certainly not to the tune of £650 or so. And neither may you, I don't suppose (double negatively), there being other family members having claims of greater, lesser or equal importance upon the family loot at any particular point in time. In other words, personal expenditure of such magnitude (i.e. £650 or so for 50 self-published books) simply had to be justified and/or derived from other sources. (Incidentally, I'm not whinging about this: it's a discipline I joyfully embrace. Well, no – not "joyfully", but *willingly*, certainly. Because I really do believe in the need to justify major expenditure from jointly-held accounts. Quite apart from any other consideration, I think it sharpens the mind.)

I repeat . . . How was I going to meet this bill?

Maybe I could have stayed away from the pub six nights out of seven, saving – what? – £15 per session, at which rate, say (6+ weeks of non-boozing: 44 sessions), would have seen the necessary £650 in my pocket, not to mention a much slimmer photographic portrait on the inside back cover of my book.

But I had already sworn off those six sessions per week (that is to say, catching last orders down the Old David's, Middleton) during a previous burst of personal expenditure. So, here's what I resolved to do instead in order to make good the bulk of that £650 shortfall: I took a long hard look at my library of books – a good collection, comprising (in addition to non-fiction) half as many fiction titles as are at present contained in Manchester's new North City Library, and I asked myself this question: 'Which of these books am I never going to read again? And which of them am I never going to get around to reading in the first place?'

Then, girding up my loins, so to speak, I logged on to Amazon Marketplace. (N.B. Do this in any case, because you're going to need Amazon Marketplace soon enough to help you sell your self-published book around the world.) And I supplied Amazon Marketplace with the details they required (i.e. bank account number etc.) whereupon (Amazon does *all* the work very efficiently and trustworthily, too – including the banking) I raised as much as £400 from the sale of "unwanted" books. (I speak figuratively: of course, I certainly wanted those books; but I wanted my own self-published book even more.)

Perhaps 25% of this booty went in postal costs, so I still had a sub-total of £300 left in the kitty – at which point (scotch whisky drowned with soda being my tipple nowadays – a stinger, or, more correctly, *stengah*) I issued my five kids with strict instructions regarding Father's Day, birthday and Christmas: specifically, pint bottles of whisky X 3 X 5 equals 15 bottles of whisky p.a. equals £150 minimum to add to the £300 already in my sky. Grand total raised: £450.

The shortfall of £200 was more easily made up from other economies and I was on my way. So perhaps readers should be prepared to do something similar (or different).

With regard to selling books via Amazon Marketplace:

- you will, in any case, shortly need access to Amazon Marketplace in order to sell your own self-published book around the world (see below); and

- any book you sell at this stage, if too badly missed, may usually be retrieved via Amazon Marketplace and/or www.abebooks.co.uk .

Furthermore, you may perhaps take comfort from the fact that I have only ever given one book a second thought since I sold it. This was *Three Lives for Mississippi* by William Bradford Huie, which went to a good home in Scotland. It's a great book by a great journalist. This first edition of the book, with a publication date to match, was uncannily redolent of the unconscionable racial tensions in the American Deep South during the 1960s, William Bradford Huie being no stranger to heroic reportage above and beyond the call of duty. Once upon a time, 'tis said, he assumed a role as Benjamin "Bugsy" Siegel's long-term butler so as to get an exclusive gangster-based exclusive.

Ooh, er, you may well say.

What retail price should you put on your book? Let's face it, the self-published author is in a no-win situation whatever he does. Most paperback novels at the time of writing retail at £6.99. So, if you charge any more than £6.99 for your book, there is bound to be customer resistance to sales. But if you retail your book @ £6.99 and you've bought in a first run of only 50 copies at a cost of approx. £650, you will be on a loser even before the book shop or wholesaler takes its commission on sales. In other words you'll be making a loss before you start, and not a profit. And, if you don't make a profit, you run the risk of having HM Inspector of Taxes put the boot in by treating you as a hobbyist rather than a working author. Consequently, HM Inspector of Taxes may not permit you to set your expenditure against income.

DD: *Jeesh!* Bugsy Siegel was a puddy-tat by comparison!

BK: I couldn't possibly comment.

DD: Listen, suppose I buy in a few thousands copies for the first run. That'd fetch the item cost right down, wouldn't it?

BK: Well, yes, it would. But apart from the difficulty you'd have storing thousands of books, just remember what Limited Edition Press has to say [Appendix 12] in answer to Question 18 of my questionnaire . . .

> 18. If I were to order a few thousand copies, say, would the cost per copy be more advantageous to me? LEP: *Yes, but don't order more than you know you can sell.*

DD: Ooh, er . . . So, how should I proceed? I mean, is there nobody amongst the self-published authors you know who ever orders thousands of copies.

BK: Well, yes, there are. Three of them, to be honest – well, four really. Brian Hughes, MBE always orders in quantity; Fr Brian Seale ordered quantity as a first print-run; and Martin Purdy and Ian Dawson made sure they ordered quantity for the first print-run of *Doing Our Bit*.

DD: What do you call quantity?

BK: Anything in four figures . . . 1,000, 1,500, 2,000, 3,000.

DD: So, how do *they* get away with it? I mean, they don't have books left on their hands, do they?

BK: No, they don't. Well, eventually they don't?

DD: There you go then

BK: Yes, but those authors all have access to a public and they know it. So, they're pretty confident from the start that they'll be able to shift a shed load of books, knowing a certain number of sales are guaranteed.

DD: *Guaranteed?*

BK: Well, sort of. You see, Brian Hughes is well-known in boxing circles at home and abroad; and the Salford Diocesan Almanac lists the population of Fr Seale's parish as 1,500 strong. So they aren't going to let him down, are they? Meanwhile, Martin Purdy and Ian Dawson have extensive press connections in the Greater Manchester area, so they're bound to get a certain number of sales outlets and book reviews, too, such as, by way of example, a review in the *Manchester Evening News* . . .

DD: That's nice.

BK: I couldn't possibly comment, having never experienced such.

DD: Even so.

BK: What?

DD: Must be nice, that – a review in the regional press.

BK: Didn't do Billy Hopkins any harm: I know that.

DD: But there'll be nowt down for my book from that quarter for my book, you reckon.

BK: It's anybody's guess. Which is why the best way to proceed as a new writer, with no prospect of guaranteed sales or book reviews, is to order a first print run of 50 copies, say (50 copies will be no problem, believe me: don't go for 25, and ask a bit more than £6.99 for your retail price. My books retail @ £14.99 each – not ideal, I know; but the wrong side of HM Inspector of Taxes would be even less ideal.

DD: He'd probably make you an offer you can't refuse.

BK: Ooh, er . . .

DD: That's my line.

BK: Mine too where HM Inspector's concerned. But if your book sells, you can always build on your order for the second print run, the third and so on, looking for an average whole-sale price over twelve months, say. A word of warning, though. Should your first print run of 50 copies sell out overnight, leaving thousands of potential buyers knocking on your door . . .

DD: Yeah, like as if.

BK: Well, I, personally, had to build up to 300 copies pretty quickly . . .

DD: Really?

BK: Yeah, and, as I say, if you sell your first print run of 50 copies and you then want to order more books, you won't be allowed to order a second print run of 1,000, say. Nope, your printer will insist you double up on your original order until you eventually achieve a figure of 1,000, supposing it's 1,000 you want. So, if you've had 50 copies already, you can then order 100; and when you've had 100, you can order 200 – and so on.

DD: Ooh, er . . .

BK: Now, *cheer* up, because there are a couple of bits of good news about small print-runs of 50 copies or so.

DD: Like what, for instance?

BK: Well, in the first place they're dead easy to store; and, secondly, they soon run out. By which I mean to say that if there are any errors in the text that have been overlooked by the proof-reader, you can easily correct them before the next print-run goes out. I mean to say, imagine being stuck with a print-run of 10,000 or even 2,000 copies, say (however economically-priced they are) if those same copies contain several glaring errors.

DD: Right. So, it's the proof-reader's job to sort it, is it? Who's the proof-reader when he's owt?

BK: You are in the main.

DD: Ooh, er . . .

BK: Just for once, you do right to say, '*Ooh, er*', my friend. Because proof-reading is one of the trickiest jobs in the entire self-publishing shebang.

DD: Ooh, er . . .

EIGHT: PROOF-READING

Subsequent to your detailed perusal of the FAQs of umpteen POD companies, in addition to being armed with the 50+ questions suggested to you in the previous chapter (not to mention the previously-listed 25 specifications in respect of self-published fiction), you should now know the POD company or local printer with whom you intend to self-publish your debut novel. If so, congratulations are in order – which is not to say, of course, that all the hard work is behind you at last. Because the most difficult job you will need to do once you've selected the publisher you propose to entrust with your work is the actual proof-reading of the document itself. Furthermore, you will have to proof-read it as many as three times perhaps before ever your self-published book sees the light of day.

First of all, there will be the extra careful proof-reading of the document to be done before ever you send your work off to the publisher. Then, you will be called upon to read it again (perhaps in hard format) once your publisher has got it ready for the printer – and you may even get a *third* bite of the cherry if your publisher gives you (as does mine, I'm glad to say) sight in hard format of the final document prior to directing the publisher to go ahead. Each of these stages is to be dealt with in marginally different ways, amendments to the document being permissible to whatever degree is permitted by your publisher at each stage. And believe you me, the job is a real chore, perhaps the most difficult chore you will have come across since first putting pen to paper.

Why so?

Well, the problem is that proof-reading is such a multi-faceted task when linked to a personal re-reading, and this is why many writers look to a professional proof reader to do the job for them. This would cost, of course. So, some writers look to their nearest and dearest to wield the red pen. Others (myself amongst them when it came to *Manchester Kiss*), may be able to rely upon their publisher in the matter. (Prior to that, 75% of *Every Street in Manchester* being in a Manchester vernacular, I had felt loath to farm it out for proof-reading of any kind. A mistake on my part, I now think.) You see, the problem in the main when it comes to a personal proof-reading of your debut novel is that you need to read it for a wide variety of reasons, each of which requires a different reading speed and type of reading skill. For instance, checking punctuation, grammar, spellings, and syntax requires a "clinically" slower, stop/go type of reading skill, whereas looking to get a sense of the narrative voice or of the pace and flow of the story requires an entirely different kind of continuous reading technique. Also, you will invariably find yourself setting off to do one job (checking spellings and punctuation, say) and ending up doing another (reading it as a story, say). And to make matters even worse, because you wrote the Thing, you'll know every word that's coming in a sense. So there'll be a tendency to glide over errors in dire need of correction because you, being the very person who made a mess of things the first time around, may very easily make a mess of things once again.

So, how should you tackle this problem? Because tackle it you must, the reason being that immediately your book is in print, *any* and *every* mistake in it will stand out like the House that Jack Built in a child's pop-up story book, the only difference being that a child's pop-up story book does not simultaneously feature a Back Street Bario Mariachi Band playing *The March of the Gladiators* on mildewed trumpets, whereas (if you get things wrong) your error-riddled *major opus* will certainly seem as if it is doing so – stereophonically, woefully out of tune, and at top blast, too.

Yep, it really will feel as bad as this, if you get it wrong, believe me.

So, the very first rule of the game is that you must slow the process right down. I mean to say, what's the hurry exactly? Two thousand years of European civilisation have stumped along quite nicely without your masterpiece to inform or amuse it. So the odds are we'll get along without it quite nicely for another week or two. Also, your publisher has only been tentatively approached at this stage, so he's not cracking the whip as yet. (At least I hope he isn't, or he's not the boy for you.) So, it's obviously down to you. That is to say, you've finished your debut novel, and now you just can't wait to foist it on to an unsuspecting public. Well, I am sorry to disabuse you, but the proof-reading simply *must* be done. So you really must slow everything right down to STOP. (Later, once your book is in print, you'll be glad you did.) You heard me: STOP. You're the only one who's trying to rush the process, so stop – S-T-O-P: STOP.

Now, if by any chance you were the poet Vergil – P. Virglius Maro, to list him formally – author of the Aeneid and brown-noser to the Julian (Julius Caesar's) family (and, thank God, you're not, by the way, since his Homeric similes no longer cut the mustard, to mangle rather than mix metaphors) – if you were the poet Vergil, by any chance, you would (it has been said of him) put your *major opus* away for nine long years prior to attempting to proof-read it. But that's far too long, I fully agree, before you drop cork-legged at the news. Even so, the *principle* is sound. So, what's best for you personally to do at this point? Well, I would suggest the following:

1. Adjourn to the Costa (or some such) and do anything and everything but proof-read your novel. And take as long as you like (or can afford) about it too – a week, a fortnight, a month, a year. Whatever you do, take at least a fortnight before the first proof read – even if the entire fortnight is perforce spent impecuniously in your greenhouse or garden shed.

2. Then create a spare copy of your 11pt TNR document in 16 pt TNR and save it separately.

3. Having saved the spare copy in 16pt TNR text, run it off in hard format and re-read the entire document correcting and highlighting as you go. And, finally:

4. Refer to your original 11pt TNR document, amending it according to the corrections to the spare document in hard format, and Save As.

5. Then run through the document again, should you care to.

Because this is the document you will be referring to your publisher.

'YIKES!' you say?

Okay, do nowt – and live to regret it. Because, the extent to which you now short-cut the proof-reading process will invariably be in direct ratio to the extent to which you will immediately perceive all those errors of grammar, spelling, punctuation, syntax etc. in your self-published book immediately it comes off the press.

It gets worse, by the way.

Once you've done the initial proof-reading and are readying yourself for the off (probably when you are about to initiate the transmission of your document to your chosen publisher), you will in all likelihood contract a dose of what Ernest Hemingway used to refer to as 'The Artist's Reward'. This is a really horrible feeling, debilitating as Montezuma's Revenge, though without the side effects. And, in this rare moment of unparalleled perspicacity, dear reader, everything you've worked for, written, re-written and achieved over the past six, nine, twelve months – all this will be perceived by you, its creator, to amount to nothing more than a crock of [BLEEP – Ed.]. Pray take heart when so afflicted. Because you will only feel this way if your work has some merit, however minimal. Because it would never occur to a [BLEEP – Ed.]-writer that his work might be anything other than the real McCoy.

Still, onwards and (hopefully) upwards. Because, having recruited your chosen publisher and given him the final go-ahead, you will have, as I've said, one or even two further proof-readings still to do.

Things are really going to take a bit of getting used to if and when you receive the document in hard format from the publisher. Because the hard format document you last worked upon will now be in A5, not A4 – and the page numbers will now read consecutively, inclusive of blank pages. So make careful and extensive use of all sections of *Write It Self-Publish It Sell It* that refer to this [Appendix 11 *et al.*], paying particular attention, by referring to your A4 hard format document *alongside* the A5 hard format document from your publisher, to the beginning and end of each A5 page, ensuring none of the text is missing. This is the main point of the exercise really. However, there may be some adjustments needed to accommodate spacing and such which may not have made the transfer from A4 to A5 too well. For example, the odd asterisk may be required at the (different A5) end or beginning of a page; similarly, where asterisks were perhaps required in the A4 document, they may now need erasing in the A5 document.

Again, the counsel of perfection is to take time out and read it all again. Time is of the essence – but only in the sense that you really must take time out to attend to all these things as opposed to rushing them in order to see your name in print, then perhaps rueing the fact that, due to rushing the proof-reading, your name now accompanies more mistakes than you've ever previously noticed between the covers of a book – and wishing in vain that you had taken the trouble to do the proof-reading properly when you had the chance to do it. For instance, do not expect your publisher to permit you to re-write whole swathes of text at the last moment. The last moment, as I call it, is for minimal tweakings to the document. You really ought to have made any amendments whilst you still had the chance to make them. That is to say, before ever you first transmitted your A4 document to your chosen publisher. Having said this, all may not be lost even now. That is to say, your publisher may still permit you to make changes to the text and, by the same token, of course, he may well decide to bill you for making them.

NINE: TAKING DELIVERY OF YOUR FIRST PRINT RUN

This is the day that the Lord hath made! The day scheduled (nay, *ordained*) for the 50-strong first print-run of your self-published book to be delivered to your front door, and you . . . you have been up since first light, have you not?

Stanley knife to hand, new blade at the action end, a suitable table top storage space abaft, you are in your starting-blocks, as it were, as dawn turns to day, to mid-morning, to noon, to afternoon, to . . . well, to whenever that call of nature that's been nagging you since you imbibed a Cup-A-Soup at noon becomes insistent enough to necessitate a retreat to your *ensuite*, whereupon, as if on a given signal, the carrier's two-ton truck screeches to a halt in the street outside your front door and it is She Who Has the Casting Vote At Your Present Address who is called upon to sign for *your* delivery (signature; capitals too) and *wrestle* the Thing (or, more specifically) 50 cardboard-encased copies of the Thing within your portals.

Jeesh!

Thus, does a sack truck go to top position on your weekly shopping list. But at least they're here. So – *hup!* – on to the table top storage space with them, *en garde* with the Stanley knife. *Et voila*: one gaping rectangular box containing two smaller rectangular boxes – and so, out with them, on to the table top with them, and away with the outer container. Two D'Artagnan-like slashes to the tops of each smaller box, a tug at the parcel tape, and – *lo!* – the golden hoard greets your eyes.

Heaven!

First comes the head count: 50 books were ordered; have 50 turned up? Yep, 50 books, all present and correct. Well, er, they're present, of course – but you simply cannot say correct until you've perused them. Because what you cannot be expected to suspect as yet, tyro self-publisher that you are, is that every publisher in the land is required, under an innovative job creation scheme funded by central government ('tis also suspected), to employ a hobgoblin below stairs – a Printer's Devil, as it were, and it is the Printer's Devil's task to assume full responsibility for providing each and every customer with his fair share of books, the pages and/or covers of which are perforce:

❍ back-to-front;
❍ upside down;
❍ creased, ripped or otherwise mutilated in upwards of a dozen different ways; or

- illegible on account of dog fat-impregnation of print rollers *et al.*; and/or
- creased consequent upon their having been utilised as vertical packing in transit.

So, now comes the very necessary careful perusal of which I spoke, and which is, of course, very easily achievable with a print-run of only fifty books. Check for all the aforementioned major faults and put to one side any books which have obviously been in receipt of the Printer's Devil's especial attention. The publisher must be told about these and the shortfall must be made good.

With regard to other faults, if any, proceed in a businesslike manner. Books with major faults, or which reveal major departure from your mutual agreement, must be listed and discussed (e.g. an incorrect image to the front cover; the wrong colour to the front cover; text other than the TNR you specified). Obviously these are never acceptable. But a missing full stop on page 223, for instance – well, perhaps you really ought to settle for such an omission as evidence of your continuing goodwill.

Suppose, however, you and your publisher are in agreement that, say, five books in your 50-strong order are not up to specification for any reason, then there are various options open to you:

- you may certainly demand that 5 replacement books are forwarded at the publisher's expense, in which case,

- the publisher may permit you to keep the 5 faulty books so as to save himself the cost of p&p that would be involved in returning the books to HQ;

- he may request that you send the faulty books back at his expense; in which case:

- you might consider offering the publisher a knock-down price for the 5 books, knowing as you do so that the prospect of the p&p expenses he would incur in recalling the books lends strength to your arm;

- and the publisher may well agree, or may ask for a slightly higher price, or refuse point blank. But whatever happens, do not pay more than a pound or two for sub-standard stock.

Why ever would you want or need substandard books in the first place?

To be honest, you *don't* want them? But, if you don't take them, they'll only be binned or pulped, and then they'll do you no good at all. But substandard books may sometimes be put to good use, dependent upon how substandard they are. They'll never be put on sale, of course, except at ridiculous knock-down prices. But from time to time I have managed to put substandard books to good use – well, certainly to better use than binning them or pulping them. For instance, substandard copies are eminently suitable to being:

- utilised as a working copy, should you perhaps be tempted to proof-read further;
- given to an impecunious student relation, say, should he express an interest in your work;
- donated to a charity (they're always at the door, and you surely have your own favourites amongst them);
- given as a bonus, say, to a buyer who perhaps makes multiple personal purchases from you;
- left in the hotel library at the end of your holiday on the Costa.

NOTE None of the above observations about substandard stock is to say you should be less than honest with your publisher. If, notwithstanding the ministrations of the Printer's Devil, your delivery proves to be all present and correct, you should be just as eager to convey this fact to your publisher as soon as possible.

Incidentally, the very first copy of your books to be disposed of after the stock count should be dealt with in the following way and on the same day the delivery turns up:

- place it in a Jiffy bag addressed to yourself at your home address and

- mail it from the local post office, explaining that you require the envelope to be clearly postmarked and also a Certificate of Posting bearing the date and location of posting. Recorded delivery is advisable but optional.
- Then, when the envelope is subsequently delivered to your home address, file it away, unopened and safely, complete with the certificate of posting.

This is the generally accepted means of further protecting your copyright, and the local post office personnel will not think you've lost your marbles. They have seen it all before. But do make quite sure you protect yourself in this way. Because, despite the widespread, oh-so-confident, mutually back-slapping reassurances of broadsheet-approved literary types who come out of the woodwork whenever the question of suspected plagiarism by one of their number is mooted in the press, stuff *happens*. This is not to say I necessarily believe another writer of my acquaintance who claims to have first suggested the idea of a major TV comedy series for which somebody else received the credit; nevertheless I am aware that things like this *can* happen. For instance, what I can say, and quite categorically at that, is that a certain famous author, now deceased, once helped himself to a literary device of my own. Oh, he can retain his anonymity, for what it's worth, just as his book retains the device, for what that's worth. Because I binned the novel which featured the device thirty years ago, immediately it was rejected by said famous author's literary agent. Besides, it wasn't much of anything really – a passing reference to a certain painting by a certain painter in a certain narrative situation in a certain location subsequent to a particular eventuality. Even so, it was *my* device, and the professionally bankrupt hack pinched it for his own purposes. As luck would have it, I have never since felt the need of that particular literary device. But, yeah – stuff *happens*. You have been warned: so be careful.

By the same token, always make sure you seek permission to quote another author's work (for an epigraph, say); and, should permission be granted, ensure too that you publish a suitable acknowledgment within your book. Apropos of which, waste not one second of your precious time on quotations by US authors, since such would entail your needing to obtain permission from an American publisher. Remember how Stephen King and John Kennedy Toole were treated. What makes you think you'll fare any better?

TEN: THE LEGAL DEPOSIT SCHEME

NOTE *As part of the agreed package your publisher may undertake on your behalf to fulfil the mandatory requirements of the Legal Deposit Scheme. If this is not part of the agreement, simply proceed as indicated: it's a chore, though no great one.*

As and when a new book is published in the UK (as, for instance, is the case with your recently self-published novel), a copy of that book must be lodged with each of six legal deposit libraries which, collectively (see below), maintain the national published archive of the British Isles. This arrangement goes by the name of the Legal Deposit Scheme, and it is a strict legal requirement. So take no notice whatsoever of any soft-soaping POD company, angling for your business, which pretends that, as part of its package, it will do you the very great favour of depositing copies of your book with the six libraries on your behalf. Should your publisher, offer (as does mine) to undertake this job on your behalf, then you may depend upon it that there is no way he will be doing the job as a favour. In the first place, as I've said, it is a legal requirement and, if your publisher volunteers to do the job for you, he will bill you for it. Why ever should he not? It's an extra job of work to be done and it's a job of work that will necessitate additional expenditure of time, effort and cold cash, too, for p&p. Even so, do not be taken in by any pretence of a favour's being done – in fact, cross any such POD romancer off your list on the grounds that, if you can catch him out in one lie, he is probably lying to you about other aspects of the self-publishing process that you perhaps won't clock until it's too late.

Here is how you should proceed if you'll be taking the DIY route in respect of The Legal Deposit Scheme. First of all, the six legal deposit libraries are the British Library; the Bodleian Library, Oxford; the University Library, Cambridge; the National Library of Scotland, Edinburgh; the Library of Trinity College, Dublin; and, the National Library of Wales, Aberystwyth.

Now, what, in effect, happens is this: a copy of your book must, by law, be forwarded to the British Library. Meanwhile, the other five libraries have the right to claim their own copy of the book. So, best practice is to deposit a copy your book with all six libraries without waiting for a claim to be made.

Here are the addresses to which your book should be sent: Legal Deposit Office, The British Library, Boston Spa, Wetherby, West Yorkshire L23 7BY Tel: 01937 546268 e-mail: legal-deposit-serials@bl.uk Web: www.bl.uk

The other five legal deposit libraries employ an agent to collect books on their behalf. So five copies of your book should be sent to: Copyright Libraries Agency, 100 Euston Street, London NW1 2HQ Tel: 0120 7388 5061 e-mail: ats@cla.ac.uk Web: www.llgc.org.uk/cla

If you are based in Eire, the copies destined for the other five legal deposit libraries should be sent to: Irish Copyright Agency, c/o Trinity College Library, College Street, Dublin 2 Tel: +353 (0) 1608 1021 E-mail: lbryan@tcd.ie Web: www.tcd.ie/Library

NOTE Given the twin precepts which, in British life public life, are ultimately and inexorably applicable to:

- ❑ legislation enacted by Parliament – namely, that every legal requirement will become obsolete and/or a hanging offence immediately the populace as a whole is appraised of its existence; and,

- ❑ the dogged determination of the communications industry to prevent communication, to which end every address, telephone number, e-mail address and website in the land will automatically become something entirely different every time a toad has a wart on its nose and/or BT decides to stick another nought on it . . .

Given these twin precepts, as I say, I confidently expect all information supplied above to change on a weekly basis, if not more frequently. Therefore, I do strongly advise readers looking to fulfil the requirements of the Legal Deposit Scheme to endeavour to contact each relevant institution for up-to-date information prior to casting six copies of their self-published book into the void.

Incidentally, it is possible, I suppose, that a reader of a more cynical frame of mind than the rest of us (if bird so rare there be) may harbour the suspicion (as does a self-published acquaintance of my own, by the way) that, in bagging half a dozen self-published books from him, the aforementioned legal deposit libraries are, as my self-published acquaintance colourfully puts it: 'A gang of [BLEEP – Ed.] freeloaders!'

For myself, though, I put it to you that a very different point of view invites our consideration. By which I mean to say that, in 'bagging those half a dozen copies of your self-published book, free-of-charge', the dreaming spires and the other academics of that venerable ilk are actually doing you, my supra-cynical acquaintance, and the rest of self-published mankind a great, albeit no doubt involuntary, favour. Because, by their gracious acceptance and subsequent inclusion in their respective inventories of his/their/*our* self-published book(s), they do thereby simultaneously accord each of us additional, not to say ultimately dependable protection with regard to copyright.

So, perhaps we ought to thank them . . . There again, perhaps we ought not.

ELEVEN: NIELSEN BOOKDATA & AMAZON

NOTE *As part of the agreed package your publisher may undertake to carry out on your behalf the necessary task(s) specified below in respect of book title registration. Should this not be the case, proceed as indicated. You will find Nielsen personnel are helpful and properly professional.*

❑ NIELSEN BOOKDATA

Every book published for re-sale in the UK must by law have its own ISBN number (International Standard Book Number) and, once it has been allocated an ISBN number (*and* a Barcode, *please,* or no book shop is going to touch it), the book should then be registered with Nielsen BookData. Because no book shop in the country will have access to your book until such time as it is registered with Nielsen BookData. Of course, if you are self-publishing your book for private use only – i.e. for the use of family and friends – and *not* for re-sale to the general public, then there is no legal requirement for the book to be allocated an ISBN number or registered with Nielsen BookData.

But with regard to registering your book with Nielsen BookData subsequent to its having been allocated an ISBN number, most POD companies will as a rule attend to this task for you as part of their package. If not, you will need to register the book yourself.

Ah, dither ye not, old bean: this task is easy-peasy.

Simply telephone Nielsen BookData, ISBN at the ready should it be needed, and ask to be allowed to apply for registration, whereupon Nielsen BookData will e-mail you an application form by means of an attachment. Then, you may either apply on line or download the document in order to complete it and post it back to Nielsen BookData via land-mail. Nielsen BookData will want to know the name and address of the book's distributor. If the distributor is not your publisher, but yourself, make quite sure that Nielsen BookData is appraised of this fact. So have every bit of information about your book to hand just in case.

Then, once you have made application to Nielsen BookData for registration, it usually takes something in the order of three weeks or so for Nielsen to effect the registration. Do *not* contact Nielsen further in this matter, making repeated enquiries about the registration process as it affects your book. The point is you will know *immediately* your book has been registered.

How?

Because *immediately* your book is registered by Nielsen

BookData Amazon will pick up on it, as it does with all such book registrations – and, as soon as you see your book title advertised for sale on Amazon, you will know, too, that the registration with NielsenBookData has successfully taken place. So, if you care to do anything further in this matter during the time subsequent to applying to register your book with NielsenBookData, simply run a daily check on Amazon – something that is well-worth doing, in any case, since Nielsen BookData may register your book before the three weeks is up.

NOTE Once you see your book title advertised on Amazon go back to Nielsen BookData and enquire if everything is now in order at their end, enabling:

- book retailers to contact you with a view to ordering your book (I advise this lest, as an absolute beginner, you have inadvertently triggered something in the system which might tend to preclude this happy event); and,
- ask to be connected to Nielsen Technical Support Services and then ask them to arrange to connect you to the Nielsen Teleordering Facility.

❑ THE NIELSEN TELEORDERING FACILITY

Simply stated, this is a pretty nifty system by means of which Nielsen will transmit direct to your PC after close of business each day orders from all the wholesalers and book shops in the UK who wish to order it. The Nielsen Teleordering facility operates 7 days a week, 365 days a year – and it's free-of-charge. All you'll need to do is check with Nielsen every morning. Nielsen will arrange a specific site and password for you. Thereafter, once you receive an order, mail the goods, together with your invoice, to the wholesaler identified alongside the order. Should you *not* be connected to the Nielsen Teleordering facility, orders will be forwarded to you via land mail, a slow process, as you are aware – and not altogether trustworthy.

Here are the contact details you'll need: Nielsen BookData, 3rd Floor, Midas House, 62 Goldsmith Road, Woking GU21 BL0 Tel. 08707778710

Customer Services: Tel. 01483 712 325
E-mail address: customerservices@nielsenbookdata.co.uk
Technical Services: Tel. 0870 7778713
E-mail address: help@nielsenbookdata.co.uk
Publisher Help Desk: 0845 4500016
E-mail address: pubhelp@nielsenbookdata.co.uk
Trade Data: 01 483712440
E-mail address: tradedata@nielsenbookdata.co.uk

- ❑ LISTING YOUR BOOK FOR SALE ON AMAZON

NOTE *Your publisher may tell you he will list your book on Amazon as part of the agreed package. But what really happens, as I've indicated above, is that, within three weeks or so of his perhaps making application to Nielsen BookData your book title will, in fact, become registered with Nielsen BookData, whereupon Amazon will immediately pick up on this fact of its own accord, subsequent to which your book title will be listed on the Amazon website quite automatically. All that then remains to be done is for the person who registered the book with Nielsen BookData (either you or your publisher) to upload to Amazon:*

- *further details about your book (e.g. blurb, reviews etc.) together with*
- *a copy of the cover illustration.*

Should you personally be the person responsible for uploading these details and the cover illustration, simply proceed as follows once Amazon has listed your book title.

If you want your book to be listed for sale on Amazon, (and I strongly recommend that you *should* want this), you won't in any case have much choice in the matter, because either your publisher or you personally are going to need to register your book with Nielsen BookData, and approximately three weeks later, as we have seen, Amazon will duly list your book on site, taking its information from Nielsen BookData. (I apologise for reiterating this point, but it galls me to see some publishers pretending their input in the matter extends to more than a bit of tinkering subsequent to submitting a registration application to Nielsen BookData.)

With regard to your book's listing with Amazon, it is not that sales will necessarily be plentiful, or even interesting. But readers use Amazon in much the same way as potential customers check out the price and availability of other consumer goods in the Argos catalogue – and you never know, you may get a good few sales. You'll certainly get *some* sales, though not necessarily via the Amazon Advantage bookselling facility (see below), which I personally would not recommend unless your publisher is also your distributor – in which case, again, you won't have much choice in the matter, because that's the way your publisher will choose to sell your book. Should you act as your own distributor, however (which is the way I operate, as I've said before), I would seriously recommend (see below) that you sell your book via Amazon Marketplace at approximately a third less than the 60% commission rate applicable to sales via Amazon Advantage.

Anyway, at this point in the procedure (that is to say, three weeks on from your initial contact with Nielsen BookData), details of your book should have already appeared on Amazon, though (unless your publisher is also your distributor) they will be very rudimentary and will not include:

- a blurb and other relevant details other than basic bibliographical details listing the name of the publisher, the number of pages etc. or,

- an image of the front cover of the book;

So, really, I should not perhaps have said "if you want your book to be listed on Amazon", but, more precisely, "should you want your book to be *more appropriately and professionally listed on*

Amazon", and I do strongly recommend that you *should* want this, then you will need to arrange to list, in accordance with Amazon's instructions in the matter:

❍ a blurb and other relevant details, including any reviews the book has received,
❍ an image of the front cover of the book.

NOTE I repeat: *as part of the agreed package* your *publisher may undertake to carry out on your behalf the necessary task(s) specified below. Should this not be the case, you should proceed as indicated, or get a PC-proficient pal to do this for you. Thankfully, upon request, my publisher was willing to transmit each of my cover images to Amazon on my behalf.*

❑ HOW TO ENTER A BLURB AND OTHER DETAILS

Follow Amazon's simple instructions on line with regard to entering further details about your book, including reviews you have seen in the press – and ask any customers you know personally to enter customer reviews of their own. There's no need for anybody to be concerned about their finesse as a potential reviewer. One of my favourite comments about *Every Street in Manchester* came from an old friend who volunteered without prompting: 'It made me laugh, it made me cry, but most of all it made me happy.' I ask you: which *Gruinard* or *Thames* book critic could have waxed more lyrical?

After you have successfully uploaded your details to Amazon's server, send an e-mail to book-catalogue-dept@amazon.co.uk. For a speedy response, Amazon advises that you write "FTP Upload Details" in the subject line and the names of your files and their contents in the body of the message. This will ensure that your data is retrieved and processed promptly.

❑ SUPPLYING AMAZON WITH THE COVER IMAGE OF YOUR BOOK

For images saved electronically, Amazon's formatting requirements, as they will tell you should you care to double check with them, are as follows:

* JPEG or TIFF format
* 648 pixels tall
* RGB colour
* 72 DPI
* Cover image file must be named by the ten digit ISBN, i.e. 1234567890.jpg
* Interior image files must be named by the ten digit ISBN and interior number from 1 to 8, i.e. 1234567890.interior01pg; 1234567890.interior02.jpg; 1234567890.interior03.jpg
* Cover image should be full front view of cover, no borders

The user login and password for Amazon's FTP server are as follows:
login: catalogue
password: Letdre99

Finally, Amazon's FTP address is ftp-1.amazon.com. Please note that the security system on Amazon's server is case-sensitive, therefore make sure you capitalise all appropriate letters in the password.

But if the foregoing instructions are, to your way of thinking (as they are to mine) just so much Double Dutch to the tune of a Gobbledegooked Spanglish Patois with Umlauts Added, get a PC-potent buddy to do the honours – or your publisher, if you have a publisher like mine.

❑ HOW BOOK SALES ARE EFFECTED VIA AMAZON MARKETPLACE

NOTE *Should your agreed package specify that your publisher will act as distributor for your book, he will deal with Amazon Advantage, not Amazon Marketplace – and, should such a package be agreed between you, this would prevent your personally offering for sale any other than second-hand or damaged copies of your book via Amazon Marketplace. My publisher does not act as a book distributor, so whatever copies of my books I sell via Amazon Marketplace I sell on my own initiative.*

Once your titles are listed on Amazon, Amazon can begin to take orders for it. Here's how their ordering system works for someone like me who is his own distributor. Amazon will order books from you on a per-order basis via Amazon Marketplace.

What then happens in the Amazon Marketplace scheme of things is that a p&p charge of £2.75 is applied to each book sale. So, for example, in the case of *Manchester Kiss*, say, which retails at £14.99, you might expect the total cost of the book to the customer to be £14.99 PLUS £2.75 (for p&p), which equals £17.74.

However, this is very far from being the end of it. Because it is possible, I suspect, that Amazon would prefer you to use, not Amazon Marketplace, but the ultra expensive Amazon Advantage sales facility instead, where you would need to pay a whacking-great commission rate of no less than 60% in total.

Yikes!

Ah, but what you will find with books such as your own that you choose to advertise for sale via Amazon Marketplace so as to avoid the ultra-expensive Amazon Advantage is that Amazon will now effectively scupper your chances of selling any books via Amazon Marketplace:

- by applying an extra mark-up of £1.99 per copy to the advertised retail price of your book on the grounds that this represents a "stocking charge" – so your book (taking *Manchester Kiss* by way of example once more) will end up costing potential buyers (wait for it!) £14.99 PLUS £2.75 postage PLUS £1.99, which equals a grand total of £19.73 – that is to say, a full 31% more than the book is on sale for on the shelf in Waterstone's; and,

- by intimating, too, that delivery will take from 4-6 weeks ("usually dispatched in 4 to 6 weeks", says Amazon).

And the really annoying thing about this, I've found, is that:

- I personally do not NEED or REQUIRE the extra £1.99 LESS Amazon's commission, and:
- any order I receive from Amazon Marketplace invariably goes

out by first class return post, provided the Royal Mail, in turn, doesn't then propose to rip me off for more than a quid per book for inland postage.

However, the argument is academic because Amazon Marketplace policy will invariably prevent any meaningful sales of your book via Amazon Marketplace unless your potential customers are also rabid lunatics who:

- ❍ don't mind paying through the nose when your book may be had from Borders, say, for £4.74 less than the inflated Amazon Marketplace price;
- ❍ don't mind hanging about for (a putative) 4-6 weeks for a book they are paying £4.74 more for than Waterstone's and Borders are asking for your book.

Most unconvincing are Amazon's stated reasons for these tactics, their being readily available to readers via the Amazon website. So if you care to do so, please refer to Amazon's Online Publisher's guide at www.amazon.co.uk/publishers. And perhaps look up www.amazon.co.uk/advantage too, though there's no way in the world I'm going to recommend you use Amazon Advantage.

So, how *do* I recommend you sell your book on Amazon? Because I certainly *do* sell some books via Amazon. Via Amazon Marketplace, that's how. Because, via Amazon Marketplace, provided you do it 'My Way'. Yep, if you do it 'My Way', you will assuredly be able to arrange things so that your customers:

- ❍ pay not one penny more than they'd expect to pay in a Waterstone's or Borders;
- ❍ pay not one penny piece for p&p, as it were;
- ❍ luxuriate in the added assurance of first class delivery by return post.
- ❍ Meanwhile, you personally will end up paying a pretty reasonable commission rate of approximately 39% – which is

much more reasonable than that swingeing Amazon Advantage 60%, I feel sure you will agree.

How is this to be effected, though?

Well, for example, suppose you look at the page on the Amazon website that purports to advertise *Manchester Kiss* for sale at a retail price of £14.99 PLUS £1.99 "stocking charge" PLUS £2.75 for p&p – a total cost to potential customers which, I certainly don't recall that anyone has yet been daft enough to pay for the book. (Incidentally, what a relief it is to realise, by the same token, that my readership is utterly bereft of nutters.) Well, on that same page, you'll also notice one or more copies of *Manchester Kiss* that are offered for sale by one or more individual booksellers (including Amazon), these books being variously described as "New", "Like new", "Very good", "Good", or merely "Acceptable". Well, this is precisely where I sell copies of my book(s), describing them thus: "New, autographed by the author, complete with generic bookmark, despatched from the UK by first-class return post". And this is the only way in which you, too, will be able to sell your book on Amazon at a reasonable commercial rate. Here's how the deal works out . . .

I know the charge for p&p will be £2.75, so I subtract £2.75 from the asking price for the book, this being £14.99, as you are well aware, whereupon I get a subtotal of £12.24. So, I advertise *Manchester Kiss* for sale @ £12.24, which ensures that it is now on sale on Amazon for the same price (£12.24 PLUS £2.75 p&p equals £14.99) as it is in Waterstone's and Borders.

Now, should an order materialise, when Amazon takes its commission on the sale price of £14.99 (i.e. £3.02 PLUS £0.45VAT equals £3.47), I am left with a subtotal amounting to £11.52. So, if I pay 25p for a Jiffy bag (I often do better in the £1 shops, by the way) and 98p to the Royal Mail, my costs for p&p will be £1.23. Subtracting £1.23 from the £11.52 Amazon will pay into my bank account leaves me with a grand total of £10.29 – which, if you do your sums correctly represents roughly 39.559706% commission paid on a book which costs my customer £14.99.

QED, methinks. Because Amazon Marketplace PLUS that iniquitous £1.99 levy moves *no* books whatsoever; and Amazon Advantage would leave me with less than £7.52, post paid, in my pocket.

Of course, I'll need to advertise another copy of the book immediately a customer orders the copy that's been on sale – something I need to do at the moment, to speak truly, having shifted a copy in this way only yesterday. But it's just got to be better than paying 60% commission, hasn't it? And it is reassuring, too, to realise I do Waterstone's and Borders no injustice in the process, because I'd need to pay them commission on sales at a pretty comparable rate.

Happy Amazon Marketplacing, ye canny self-publishers!

TWELVE: SETTING UP YOUR ACCOUNT WITH THE WHOLESALERS

NOTE *If the agreed package with your publisher specifies that he will be acting as the distributor for your book, there will be no need for you to set up accounts with the book wholesalers; accordingly, neither will there be any need for you to take aboard any of the information which follows concerning invoices and packaging since you will not be doing any of it. That is to say, the information, advice and opinions set out below are intended to assist any self-publisher who, like myself, handles his own distribution.*

By this stage in the proceedings, if you are the sole distributor of your own self-published book, you will have already dealt with a company whose name you had perhaps never heard of (i.e. Nielsen BookData). And it didn't hurt too much, did it? So, the imminent prospect of your now needing to contact a minimum of three book wholesalers whose names have perhaps hitherto and similarly been unknown to you (viz. Gardners Books, Bertrams Books and Askews Library Services), will hold no terrors.

Because the plain facts of the matter are these:
1. Many of the book shops you will want to do business with (perhaps most of them: e.g. Waterstone's and many of the independents) will, should you succeed in persuading them that it makes sound business sense to stock your book, need to place their orders with you, the sole distributor, via one of the several book wholesalers acting as their intermediary (e.g. Gardners Books, for example, whose contact details are listed below), the point at issue here being that it is hardly worthwhile for Waterstone's and other book shops to open a separate account on their own behalf with a distributor (i.e. you) who has only one (or two) book title(s) to offer; in addition to which

2. the vast majority of the public libraries you are hoping will want to include your book in their respective inventories will need to place their orders with you, the sole distributor, via Bertrams Books of Norwich or Askews Library Services of Preston.

Gardners Books, 1 Whittle Drive, Willingdon Drove, Eastbourne East Sussex BN23 6QH
Tel. 01323521777
E-mail: custcare@gardners.com Website: www.gardners.com

Bertrams Group Ltd., 1 Broadlands Business Park,
Norwich NR 7 0WF
Tel. 0870 4296600 Freephone: 0800 333344

Askews Library Services, 218-222 North Road, Preston,
Lancashire, PR1 1SY
Tel. 01772 555947 E-mail: enquiries@askews.co.uk

❑ YOUR INITIAL APPROACH TO THE BOOK WHOLESALERS

Simply telephone Customer Services in the first instance. (N.B. To avoid unnecessary reiteration, this is the way you should approach each of the three named book wholesalers: Gardners of Eastbourne, Bertrams Books of Norwich, and Askews Library Services of Preston), and explain the situation to them, that is to say:

❍ you are the self-published author of a recently-published book which is registered with Nielsen BookData and has an ISBN number;

❍ the publisher's name is (whatever it is), and you (name) are the sole distributor, therefore

❍ you wish to set up an account with Gardners, Bertrams and/or Askews, as applicable.

At this point in the proceedings, as is the way of things with unsolicited telephone calls of any kind, the operator on the Switch will transfer you to the appropriate department (e.g. Local Books or some such) and, having rehearsed what you want to say, you will now be invited to tell your story all over again.

Office staff at Gardners, Bertrams and Askews are thoroughly professional, so you should have no concerns on that score. So, given the nature of your request (i.e. the opening of an account with the wholesaler), make sure that you appear similarly professional to them. For example, one point you will need to discuss with the wholesalers is the percentage discount you are prepared to offer them. You'll find the Society of Author's Quick Guide 18: Self-Publishing and Print-on-Demand helpful in this, though their suggested discount rate of 35-45% is a bit generous to my mind when you consider you will be offering to welcome orders for single copies from the wholesalers. Try for 30% (or even less), but don't stick your neck out and risk losing their interest. Don't forget, too, that you may bill the wholesaler for p&p on any order though, personally, despite the heavy postal charges currently decreed by the Royal Mail, I invariably contrive to subsidise any swingeing postal charge in excess of £1 per book.

Have all the necessary details ready to hand: everything the wholesaler can possibly want to know about you and your book – e.g. your bank account details, the address to which book orders should be sent etc. And don't be fumbling around trying to find the ISBN number rather than having it already written down within sight. Also, if by any chance you already enjoy the easy ordering method afforded by the Nielsen Teleordering facility, this is something the wholesaler will definitely want to know about. Try, too, to have the wholesaler agree to pay you via BACS payments rather than by cheque. Then make sure you make a note of any account or other reference numbers you are given, and that you understand exactly how things may now be expected to proceed. Should you perhaps expect some documentation in the post, say? (e.g. a BACS application form to fill in; any business agreement to be signed.)

When the time comes for you to ask the various bookshops and public library services to stock your book, you'll find many of them (Waterstone's in particular) will submit their orders to you via Gardners, whereas it will be Bertrams and Askews which will contact you with regard to orders emanating from the respective public library services. What this means, in effect, is that, no matter how keen most book shops or public library service may be to stock your book:

- their order will usually be submitted to you via their contracted wholesaler;
- you, in turn, must forward the book to the contracted wholesaler together with the invoice;
- eventual payment of the invoiced amount will be transmitted to you by the contracted wholesaler.

Eventually, you will find this way of doing things is useful in that you will know exactly where your invoice will end up – that is to say, with the wholesaler, because *you mailed it to the wholesaler*. But in many other respects, the arrangement can be a pain when it comes to dealing with the book shop and/or the library service itself. For example, you may live next door to your local Waterstone's branch or down the road from your local branch library, but you'll still have to mail their book orders and invoices to the wholesaler's address – and the wholesaler will still have to mail the book orders on to your local Waterstone's branch and/or public library, as the case may be – which is obviously an irritating waste of time and money.

❑ ONCE YOU HAVE SET UP AN ACCOUNT WITH THE BOOK WHOLESALERS

❍ RECEIVING ORDERS FOR YOUR BOOK Assuming you are party to the Nielsen Teleordering facility (and you must ensure that you are), site access is via your PC, using the key/password that Nielsen have assigned to you. You really must get into the habit of checking your PC for book orders every morning immediately you are up, dressed and ready for action. Because book orders are transmitted overnight after close of business. (Failing access to the Nielsen Teleordering facility, wholesalers will submit orders to you by land mail.)

Should an order materialise via the Nielsen Teleordering facility, it will register as a small green square representing a day of the week on a calendar listing the month in question. So, any book order emanating from a wholesaler as I write these words would manifest itself as a small green square on the 17th day of the month of December (as, indeed, one has, in fact – from Gardners), whereupon I left-click on the mouse where indicated and fuller details appear, listing the wholesaler (and his address) whence the order originated; together with an order number; a date for that order; the name of the book title required; it's ISBN number; a reference number; and the number of copies required.

❍ INVOICING ORDERS FOR YOUR BOOK Since you are not some swish multinational company with money to burn, you should send your invoice out with the order rather than later. This will give you an immediate saving on postal charges, or so you hope. (See below.)

1. Buy a carbonless triplicated invoice book from Staples or elsewhere. They're inordinately expensive, but a duplicate Invoice Book will not do the job you need it to do. Alternatively, rig some DIY triplicated forms up on your PC.

2. The very same day you receive a book order via the Nielsen Teleordering facility retrieve the required item (or items) from stock and write out the invoice.

3. Enter on the invoice every detail that appears on the book order PLUS your name and address PLUS a reminder of the 30 days settlement period (minus a reminder of your sale-or-return offer lest it prove too tempting). Most importantly, list the name of the book and its ISBN number.

4. With regard to the reconciliation of figures, enter:
a) the cost of the item or items;
b) LESS the amount of discount agreed between you and the wholesaler
c) PLUS the cost of p&p
d) the total amount due.

5. Tear the yellow duplicate from the invoice book, leaving the original white invoice form in place together with the pink triplicate form. This pink triplicate form will now serve as your reminder until this invoice has been paid.

6. Fold the yellow duplicate and place it within a blank sheet of paper or a section of multi-punched polythene pocket. Why? Because the invoice book is carbonless and the yellow sheet is therefore capable of making a mess of the book you intend to mail.

7. Place the protected yellow invoice inside the book leaving just a flap folded to the outside of the book by the front cover.

8. If using a Jiffy bag, slide the book inside the envelope with the yellow invoice showing towards its opening flap.

❍ WHY BE SO FINICKY ABOUT INVOICING? Because:

a) with regard to the details on your invoice, *you want to get paid*; and
b) with regard to the way the invoice is packed, *you want to get paid.*

To be absolutely fair to the book wholesalers, every properly completed invoice will eventually be paid, the majority of them as and when payment falls due. But there may be occasions, too, when it may occur to you to suspect that delayed settlement is perhaps a book wholesaling business practice. Ah, not so, dear reader. No, those (thankfully rare) occasions when you may be constrained to submit a duplicate, or even a triplicate invoice, before payment duly materialises . . . Well, those occasions are, as I say, thankfully rare, and are ('tis thought) a direct result of another little known, still less popular, government-sanctioned job creation scheme. For the fact of the matter is ('tis said with tongue planted firmly in cheek) that there lurks below stairs at the premises of book wholesalers a species of troglodyte, or rather, Paper Tiger. Luckily (for us), the beast is part-time and peripatetic, for the Paper Tiger in question cannot be relied upon to open the parcel of books you mail to the book wholesaler with its teeth for 365 days in the year, devouring all wrapping paper, parcel tape, polythene, and invoicing, yet not the book itself, since by the time it's got its teeth on this (*hic'*), it will be suffering from deep-seated dyspepsia and couldn't bring itself to touch another thing (*hic'*), whereupon your book will promptly arrive at Accounts (*burp'*), un-invoiced. Hence, payment will not arrive on the due date on occasions such as these, necessitating despatch of a duplicate invoice and, very occasionally, the aforementioned triplicate. So pack your invoices carefully, please do.

❍ WHAT DOES 30 DAYS SETTLEMENT MEAN EXACTLY?
My invoices read, "Terms: 30 days". So if an invoice is dated 18 November 2007, I don't expect to receive payment until *the end of the month* after the 30 days has passed – which takes us to the end of December 2007 in the instance quoted. And, even then, I may not receive payment for another couple of weeks, dependent upon the book wholesaler's favoured day for settling monthly accounts. So, again, in the instance quoted, I wouldn't think of querying a "missing" payment until 18 January at the earliest.

❍ DESPATCHING MULTIPLE COPIES OF YOUR BOOKS
You really must accept orders from wholesalers for single copies of your book. Look at it this way: what a relief it is that *somebody* wants to order a book by somebody who is as yet a nobody. However, given the current swingeing postal costs decreed by the Royal Mail, it is no longer true to say that mailing single copies is

the most expensive way to do it. Personal experience tells me that, one copy mailed is just about manageable in a financial sense, but that any number of books from two to nine copies is nowadays inordinately expensive to post. So try to find some magic number of books favoured by current postal rates that you might consequently offer to the book wholesalers at a bigger discount – e.g. 10 copies @ 40% discount; 24 @ 50%. For two or three copies, however, you may just have to bite the bullet, its being a sheer chore to pack three books singly.

With regard to packaging, it can be a real problem finding the right kind of cardboard wrapping in which to mail multiple copies of your books. However, you may care to contact a really friendly and efficient West Yorkshire company, as follows: D & M Packaging Supplies Ltd., 5A Knowl Road, Mirfield, West Yorkshire WF14 8DQ Tel. 0194-491267
e-mail: packaging@dandmbooks.com

D&M, also trading under the name Brodart, supplies book covers, packaging and various cleaners and repair materials to public libraries. Certainly, their catalogue is well worth a look, and I've made good use of their clear plastic book covers in the past (more about which anon), and also their book packaging materials on occasion. I remember working out that a single packaging item could, at a pinch accommodate half a dozen copies of *Every Street in Manchester*.

On the other hand, it will not have escaped the attention of cheapskates (such as myself) that the reinforced cardboard boxes that contain a dozen litre packs of milk down the local supermarket make an excellent packing case for books in transit, always provided you:

❍ trim them;
❍ invert them, positioning the lettering to the inside; and,
❍ pre-wrap the books in clean paper prior to packing them.

Henceforward, too, you must never ever discard any Jiffy bags, cardboard cartons or large envelopes that you receive in the mail, for such things are akin to treasure trove to a self-publisher who is also a distributor of his own self-published books.

THIRTEEN: GETTING YOUR BOOK INTO THE LIBRARIES

NOTE *Even if the agreed publishing package between you and your publisher specifies he will act as distributor for the book, it is most unlikely that he intends to contact any public library service on your behalf. Therefore, it is strongly recommended that the publicity campaign delineated below in respect of the public library system throughout the UK should be initiated by every reader of this book immediately he is in receipt of the first print-run and has set up accounts with the book wholesalers listed above.*

Make no mistake about it, the public libraries can wield much influence and power in getting your book out into the public domain. Given that the normal route to widespread distribution of your book title is closed to you by reason of the intransigence of mainstream publishers and broadsheet disdain, you are perforce looking for a groundswell of interest developing from the grass roots readership up. Only the public library system has the potential of delivering the goods in this regard. So, something you must not fail to do once you have set up accounts with the various book wholesalers (by means of which you are, of course, contriving to ensure that your self-published book will now be available to any customer who may require it) . . . what you really must not fail to do is to contact every library service in the UK.

You heard me a-right: you really must not fail to make contact with every library service in the UK.

DD: *Gulp!*

You must make contact by e-mail or snail mail, whichever you prefer. Enclose or attach a press release supplying details about your book, together with a politely worded suggestion that your book title ought to be considered for acquisition by each library service you contact, simultaneously suggesting reasons why this would make eminently good sense. Try to think laterally in this respect.

For example, in addition to indicating the apposite title of my debut novel in the press release I sent to the Manchester Library Service, I went on to mention the fact that I had lived and worked in the city for the greater part of the last half century. And when I subsequently contacted the Devon and Torbay Library Services, I emphasised the point that the main protagonists in the book enthuse about holidays taken in Devon, particularly in St Marychurch and Babbacombe – which location they regard as their personal Shangri-la in much the same way as Jack Kerouac's *On the Road* looks to California and the character, Ratso, in James Leo Herlihy's *Midnight Cowboy* sets his cap at Florida or die (and *does*, in fact, die, you may recall). Similarly, I made sure the Pennine Way episode in *Every Street in Manchester* was duly noted when seeking to influence librarians in Yorkshire, West and North.

The person to contact in each library service is the Library Acquisitions Officer, or address your communication more generally to the Fiction Selection Panel. But dither ye not. Nomenclature such as this will be close enough to afford access to the person you need to contact. Also, you will generally find the Library Acquisitions Officer is to be found at the Central/Main Library in the biggest town in the area served by each library service. And, should you inadvertently misdirect your approach, there is still a good chance that another librarian will re-direct it, in addition to cheerfully advising you of this fact. On no less than two occasions (courtesy of branch librarians in Failsworth, Oldham, and Leigh, Lancashire) I had good reason to be grateful for such gratuitous kindness. Meanwhile, only one library service in the UK (its name only available to close acquaintances in moments of hilarity down the pub) declined to communicate with me, quoting the Data Protection Act.

Lord, love us!

Still, dither ye not. True, you have an arduous task before you, exhaustive and exhausting too. And it is not a job to be done overnight. Rather should you tackle it over a few months – perhaps over a calendar year. It is a job to be tackled in logical progression, too.

Begin with the library service in the town or county where you live, then gradually broaden your approach to include library services in towns or counties contiguous to your own. For example, the library service serving Middleton, where I live, is Rochdale, so the Rochdale Library Service was the obvious first port of call, Manchester Library Service being a close second. Then, in the same e-mail/land mail campaign (that is to say, immediately my book was available via the wholesalers), I went on to contact Library Acquisitions Officers in Bolton, Bury, Oldham, Salford, Stockport, Tameside, Warrington and Wigan. I have since learned that just one of these library services declined to stock the title; whereas Bolton Library Service in particular proved to be very generously interested from the start.

Of course, given their propinquity to my home address, the Rochdale and Manchester Library Services were easy to contact, a simple visit to a couple of nearby libraries yielding the relevant details and personnel I would need to approach. And I feel sure you'll be able to do something similar on your own home patch. But what will you do about library services that lie further afield. Take, the Torbay Library Service, for example, to which I previously referred. How on earth did I manage to make contact with Torbay?

Again, good reader, dither ye not. For help is at hand in the shape of a truly comprehensive and wide-ranging UK Public Libraries website that is freely available to you via the internet, compliments of its designers, those twin benefactors of literate humanity whom I hereby acclaim by name: librarians Sheila and Robert Harden.

Who?

Never mind that for the moment. (Further accolades anon.) Because, wonderful to relate (*mirabile dictu,* if I may wax Latinate in unbridled delight at what I am about to reveal to you), these, my/your/*our* benefactors, the Hardens, dear reader, have designed a website which will afford you immediate, ready-to-hand – indeed, *blanket* e-mail/land mail and telephonic access to every single library service (and, thereby, every blinking branch library) in the UK.

To self-publishers such as we the Harden's UK Public Library website is, not to put too fine a point upon it, *worth its weight in 22 carat gold of Ophir with diamond-encrusted knobs on top.* Therefore, you will readily understand that it is with tears in my eyes that I now realise (Ah, too late! *Sob!*) that I really ought to have stung you for twice the asking price for *Write It Self-Publish It Sell It* whilst I still had the chance to do so. Because, as matters now stand, I find myself constrained to hand you a bibliophile's version of a gold ingot for free. (Cue: *copious lachrymose lamentations tantamount to a flash flood of tears sufficient to saturate the document before me.*) You ready, then? You ready for it? The Harden's all-encompassing UK Public Libraries website? Hey, too right, you are. Here we go, then – simply enter:

www.harden.dial.pipex.com/ukpublib.html or, indeed:
www.harden.dial.pipex.com/weblibs.html

Et voila!

Now, read 'em and weep! (To tell the truth, I never did understand what this means.) So even more appropriately with regard to Sheila and Robert Harden's UK Public Libraries website: read it and *drool*!

Here's what Robert Harden modestly allows: 'Though our site is handy for self-publishing authors on a tight budget, for those with more spare cash than spare time there is the mailing labels/ database from Facet Publishing.' More details at:

http://www.facetpublishing.co.uk/listrental.shtml

Right, enough festering, you gold-diggers, glorying in such unwonted largesse! Back to work – though work that is suddenly a much more attractive prospect, courtesy of Sheila and Robert Harden's superbly splendiferous website and to their further unbridled generosity in respect of the contact details for Facet Publishing.

So, taking each prospective task in turn:

❍ Immediately your book is available for sale, contact, as previously detailed, the Library Acquisitions Officer (or the

Fiction Selection Panel) in the library service serving your locality – that is to say, your town or borough.

- Then, gradually moving outwards, extend your contact zone to a contiguously concentric circle of all other towns and/or counties adjacent to your home address.

- And over the months to come (years perhaps, depending on your workload), extend your contact zones county by county, moving ever outwards in concentric circles until you've covered the entire UK.

Now, the job so far has been easy-peasy, thanks to the Harden's UK Public Libraries website, so you'll surely be up for the next task. Because, the time has come for you, self-published author that you are, to commence contacting . . . *every branch librarian at every branch library in the UK.*

Why so? What exactly is the point of that?

Well, the point of that, dear reader, is to reach out with your sales campaign to every library service in the UK (let's face it: the *better* library services in the UK) where branch librarians and others of lowly degree are perhaps encouraged to suggest book titles for acquisition from time to time. Perhaps there are no such library services in the UK; there again, perhaps there are one or two as news of the dawn of the Age of Reason finally reaches these shores – though, certainly, it won't be all the library services in the UK whilst there remains a single library service in the land where (*hah, hah*? Nay, *shudder*) the Data Protection Act (or a manifest perversion of it) chimes a sweeter chord than bibliophilia.

As the foregoing would suggest, those go-ahead, we're-up-for-it, cutting-edge library services in the UK may number single figures, or they may number none. We just don't know. But there are two things we may depend upon for sure:

- branch librarians are at least as interested in books and bookmen as are Borders' and Waterstone's staff; and,
- you won't get anywhere without trying.

So while you're at it (contacting those branch librarians, as I say) ask them if they also host an in-house readers'/writers' group or an Open Mike session that meets on a regular basis, or a Writers' Festival from time to time (the Reading Development Officer will be the person to contact) – and volunteer to address that group (if any), free-of-charge, provided you may bring a few books along for sale, there being no obligation to buy, of course.

Spread the word – hey, spread *your* word, as it happens, or rather, *words*. 'Go ye and teach all nations!' I tell you. 'And let distance and concern about personal expenditure not stand in your way. (These are tax deductible.) Because you're on your way by your own efforts at last; and only by your own efforts will your bandwagon continue to roll.'

Besides which, the UK library services are of nothing less than essential and continuing importance to your sales campaign, for they are the very tinder which, provided you personally continue to fan the flame, will yet launch your book from the ground level up.

FOURTEEN: REGISTERING FOR ROYALTIES PAYABLE TO YOU

NOTE *Should the agreed publishing package specify that your publisher will act as distributor for your book, he will certainly not be contacting *PLR and/or ALCS on your behalf. So you must do this on your own behalf immediately you are self-published. *Public Lending Right and the Authors' Licensing & Collection Society*

Once published, your book title, together with your personal details as its author, should immediately be registered with the two official bodies which oversee and handle the annual payment that will be made to you of any royalties that become due consequent upon readers either borrowing your book from public libraries throughout the UK, or copyright material within your book being photocopied for any purpose. Do not fail to make application for payment of these royalties.

To qualify for PLR your name should appear on the title page of your book. For its part, once you and your book title are registered, the PLR service will pay any royalties due to you direct to your bank account in February each year. Statements are issued in January.

Make application either by writing to the address below or by accessing the PLR website where it is possible to apply on line. The PLR Year runs from 1 July to 30 June, so make application immediately your book is published. This will qualify you to receive royalty payments, if any, in the following February.

Royalties are minimal (less than 5p per borrowing at present), but they *are* your entitlement and you really *should* arrange to collect any income so raised. The minimum payment per annum is £1, the maximum is £6,600. Of course, it's the likes of Catherine Cookson, Maeve Binchy, and Stephen King who will continue to collect £6,600 each, but don't for a minute imagine you'll receive nothing, provided you've shifted at least a few books. By way of example, there's no way I'll be wanting to discuss with you the £6,600 I expect to receive next year. (Joke.) But, by way of encouragement I do not mind telling you that, way back in the Spring of 2006 (at which time, remember, I had just one title to my name – and this just the *first* edition of *Every Street in Manchester*, of which I'd shifted perhaps 300-500 copies at that time, perhaps 25% of that number to public libraries (I'm guessing), I was absolutely gob smacked to receive from PLR and ALCS . . . around £100 in total.

J K Rowling received more, I know it – as did Jeffrey Archer and Dick Francis. But even so, £100-plus (before tax) is *still* seven Sunday lunchtimes *à deux* at the carvery in the Old Boar's Head, Middleton (*burp'*), or (*brrrm!*) a couple of tankfuls of petrol plus a car wash for the Hyundai Lantra Estate I was driving at the time, or [*hic'*] 11/12ths of a case of Grant's Sherry Cask Reserve whisky at a discount price from Tesco at the Sudden (Rochdale) roundabout.

No fee is payable to access your PLR rights, so address your enquiries as soon as you may to Public Lending Right, Richard

House, Sorbonne Close, Stockton-on-Tees TS17 6DA Tel: 01642 615699/01642 615641 e-mail: authorityservices@plr.uk.com website: www.plr.uk.com and also to: ALCS, Marlborough Court, 14-18 Holburn, London EC1N 2LE Tel: 020 7395-0600 e-mail: alcs@alcs.co.uk website: www.alcs.co.uk

There is no fee payable to apply for listing with ALCS (The Authors' Licensing and Collecting Society); neither is anything payable as such for the annual collection/payment service you are afforded once you and your self-published book are listed. However, ALCS *will* take a small percentage of royalties due. Similarly, ALCS advertises membership at a price, though there is no necessity whatsoever for you to join. In any case, one of the benefits of membership of the Society of Authors, which you really ought to join once you are published, is free membership of ALCS. (More of which anon.)

Incidentally, royalty payments from PLR and ALCS are not taxed at source, so income tax is payable. So receipt of your first royalties from PLR and ALCS will be a timely reminder that, once your book is selling to greater or less extent (though not before), you must inform HM Inspector of Taxes of your new source of income. Naturally, you must not forget to retain all evidence of expenditure you have incurred and will continue to incur in the matter – publisher's receipt; p&p; advertising; travel etc. Better still, get an accountant on the job, especially one who is well-versed in the business, one or two of which advertise their services in the pages of *The Author*, the quarterly magazine of the Society of Authors – which you will, of course, be joining, I trust. [See Appendix 10.]

FIFTEEN: PLACING YOUR BOOK WITH THE BOOKSHOPS

NOTE *Even if the agreed publishing package specifies that your publisher will act as distributor for your book, there is no way he will be contacting any bookshops in the matter. The extent of his involvement in the sales process will simply be to respond as and when orders are received. So you really must initiate a sales campaign on your own behalf via bookshops large and small – that is to say, via the main bookshops and the independents wherever they are to be found.*

❑ MURPHY'S LAW Such is Murphy's Law (or Sod's, as the earthier-tongued amongst us would have it) that whatever *can* go wrong *will* go wrong as surely as night follows nightfall and pratfall follows pit. In a previous incarnation, by way of example, whilst working as a trainee salesman in a tailor's shop when I was a student, I can remember being "sent forward" to service my very first customer in a state of such unpreparedness it had the routine greeting, 'Sir', lurching ungainly as an amputée across my tongue. Not unsurprisingly in the circumstances, said customer turned out to be a deaf-mute, quite incapable of communicating to me the object of his sartorial desire. And, by way of further example, I can tell you that, in August, 2005, whilst taking my first two steps as a book salesman, whose sole stock-in-trade was his own debut novel, I would find things have not changed for the better forty-three years on. In fact, the chances of communication had become twice as bad, my first two tentative visits to independent retail outlets bringing me face to face with the kind of fiction buyer whose sour-faced purpose in life seems to be to thwart any reasonable request from book salesman or customer in much the same way as a redoubt would withstand armed attack.

Neither one of these stalwarts, I need hardly add, had the slightest intention of letting *Every Street in Manchester* loose upon their shelves, or even of permitting me to state my case. Yet, despite this initial setback (I refrain from naming the independent retail outlets where folk like these are caged since what follows is the *really* important point to note), I would subsequently succeed in placing my debut novel with one of these outlets – where its successors (and sequel) remain on sale to this day. That is to say, I would eventually contrive to place *Every Street in Manchester* exactly where I sought to place it in the first place – and, subsequently, *Manchester Kiss*, too. Because:

- just as I take no notice of any publisher/literary agent who summarily rejects my typescripts, neither do I take 'No' for an answer from any other closed minds in the book trade; and,
- the human doorstops to whom I refer above are in any case, "fiction buyers of the rarer kind".

That is to say – well, certainly, if I exclude one of them from the equation (his place of employ was subsequently fire bombed one night, and I do wonder why – or, rather, *who*) and milady (more recently sighted hosting a book-signing in the Northern Quarter at which a skulk of tattooed guests toasted an effluently-mouthed author with wine glasses in both fists, the ambience about them curdled with invective and the whiff of cheese munchies), certainly if I exclude know-nothings such as these, I have generally found fiction buyers to be welcoming and friendly, and interested, too, in conversing about books (not just my books), in addition to their being highly-qualified for the job they do and (best of all) willing to give my two books a go. Let me put it like this, any fiction buyer who is mannerly enough and patient enough to permit me to state my case will invariably be kind enough to order one or two copies of each title, four or five perhaps (thank you, Ottakars, Oldham, of blessed memory: nowadays Waterstone's) – and a full dozen or more (thank you, Borders, Manchester Fort) if the books happen to have a sales history in that particular location.

Why? And what, if any, are the magic words?

Well, the magic words are ever (just as they are with commercial publishers) 'sale-or-return'. You really must stress the sale-or-return basis of the sale. You will not be taking cash upfront, please note. You will invoice for payment at a future date (say, 30 days) – and you will leave your books on a sale-or-return basis.

Dither ye not. Only on one solitary, sad occasion have I ever been asked to take books back. (By a dimwit who had hidden the books rather than display them and then whinged because only 10 out of 30 had sold. Not a bad result in a month, given the adverse circumstances, it seemed to me.) Indeed, why on earth would I ever need to take books back if the fiction buyer has submitted a sensible order in the first place. That is to say, any halfway decent book shop can shift a couple of copies without even trying.

Thereafter, such fiction buyers as have been gracious enough to hear me out will usually re-order fresh stock when the books I've left with them sell and (here's a mark of good professional practice with some Waterstone's branches, I always think) will *share* surplus copies they have to hand with neighbouring branches as and when they may be required for book signings etc.

❑ STOCK LEVELS By way of reciprocation, of course, I make sure I keep in touch with Waterstone's and Borders to check on their requirements and, whenever possible, I visit the branches in person. My first concern in doing so is, naturally enough, to verify stock levels. Because – well, for example, Waterstone's branch practice would appear to be that any subsequent re-order is automatically triggered when the branch has just one copy of a title remaining, whereas I personally regard "one copy remaining" as a danger signal.

Why so?

Well, that one "remaining" copy may have been mislaid somewhere, or left in the stockroom perhaps; may have fallen behind the other books on the shelf; or (heaven forfend!) may have been nicked. And any one of these eventualities might lead to an undesirable malfunction of the automatic triggering of a re-order of my book titles, since the (missing) book might feature on the branch inventory for evermore.

However, there is a secondary, albeit similarly important reason for my regular visits to Waterstone's and Borders branches which stock my book. And the other very important reason for my regular visits to Waterstone's and Borders is so that I may check for any shop-soiled stock.

❑ SHOP-SOILED STOCK The point at issue, here, is that, of course, potential customers need to pick up and leaf through my books on the shelves before they know whether they'll want to buy. And so (certainly over a period of a few months, say) some of the stock may, to greater or less extent, become shop-soiled. And, believe me, I am at all times eager to repair or replace shop-soiled stock for Borders and Waterstone's, both – and, indeed, for any other bookshop or sales outlet stocking my books.

Why on earth would I want to do that? Because it makes eminent good sense to do so. That's why.

As I have already indicated, every book I supply to the bookshops (Waterstone's, Borders, the independents) is necessarily supplied on a sale-or-return basis. (I pause at this juncture in order to emphasise that, if you don't sell your book on a sale-or-return basis, you will never sell *any* books.) So the plain fact of the matter is that any book shop is within its rights if it asks to return my books at any time after the 30 days on the invoice has passed. So any bookshop that does *not* initiate such a demand after 30 days is being more than decent about it in the first place. Even so, it simply cannot profit me in the long-run to take unfair advantage of such decency. That is to say, if the stock I have sold to Borders, for instance, becomes shop soiled, no customer is ever going to buy it – and, if no customer buys the shop soiled stock from Borders, Borders is never ever going to reorder *fresh* stock from me. So shop soiled stock is dead stock – as dead to me as it is to Borders in the instance given. Ergo, I am eager at all times to repair or replace shop-soiled stock.

How repair it? Well, I've done this on occasion with very marginally shop-soiled stock, using the plastic book covers I purchase from Brodart. You know the kind of cover: your public library uses them too, In fact, this is precisely the reason I decided to get hold of some Brodart plastic covers in the first place, having noticed a copy of *Every Street in Manchester* in my local library (temporarily resting-up between Brian Keenan and Garrison

Keillor: good company, indeed!) and looking very much like a new book (in its plastic cover) despite date stamping to page 3 indicating that the book had been loaned out on no fewer than twenty-two occasions.

Okay, but will I really *replace* shop-soiled stock. Yes, I will. I willingly exchange shop soiled stock for new copies. More than likely, repairing the books I take away with Brodart covers when I get back home, and using the repaired books to some lesser purpose than selling via Waterstone's or Borders. [See below: The Author's Personal Input into Marketing.]

Note, though, that there is one particular class of books which is never sold to bookshops on a sale-or-return basis. And these are those personally autographed copies left on hand with the branch subsequent to a book signing. (More of which anon.) Nevertheless, I personally remain more than happy to exchange these books, too, for newly-autographed copies, should the old stock subsequently become shop soiled. Because shop-soiled stock is dead stock, as I have said – as dead to you as it is to the book shop and to prospective customers, too. So, always be prepared to:

Repair and/or replace with a smile on your face.

WITH REGARD TO CONTACTING FICTION BUYERS IN GENERAL

❍ Choose a regular time to approach fiction buyers in the various bookshops. Once a month, say – whatever you (and they) feel comfortable with. But do stay in touch with the bookshop contacts you've made.

❍ Should you telephone or mail prior to visiting? Go with your personal inclination, of which mine is to take a chance on just dropping in for a visit. Sometimes it works; sometimes it doesn't. Even so, I have an in-built aversion to telephoning first only to be told that the fiction buyer is "in a meeting". And a visit to the book shop, even if the fiction buyer is unavailable, does at least enable you to check on the status and condition of your title, and might yield news of a different kind. Perhaps the fiction buyer you know is due to move to another branch, in which case you'll need to know who the new fiction buyer is.

- Don't expect to get hold of or have a meaningful conversation with a fiction buyer (and this goes for all bookshops) early in the day, at lunchtime, in the evening, or on Saturday, Sunday and/or a public holiday. Contact with fiction buyers is best effected on weekdays between 10.00am and noon, and 2.00pm to 4.00pm – and perhaps leave Monday out, too.

- Have a small supply of books with you in an attaché case: for illustrative purposes and just in case you are invited to leave some stock. (Pilots' flight bags will hold approximately a dozen books, a smaller executive case, six.)

- Have your bookmarks, invoice books, a calculator and a pen with you. Don't gush with an offer of 50% discount rate as soon as you get your foot in the door; ask instead what commission rate the fiction buyer will require. If they really do require (*Ouch!*) 50%, you, in turn will require them to take a shed load of books. More likely is it that the required commission rate will be between 30% and 40%, and the number of copies ordered from 2 to 6. Believe me, 6 would be a real achievement on first acquaintance.

- Don't take 'No' for an answer; go back another day in perhaps a month's time. You might get hold of a different fiction buyer. I mean to say, why should the shop *not* take a small supply of your book *on a sale-or-return basis*. Repeat: always, always, *always* mention the fact of that sale-or-return basis – and, if you wish, your intention of replacing shop-soiled stock, though this aspect is perhaps best left to be discovered during what will hopefully be a long and happy association with the book shop in question.

- Play the game exactly like some people play the dogs: they double up on each bet, then go home immediately they have a winner. Leave the doubling up in the lap of the gods, but go home immediately you have a winner. That is to say, go home immediately subsequent to making a successful placement of books at a book shop new to you. Because it really is important to conclude your "sales round" on a positive note. It can make the world of difference to how you feel about selling – to how you feel about going out and selling on the next occasion.

❑ PLACING YOUR BOOK WITH WATERSTONE'S First of all, contact Waterstone's HQ so as to introduce yourself and supply the full relevant details about your book: Waterstone's Booksellers Ltd., Head Office, Capital Interchange Way, Brentford, Middlesex TW8 0EX Tel: 0208 742 3800 Website: www.waterstones.co.uk Also, request from Waterstone's HQ:

- permission to approach Waterstone's branches with a view to their stocking your book; and,
- a list of Waterstone's branches.

Once appropriate permission turns up together with a list of branches, select Waterstone's branches in your area to approach in respect of asking the fiction buyer to stock your book. The rules are as above, except that:

- Waterstone's will not accept a supply of books in-branch;
- if Waterstone's has an account with your distributor, the branch will order direct from the distributor;
- if Waterstone's does not have an account with your distributor (that is to say, if you are, as am I, the distributor), the branch will need to order via Gardners. [See Setting Up an Account With the Wholesalers, above.]
- In the event of such an order being made via Gardners, then Gardners will order your book from you, who will invoice Gardners and forward the book to Gardners in Eastbourne, who will then forward the book direct to the Waterstone's branch which ordered your book, and it is Gardners which will eventually pay you.

NOTE On making your first placement of books via a Waterstone's fiction buyer, ask him to check that everything is in order with the way Gardners is listing your book for sale. Mistakes can happen, and you certainly do not want your book listing in some odd manner which would preclude its selling successfully. Check also with Gardners itself on returning home. (This is a fail-safe double check. The thing is, as a beginner, there may be some specification you inadvertently failed to make; and it is only too easy for someone at the other end inadvertently to click on some wrong key on a computer keypad and thereby unwittingly affect your book's availability to the world at large.)

❑ PLACING YOUR BOOK WITH BORDERS To be perfectly honest, I have only ever dealt with two branches of Borders, one at Manchester Fort (more of which anon) and Borders at Manchester Trafford Centre (which was, in actual fact, a branch of the related Books Inc. wearing Borders' livery) Both contacts have resulted in friendly, businesslike relationships, according to which I was welcomed from the start, my main dealings being done at Borders, Manchester Fort.

I first became acquainted with Borders, Manchester Fort*, when staff supplied the book-buying service to the Midland Hotel for the Portico Literary Prize Presentation Dinner in November, 2006. What a go-ahead bunch of people they are. On the young side in the main, they service a massive hangar-like bookshop in an area of the city which was previously known for scrap-yards, motor factors and wholesale goods suppliers.

*The "Fort" nomenclature, as one ex-Brum Borders fiction buyer tells me, stems from a Fort Dunlop-backed investment venture which expanded to various other sites within the UK. This ex-Brum Borders fiction buyer, incidentally, is the same man who persuaded Radio Manchester to field a fortnightly book review on which *Every Street Manchester* was featured by request of a Bolton library readers' group.

Borders, Manchester Fort, is very handy in several respects:

- There is ample parking, so I don't have to lug a bagful of books around town.

- There are several members of staff, not just one, who are

authorised to make a decision about whether I may place fresh stock with them.

❍ Knowing my books are left with them on a sale-or-return basis and that I regularly service shop-soiled stock, Borders is not unadventurous about the number of copies of my books it will take into stock. A dozen of each title, say, does not faze them.

❍ It's always a pleasant experience to visit Borders, Manchester Fort, whether I place stock with them or no. Because hangar-like though the premises is, the atmosphere has all the warmth and welcome of a village store. A Starbuck's coffeeshop is a feature, too.

❍ When I do place stock with Borders, it is taken direct from me in-house, so what I do is to leave the requisite number of books PLUS an invoice for those books.

NOTE The potential downside of the arrangement is as follows:

❍ it may take some time for the stock I leave with Borders to make it from the stockroom to the book shelves (they hold massive stocks). But the branch is conveniently nearby, so I check up on a weekly basis, tootling down there on Saturday mornings.

NB Borders HQ, 122 Charing Cross Road, London WC2H 0JR Tel. 020 7379-7313

❑ PLACING STOCK WITH INDEPENDENT BOOKSHOPS Do this any which way the bookshop indicates, either via Gardners or over the counter. The rules apply as per the sections above.

❍ Think laterally about sales points, too. For instance, your local newsagent, art gallery, museum – maybe pharmacist and undertaker, too, may be only too happy to sell your book for you.

❍ Consider wrapping your books in plastic punched pockets to keep them clean.

- Leave just four books at a time and offer commission of 25%: this way there will never be any mix-up about monies due.

❑ PLACING BOOKS WITH THE MAJOR SUPERMARKETS (YEAH, LIKE AS IF)

- Unless you can afford for the major supermarkets to sell your book @ around £3-plus per copy, which means, of course, that . . .

- you will have to be selling your book to the major supermarkets @ around £2 or so per copy, which means, of course, that . . .

- you'll have to be buying your book from your publisher @ around £1.00 or so per copy, which means, of course, that . . .

- pigs by the litter have, indeed, gone for take-off from Manchester Terminal 2.

- So just don't bother trying.

Let's face it, there are novelists of major importance who don't sell their books via the major supermarkets. Because the major supermarkets sell books in much the same way as they sell near sell-by date stock – as cheaply as possible before it gets left on their hands. Not to put too fine a demographic point on it (if I may for a moment speak as a concerned ratepayer and voter), the major supermarkets are *in* the community but not *of* it. So, I don't believe it is even worth trying to place a local book by a local author with any of the major supermarkets.

Of course, if you are as dumb as I was when I began marketing my debut novel (or dumb enough not to heed this hard-won advice of mine) you may presume to make contact with Super Duper Mart HQ (let's call it) – and you may even get to speak to the person responsible for book sales at Super Duper Mart HQ, and the person supposedly responsible for book sales at Super Duper Mart HQ may even deign to speak to you. Indeed, the person responsible for book sales at Super Duper Mart HQ may even utter words of encouragement which cause you to forward a copy of your debut novel to the person responsible for book sales at Super Duper Mart HQ, whereupon . . . (Cue: *a cold wind whistles across the north of England, with tumbleweed travelling at ground level on a horizontal trajectory across the Irwell Valley, where distant traffic flow can be heard on the M62 and the M60, eastbound and west; an owl hoots; the clock on Middleton parish church strikes thirteen . . .*)

Whereupon, one month on, you telephone the person responsible for book sales at Super Duper Mart HQ, whereupon, too, you discover the person supposedly responsible for book sales at Super Duper Mart HQ has developed a bad case of Sloping Shoulders (let's call it), so you are, instead, put through to a person *partly*-responsible for book sales at Super Duper Mart HQ, who promises to look into the matter, whereupon . . . (Cue: *close study of cuticles, some wide-mouthed yawning, a bit of blinking as if trying to stay awake, shuffling of shoe leather, puffing and panting on occasion, a solitary stray fart, arms folded, arms akimbo, a pained facial expression, tumbleweed drifts across the Pennines, a passenger train rattles towards Manchester along the West Yorkshire line . . .*)

Whereupon, one month on, you telephone the person partly-responsible for book sales at Super Duper Mart HQ, whereupon, too (*yawn*), Mr Sub-Sloping Shoulders (let's call him) tells you that he has made his enquiries and, with Christmas being almost upon us now, it is far too late in the year for Super Duper Mart to stock your debut novel at any branch in the UK . . . Yes, as a matter of fact, he does know there are umpteen branches of Super Duper Mart in the Greater Manchester conurbation where customers may be more than interested in a book called *Every Street in Manchester* . . . And, yes, he quite understands that you have been waiting since August for this negative response . . . And, No, that copy of your debut novel (price £14.99), he cannot return, due to its having been misplaced somewhere in the system . . .

Whereupon, you ask She Who Holds the Casting Vote at Your Present Address if she has a use for a £15 Super Duper Mart gift token, as she quite naturally has . . . whereupon you request a £15

Super Duper Mart gift token from Super Duper Mart HQ (the price of one copy of your book), and a £15 Super Duper Mart gift token duly arrives without further ado – a welcome contribution to the Christmas festivities. But, let's have it right, you've done a helluva lot of work for that £15 Super Duper Mart gift token. So, as I say, with regard to placing your book with the major supermarkets – it's just not worth trying. Because, as the man said (said man in this instance being Bill Keeth), there are more ways to skin a Super Duper Mart cat. [See below.]

❑ PLACING BOOKS WITH W H SMITH Oh dear! Least said, soonest mended, as the same man said. Said man being Bill Keeth again. Because I gave up with W H Smith, just as Mark Etherington tells us he did.

Mark Etherington, author and self-publisher of *The Best of British*, a fast-selling booklet humorously comparing UK and US idiom (see his website: 'The Very Best of British – How to Publish Yourself in the UK') explains himself like this: "I gave up with W H Smith . . . I did all the right things, got the right buyer, had a chat, sent him a book and called back. He would not take it. After selling 20,000 copies I tried again but [the buyer] still was not interested."

I gave up with W H Smith, too. That was over twelve months ago – and please don't imagine I had sold no books via W H Smith: I sold plenty, believe me. But the business relationship failed to progress. About which I'll say no more than this. The overall general impression I got was that trying to do business with W H Smith as a local writer/self-publisher is akin to attempting to deal with "an absent principal". Because individual branches would refer me to head office whilst head office, in turn, would refer me back to the individual branches. Having said which, I must say I found the staff at HQ okay, particularly Accounts. But the branches were hard work – until it occurred to me to upsticks so as to initiate a new approach to sales via W H Smith, which in some instances would suit sales via Super Duper Mart too. [See the next chapter.]

SIXTEEN: YOUR PERSONAL INPUT INTO MARKETING

NOTE *Even if the agreed package specifies your publisher will act as distributor for your book, he will not be marketing your book in any proactive sense. It really is up to you to publicise and actively market your book from the start.*

The more you put into marketing your book, the more copies you will sell. It's as simple as that. Think about it.

- ❍ Did Chris Tarrant ever walk up your garden path, knock at your front door and give you a million quid for *not* taking part in *Who Wants to Be a Millionaire*?
- ❍ Has HM the Queen ever pinned an MBE on you on her birthday in recognition of your having lived as a recluse for the past twenty five years?
- ❍ Did Sir Alex Ferguson ever field you in his First XI on the strength of your unparalleled experience as a couch-potato?

Nope with knobs on! And you know it. And it's exactly the same with your self-published book. No one is going to break your front door down to get hold of a copy. Anyway, you've taken delivery of the first print-run of your debut novel now, so you can't suddenly start pretending you're a wilting violet. You've simply got to get out there, tell people about the Thing and get them to buy it. Okay, you've done a fair bit of the work already. You've got a few copies into the libraries, you've got some into the shops. A reasonable achievement. Even so, it's not enough. Because your bookselling activities are going to need a bit of push before things get going properly, gather momentum – and sales of your book, hopefully, take off. And part of the reason for this is that your book, being a self-published book, begins life with a number of distinct disadvantages from the start. Let's see what these are.

Quite apart from the fact that commercial publishers will already have a working relationship with the major booksellers, who, in turn are very well aware that commercial publishers operate a trustworthy sales-or-return policy (something the booksellers don't really know about your book until you tell them), a commercially published book will have an advertising budget behind it which, even three months before it is published, will be keeping the booksellers and critics informed about when the book is scheduled to appear in print. There'll be advertising materials sent out too even at this early stage – and advance copies for the critics too. Your book, on the other hand, will limp off the press and need to hit the ground running. As I say, you and your book are really up against it. So what do you need to do? Also, what do you need in order to do it?

❑ DETERMINATION AND PERSEVERANCE These are the alpha and the omega behind the self-published author's personal input into marketing. Okay, you may easily take a wrong turning (e.g. books don't sell too well in pubs or on outdoor markets where bargain basement economy is the order of the day). But never give up. Find a better way to go (e.g. if your local pharmacy sells the parish magazine on its countertop, it may be prepared to sell a book by a local author too). Never decline an invitation to speak about your book. Accept all invitations while they're hot, no matter how daunting they may at first appear. Then plan for the event quite coolly, with pen and paper to hand. Never *put off* an invitation, dependent upon another person's convenience. Strike while the iron is hot or the opportunity may be lost forever. Think laterally about which organisations you might approach regarding book presentations, book signings, book sales – particularly, *whom* you might profitably approach, since it is always helpful to have an enthusiast on the inside. And don't imagine for one minute that bookshops are the only places where you can sell your books. Think about expansion of sales to include the local art gallery, the museum, the tourist information centre, the local newsagent, bistro, café. And, should any of these fail to show a return, perhaps re-jig what's on offer or even re-wrap it and re-present it before moving on. If any particular approach to sales doesn't work, then move on and find another. Let's face it – if you, the author, don't believe in your book enough to do that, who else will?

❑ A GENERIC BOOKMARK At the very least you should arrange to have a generic bookmark available. That is to say, you should arrange to have printed a personal bookmark giving details of your book (an image of your front cover. the title, author, ISBN number, publisher, your website, plus a contact number and a short greeting perhaps: e.g. "Best Wishes from D Ditherer" – and perhaps too, to the obverse side, a list of bookshops that stock your book). Get yourself a few thousand. (With three books under my belt, I order 10,000 at a go.) If you are PC-proficient enough you may be able to run off a bookmark of reliable quality on your PC. (This is what Billy Hopkins does, and a pleasanter bookmark I have yet to see.)

To my mind, bookmarks are a universally acceptable freebie – a perennially useful gift, an advertising tool, a calling card. A bookmark should be enclosed with each and every personally sold copy of your book (and with all sales via Amazon Marketplace), and a bookmark should be left in your wake wherever you henceforward go: your local library (leave a supply), the bookshops you visit (again, a supply is called for). But leave a bookmark, too, where you'd hesitate to leave a book – on the bus, in a taxi, in a café, at the railway station. Use envelopes for personal use which are sufficiently long enough to accommodate a bookmark – and ensure a book mark accompanies each personal mailing (even to HM Inspector). When you do a book presentation, place a bookmark on every chair. If you never do a book presentation or a book signing for a year, you should still get through a thousand bookmarks. What is not bought today, may well be bought tomorrow – particularly if tomorrow is Christmas Eve or the day before a birthday.

NOTE A bent bookmark is not a pretty sight and will be binned at the earliest opportunity, so make quite sure your generic bookmark is no longer than the height of your book.

❑ A PERSONAL WEBSITE This is a truly business-like means of contact and of detailing far more information about you and your book than could ever be encompassed in a newspaper advertisement or a book presentation. But please don't pay the earth for a website: some of these PC-wallahs have heads full of magic when it comes to invoicing. Do it yourself, if you can, or get a PC-proficient pal to set it up for you. (N.B. Limited Edition Press does work of this sort – and at a very reasonable price, too.)

What to feature on your personal website? Well, certainly, details of you and your book. But instead of my specifying its content, why not have a look at my website, and those of a few other authors? See if your favourite author has a site too. Check out these websites for a start:

www.billysbooks.info
www.brianhughesmbe.co.uk
www.michaelconnelly.com
www.thomasharris.com
www.michaelridpath.com
www.novelnovella.com
www.bernardmaclaverty.com
www.elmoreleonard.com
www.martinamis.com
www.dickfrancis.com

NOTE It's important for me that readers should be able to contact me but, given their fame, this seems to be the last thing that some of the other authors listed want to happen. Elmore Leonard, by way of example, claims not to use a PC, and keeps his distance by having his full-time researcher, Greg Sutter, working as its webmaster. By way of contrast, Michael Connelly's staff seem happy to answer pertinent questions, and the author of Manchester-based, *Our Kid*, is invariably tickled pink to hear from his readers, as apparently is Dick Francis, too.

❑ THE NEWSPAPERS You need to form a good relationship with the press – that is to say, the local press in the main. The *Middleton Guardian* has been very good to my books from the start, having been only too pleased to feature each and every development since *Every Street in Manchester* was first published:

❍ the first print-run, the second, the third – the second edition;
❍ the controversy that ensued when the book was banned by one

local priest even though another priest had praised it, going so far as to advertise it for sale from the pulpit;
- the book's shortlisting for the Portico Literary Prize;
- the first print-run of *Manchester Kiss* etc. etc. etc.

So make quite sure you key your local newspaper in about the self-publication of your own book by sending them a press release at least. (That is to say, one A4 page giving as many details as you could squeeze on to a bookmark plus a short description of the subject matter: don't overcrowd it with verbiage.)

In addition to this, there is a real need to keep in touch with the local press other than by e-mail. Call in to the newspaper office on occasion or telephone. I say this because, initially, another local newspaper failed utterly to feature my debut novel despite my providing a copy of my book, the journalist to whom I delivered it having given me assurances to the contrary. One year on, though (I could kick myself for not chasing this up earlier), this same newspaper made good the omission in fine style, the original omission being easily explained by the fact that the journalist who had taken the initial report (and my book) had immediately taken herself off to the Land of the Free.

Something else you may care to put to the local press is the fact that you would be willing to supply a copy of your book as a prize, say, a development which would, of course, necessitate a second mention in the local newspaper, which would certainly prove cheaper than paying for an advertisement.

Send absolutely *no* copies of your book to any book reviewer working for the national press unless, of course, you have a professional connection with the reviewer or happen to be related by blood or temporary amatory dalliance. Failing these, it is a complete and utter waste of time and money since book reviewers working for the national press have, since time immemorial, had their collective heads shoved firmly "where the sun don't shine" except on the Whitbread/MAN Booker shortlist.

Should you send a review copy to the regional press? Well, yes, perhaps you should send a review copy to the regional press – and perhaps the regional press should be interested in reviewing your debut novel, if only because there will surely be some interest in the fact that you are a regular reader who lives in the area. Local novelists, after all, aren't all that thick on the ground. Even so, don't hold your breath. Neither of the two separate copies of *Every Street in Manchester* (one 1st edition; one 2nd) which I duly despatched to the books' columnist was reviewed in the *Manchester Evening News*. And here I sound a note of warning, in that, despite its entirely apposite title and narrative plot, *Every Street in Manchester* received nary a mention whatsoever in the *Manchester Evening News* for fully eighteen months after it was published, during which time I e-mailed and/or telephoned the *MEN* on 18 separate occasions. In fact, on the penultimate occasion I made contact with the *MEN* (by which time my debut novel had already been shortlisted for the Portico Literary Prize alongside names of national importance, one of whom was to be treated to a full-page spread within days of my own application), a journalist on the newsdesk confidently assured me that there was: 'No story for the *Manchester Evening News* in a book called *Every Street in Manchester*.'

This is, of course, arrant nonsense tantamount to Michael Parkinson imagining he is personally of more interest to the viewing public than any one of the interviewees on his show. Even so, it had been similarly stupid of me to contact the *MEN* newsdesk in the first place, since the appropriate section to contact about self-published books is *Features* – and the same applies to all regional newspapers. As proof of which, when I eventually contacted *Features* at the *MEN* on my eighteenth attempt, eighteen months on, both *Every Street in Manchester* and *Manchester Kiss* received an extended mention therein. In retrospect, too, it had been similarly stupid of me to send review copies anywhere other than to *Features*. Because what I and my book really required was (what we got on the eighteenth attempt) *a feature about us, rather than a simple book review*. (See Alison Baverstock.)

Moral: The newspaper section to contact about your novel is *Features* – and don't ever think of giving up. It is perfectly right and proper that your debut novel should receive a write-up in the regional press, just as it is perfectly right and proper that you should persist in telling the regional press about your debut novel until such a feature duly appears.

❑ LOCAL RADIO Forward a press release. I was interviewed on GMR Radio (latterly, Radio Manchester) by the ever-urbane Mike Shaft. And *Every Street in Manchester* was subsequently featured on Radio Manchester at the request of a readers' group at a Bolton library.

A point to note about radio and TV, perhaps, is that the contact numbers (telephone and e-mail) listed in publicity may not necessarily be the contact numbers to which that the programme presenters have daily access. Accordingly, a telephone call to the switch at GMR Radio resulted in my obtaining a different e-mail address feeding directly through to the presenters' daily notice board. And this was the trick that broke the log jam as far as *Every Street in Manchester* was concerned: I received a phone call from GMR and an invitation to appear on the Mike Shaft Show later that same week.

❑ LOCAL TV Certainly, forward a press release. Television is obviously the most effective way of getting your sales message across. That is to say, you have written and self-published a debut novel and you want to say to a wider public: 'Hey, this is what it's all about, folks; furthermore, it's on sale now at all good bookshops.' Sadly, there is about as much chance of your appearing on local TV as there is of your debut novel being reviewed by the national press. Having said which, I did get to appear on Channel M, a new Manchester-based TV station concentrating very effectively on news reports about the Greater Manchester conurbation.

So, in order to assist you in deciding in advance whether your favourite local TV news magazine programme may be interested in featuring you and your debut novel, let me explain, as it would appear to me, the precise difference between Channel M, on the one hand, and the other television news channels serving the Greater Manchester conurbation, on the other. For the plain fact of the matter is that Channel M presenters are, every one of them, ready, willing and able, to get out of the studio into the highways and by-ways in search of topical news stories about local people wherever they may be found. Meanwhile, TV presenters on the longer-established regional television news magazine programmes (those same programmes that are praised to high heaven whenever the TV franchises and awards are up for grabs), well, TV presenters on those longer-established regional television news magazines programmes have only recently learned to stand up ('tis said) – formerly ('twas thought), they were physically bereft of legs to stand up upon, or those legs had perhaps atrophied due to disuse (as one cynic of my acquaintance has it). Accordingly, such TV presenters have very sensibly retained, for the use of ('tis also bruited abroad), a brace or two of journalistic gophers for the purpose of venturing out of the studio to get wet, windswept and a few news stories, not one of which (you may rest assured, Merry Gentlemen) will concern you or your debut novel whilst (and I quote last week's looniest reportage from the longer established regional television news magazine programmes "serving" my home address) there remains *a solitary one-legged pet parrot to be reported upon.*

All this is said in jest, of course. But, as UK-based US journalist Michael Carlson warns us (see "Afterword: The Novelist as Reporter": *Crime Beat* by Michael Connelly, pub. Orion): "Too often in our world journalists move from graduate schools into hermetically sealed newsrooms . . . cut off from the real lives of the people about whom they are supposed to report." None of which means you should not tell your local television news magazine programmes about yourself and your debut novel – and keep right *on* telling them, too. But TV in the UK has long been a quasi-private reserve, particularly where it is financed with public money, so, don't be too hopeful about getting on local TV if you don't have connections akin to those of the Dimbleby family or the Madeleys, Richard and Judy. (And don't even dream of making Richard and Judy's booklist if you don't already qualify for Booker/Whitbread Prize consideration – said list being (*yawn*) just more of the same.)

❑ YOUR BOOK LAUNCH Now, behave yourself! Of course, you're going to hold a book launch. You really *must*! Believe me, you are most definitely going to hold a book launch, if I have any say in the matter.

Yes, I do know, as a matter of fact, that you are the shy, retiring type, a wallflower, so to speak – loath to push yourself forward, the sort of person (let's say) who wouldn't say boo to a goose, were boos to geese *de rigeur* by the gaggle. (Aren't we *all*?) But having written a novel, you are *ipso facto* now a celebrity of sorts, however minor. Because, no matter how many thousands of novels the literary retail trade tells us are published in the UK each year (and I'll grant you it's helluva lot *more* than in the US – it really *is*), writing a novel is still a major achievement, something you don't do, or hear of being done, locally, on every day of the week – something, in fact, that most people living within these shores will never do. And, whilst there are literally millions of people living in the UK at present (something of the order of 59M at the last count), you may depend upon it that very few of them have written a novel and published it in this last twelve month period.

Okay, so you're not the UK champion novelist, so to speak – and you're not even area champion. Like myself [see Appendix 7], you may be only one of several contenders. Even so, you *are* a contender, and that's important. You are someone special in that respect – special on your own terms too. (Witness the one and only complaint of Terry Malloy, the side-lined and much abused protagonist played by Marlon Brando in the Budd Schulberg-written/Elia Kazan-directed *On the Waterfront*: 'I coulda been a *contender*!' complains Terry Malloy.') But you are at least *a contender*, so you really must have a book launch to celebrate – and sell umpteen copies of your book in the process. Besides, your mum will love it, and all your friends who've seen you muddle your way through to this achievement. And, I promise you, you will be surprised and positively delighted at the amount of interest your book launch will generate in your locality. [See David Armstrong's wonderfully upbeat account of one of his own book launches in *How NOT to Write a Novel*: his initial concerns, the thoughtful planning, the eventual small scale triumph – a very welcome (and well-deserved) social occasion for the author, his friends, family, and the town where he lives.]

You will, as I say, be surprised. I've hosted two book launches so far, one for *Every Street in Manchester*, the other for *Manchester Kiss*. On both occasions I've booked a local church hall (a different church hall on each occasion), I've invited perhaps forty or so people I know (thirty or so of whom have turned up on each occasion), I've provided some wine, red and white (a very dependable salesman is party plonk), I've spoken for forty minutes or so (as a seasoned campaigner, I am now capable of running this up to an hour), and I've sold fifteen books on each occasion (let's face it, guests tend to travel in pairs, so fifteen books is one book per couple). Which, to my mind, is no bad result. And what I list below (apart from the author, his book and his spiel) is a list of the things which I've found essential to a successful book launch:

- hold your event in a centrally-situated, ground floor level, private meeting room which is available for hire at a reasonable price (£50 tops – and you'd want a helpful body thrown in to assist you at that price) or, better still, free-of-charge;

- book the venue for an absolute minimum of two hours, so the occasion won't appear rushed;

- hold your event on a suitable midweek evening – for instance, I prefer a Thursday evening when, so I am reliably informed, Manchester United is never featured on TV: make no mistake about this, there is no competing with a crowd-puller like the Reds – unless you are, of course, an alternative crowd puller also called the Reds, or better still, the Blues;

- write, phone and e-mail everybody you know in your family, at work, in your parish, club, pub or social group (ask the local newspaper to feature the event on its diary page) – and make sure every one of your potential guests is supplied with a form or a ticket containing details of time, date and place;

- provide 6 litres of wine (and wine glasses or paper cups) for your guests: that is to say, one 3 litre carton of red; another of white, taking the surplus [*hic*'] home with you at the end of he night;

- provide no food except (should you care to do so) nibbles speared by cocktail sticks, because there's no way you want sticky hands touching your books;
- ensure there is adequate seating, heating and light for your guests;
- place a generic bookmark on each chair;
- *always*, *always*, *always* arrange for another adult to be in attendance to oversee the distribution of wine, the sale of books, general security and safety – that is to say, remember no man can simultaneously an entertainer and policeman be.
- autograph each book you sell, with or without the owner's name as per his request and enclose a generic bookmark with it;
- always leave the room as you found it;
- if the event is particularly successful, or if someone connected with the venue has been particularly helpful, it might be an idea to donate a spare copy of your book to parish/club funds, as appropriate. Regard this as an advertising pitch left in your wake to speak one volume at least about your good name – and that of your book, of course.

NOTE The wine you provide may even supply you with a light-hearted introduction to your talk in that it is said the novelist, Kingsley Amis (*Lucky Jim, The Old Devils* etc.), himself a lifelong beer drinker, was of the opinion that the three most distressing words in the English language are contained within the query: 'Red or white?'

With regard to the content of your talk, your book launch and subsequent book presentations will be pretty much the same.

❑ WHAT THE HECK ARE YOU GOING TO TALK ABOUT AT YOUR BOOK LAUNCH AND BOOK PRESENTATIONS? First of all, how many people do you expect to attend? Thirty to forty is a quorum, I'd say – reasonably cosy. But I'd reckon beyond sixty or so you'll need some amplification. Meanwhile, as we've seen, your address should last for half an hour, or anything up to an hour, if you feel confident enough.

So, let's look at things objectively. You have a reasonable brain on you or you would not have been able to write a book. Also, since the people invited to your book launch are your special guests, freely volunteering to turn up on the night, you may certainly depend upon a certain warmth of welcome to be awaiting you and to be freely given. So don't worry on that score. And, when it comes to doing a presentation for some leisure group or society, things are even better, because your audience will have invited you to address them. In any case, your audience in either instance will consist of literate, well-mannered specimens of humanity, with nary a lager lout in sight.

What is perhaps worrying you about addressing your audience is – well, to be frank, the fusty, dusty, stand-offish, holier-than-thou, pontificating nature of most public speaking we hear nowadays, from the mealy-mouthed condescension of politicos addressing the populace to the ivory-towered self-absorption of public/private sector spokespersons mouthing platitudes as humanity speeds hell-wards in handcarts. But your book launch (and/or presentation) isn't the same thing at all. For a start, you'll be talking about something that really turns you on, something you were so interested in that you've made a name for yourself by writing a novel about it – even going to the trouble of insisting your novel was turned out in a certain way.

Oh, there's loads to enthuse about there. And note, too, that "enthuse" is the operative word. Because most people are interested in hearing people enthusing about their interests and their passions. And something else people are interested in hearing about is "how a thing is done" – that is to say, that special thing that you have done – you've written a book and self-published it, too. That hooks people: look, by way of example, at all the slice of life shows on TV – airports, trawler fleets, hospitals, and so on. So the keywords are positive: 'Come on in, the water's lovely!' and the tempo should be positively upbeat.

So let's think of some of the questions you might consider answering.

1. PERSONAL Is yours a pen name? If so, why did you choose that pen name? Why did you choose the subject matter you chose to write about? What's your real job? If none, what *was* your real job?

2. THE BOOK Is the book locally-based? What's it about? Who are the main characters in the book? Are the characters made up or are they real people? Are the places real places? How long did it take you to write this book?

3. WRITING Is there any particular time of day you prefer to write? How long do you write at a stretch? Do you write every day of the year? How much do you write per day? Do you ever get stuck for ideas? Is there anybody whom you rely on to help you? Is there an unexpected downside? Is there an unexpected upside? Have any funny things happened to you? Have any weird things happened to you? How does it affect your family life? Do you intend to keep on writing? What's your next book about?

4. PRACTICALITIES How did you go about self-publishing the book? Where did you get the idea in the first place? Why did you want to do it? How do you go about getting a printer/publisher? How do you go about selling your book? What books do you like to read? Do you make money writing? When will you retire to a tax haven?

In addition to posing and answering questions like these, ask the audience if they'd like to ask any questions of their own – and don't forget to advertise to them your availability to do book presentations free-of-charge on request. All you ask is that you may be permitted to bring along some of your books for sale, there being, of course, absolutely no obligation to buy.

I could go on – and so can you. Keep it light is the main thing, I'd advise. And begin with a joke, if you can – and try and tell about the funny side of everything that's happened since you began. Another good idea (though you can't always make it happen) is to have something funny happening at the start that you can return to at the end – or that you can keep returning to in your talk from time to time. It needn't be very much at all really: e.g.

❍ an extended reference to the Kingsley Amis/wine anecdote mentioned above. And,

❍ check out www.billysbooks.info again – in particular, the additional notes the author has provided with the new paperback editions of his books, where you'll find an extended humorous reference to astrological superstition. It's the tone of the thing that counts, though your tone will, of course, be different. Essentially, don't Henry James your audience, as I call it: don't play the great author. Act normally, be approachable and completely unassuming.

Something else I'd advise you to do at your book launch (and your book presentations) is to mention, as I invariably make a point of doing, other local writers and their books. In the first place, I'm a keen fan of other local authors and their books. [See Appendix 7.] Secondly, to speak about other authors is, to me at any rate, a blessed relief from the book launch/book presentation egotism of persistently talking about myself and my work. And, personally, I don't think I'm imagining it when I say I always feel that my audience welcomes this departure too – perhaps because they know more about other local authors than they know about me, and so the members of the audience will quite naturally be drawn in to contribute their own four pennorth to the proceedings.

One thing that's a matter of personal concern to me is that, being a bit of a control freak, I tend to think I'm far too serious at book presentations. But I'm working on it. For what it's worth, though, please don't imagine I go in unprepared. I spend ages preparing and re-writing what I'm planning to say, jokes included, and I may have as many as 16 A4 pages of notes by the time I'm finished. Incidentally, I take these notes with me to the book launch or book presentation in the format as follows.

1. Upwards of a dozen separate A4-sized sheets of paper – i.e. one A4 sheet to each 3-4 minutes.

2. The text on the A4 sheets should be 16pt (repeat, 16 pt. with bold print for headings and emphasis. Why 16pt? Well, simply because your text will be as much as three feet away from your eyes when you stand up to address your audience across a tabletop.

3. Number the pages right-aligned, leaving each numeral peeping out from under the page preceding it, so a dozen A4 pages will take only 9 inches or so of space, and you may easily turn each page over as you proceed, discarding it to your left – so you'll need just 18 inches or so of lateral working space.

Once you get going it's bound to come. It will, honestly. There'll be so much of it, you will have to consider which bits to leave out – and if writing your proposed spiel doesn't come easily (Who are you trying to kid? You're a published author) use a tape recorder and handle your preparation that way.

I mean to say, there's no way you'll want to give away any trade secrets, but you must have loads of things that have cropped up since you began – some of them you wouldn't have dreamed about in your wildest dreams. Like the man says (said man being Bill Keeth, philosophising with a single malt aboard): 'You've gotta *live* it to *know* it!' Well, you've lived it all right – now tell 'em about it. Tell them about it because they're dying to know – and then they'll buy your book in quantity, and tell others about it. Remember, though, there must never ever be any obligation to buy. The real fruits of a book launch or a book presentation may not be realised until Christmas comes . . . or somebody's birthday . . . or Mothers' Day or Father's.

Keep an executive briefcase packed, ready for your book launch and book presentations, containing as follows:

❍ your presentation notes
❍ two pens minimum: *all books sold should be autographed*
❍ bookmarks: *one per chair and one per book sold*
❍ a bookmarked copy of your book for readings
❍ a display book stand: *a clear plastic letter rack from Staples will do the job*

- water/plastic cup: *a thirsty business, is public speaking*
- spare wristwatch: *it would appear rude to look at your wrist to check the time*
- comb/brush: *just in case*
- soapy flannel: *an author shouldn't have mucky hands . . .*
- dry hand towel: *or wet hands either!*
- rigger's gloves: *for off-loading boxes of books etc.*

NOTE Display your books in front of you: don't leave them boxed.

OTHER ITEMS, NECESSARY OR OTHERWISE

- your stock – one box plus a spare box perhaps
- sack truck
- folding table: just in case
- tablecloth or an old curtain: again, just in case

NOTE Book presentations will differ from your book launch in several respects:

- you will be the guest not the host of any social, parish or leisure group which requires the services of a speaker;

- you will not be providing any wine;*

- in view of this cash saving (and the fact that no commission will be payable) you might profitably consider offering your book at a discounted price – e.g. a BOGOF offer, or three-for-the-price-of two, say. (N.B. Always ask the full cover price for the book at the book launch: the provision of accommodation and victuals plus the novelty value of the occasion warrants it);

- it won't be your job to tidy up after the event.

* I used to provide wine at book presentations, too, until: a) 72 well-heeled ladies drained the entire 6 litres of wine and purchased not a single book between them in the same week as b) an altogether abstemious church group forbade me to set alcohol before them. Moral: Why bother if bother be the overall result?

❑ ADDRESSING READERS'/WRITERS' GROUPS I always regard these as particularly enjoyable occasions, coming face to face with people who are interested in and knowledgeable about books and writing as much as (perhaps even more than) I am myself.

Dependent upon the numbers in attendance (normally a lot fewer than at open book presentations – a handful as a rule), your best approach, I think, is to sit around a table, committee-style. And whether the group is billed as Readers or Writers, my instinct is to address them as writers. Accordingly, I endeavour to pitch my talk at a different level. Okay, I'll use a reading or two from my book. (I don't care to rely overmuch on readings at any event: daft, I know, but it feels as if I'm short-changing people who'll be buying a copy later.) And I'll use a point or two from my book presentation spiel. But I'm really looking to pitch the tenor of the talk at a working level, so to speak. And so should you, I suggest. That is to say, some of these people will have read your book, so they'll be looking to the significance of events in the narrative, to the real life identity (if any) of any character or institution. They'll want to know what drives you, what made you begin upon such an extended venture as writing a book. They may seek your opinion of novels as a genre. Which writers do you like? How do you get the work done? Is time of day important to you? And people such as these are much more likely to asks you questions – indeed, very searching questions that will have you on your toes, not in any worrying sense, but in the sense that they may cause you personally to analyse and re-appraise more keenly the narrative you've written.

Time passes quickly (and very pleasantly) with a Readers'/ Writers' Group. But not many books will be sold, even at your special book presentation price. This is because your hosts (fewer in number, as they are) were obviously interested in your book before they invited you and so have already bought a copy perhaps – or have, more likely, borrowed it from the library. And fair play to them, too. Because none of this matters in the greater scheme of things. These are articulate, literate people, you're dealing with, here. Whether they like you or not (and, whether they do or they don't, I tell you quite plainly I like them), they will certainly be talking about your visit before and after the event, and other potential readers who have never so much as heard your name may thereby be drawn into the keep-net of your readership.

❑ BOOKSIGNINGS All you need for booksignings is a pen, preferably two – and possibly your bookmarks. (You will, of course, have left a supply of bookmarks at the shop prior to your visit and, preferably, an A4 advertisement for the event.) The bookshop will provide books previously purchased, and you will accept no monies from customers, merely referring them to the cash point. So make sure you sign each copy before you in due recognition that books so autographed are exempt from any sale-or-return agreement. Not that the bookshop in question will be under any misapprehension about this: the bookshop in question would not, in fact, have invited you to do a booksigning did it not have confidence in the selling power of your book. On the other hand, the bookshop in question should also realise that your previous personal promise, if any, to repair or replace shop-soiled stick still holds good.

You will be afforded a table and a chair in my experience, experience which also tells me that Saturday is obviously the best time for your book signing. 10.00am till 4.00pm, say; or even 2.00pm till 4.00pm.

I do realise we're not talking J K Rowling or some such, so if I make sales amounting to double figures, I consider that I've done my bit. In fact, sales of ten books minimum will usually trigger a repeat sale of books to that particular book shop.

Sales staff in bookshops are generally on first name terms. Their thorough professionalism has received previous mention and must at all times be emulated in a reciprocally friendly fashion. Incidentally, I tend to think it's appreciated if I personally purchase a book title from the host's inventory for my own use. If I'm wrong, it certainly can't hurt, because I'm always buying books so why not support those who support me and try to ensure they'll still be in business when I next need their support?

❑ SELLING SHED LOADS OF BOOKS AT A SHOPPING MALL SALES DRIVE

Whether I shop with Super Duper Mart and/or W H Smith or do not, whether I am happy with their respective *modus operandi* or am not, whether I am eager to get hold of the sort of lines they carry or am not, I know there are two things they have got dead right. Super Duper Mart and W H Smith sell books by the score and they know exactly where to set up shop. They know the suburban shopping sites that work, they know the favourable out-of-town sites, they know exactly which shopping malls are the winners.

Think about it.

There are any number of busy shopping malls in and out of the towns where we live. But I could show you a shopping mall in a neighbouring town and adjacent to a popular tourist attraction, the ambience of which is dead in the water (an appropriate metaphor, did you but know which town I mean) or, at best, dying by degrees. On reflection, I realise, the difference between the busy shopping malls and the quiet one is that there is no branch of Super Duper Mart or W H Smith *in situ*. There is no B&Q or Currys or BHS store either: all these superstores know where to set up shop. But I am staying with Super Duper Mart and W H Smith, because they are the superstores that sell books in addition to knowing in which shopping malls to set up shop. Because what I plan to do is to sell my books riding piggy-back, so to speak. In fact, I have already done so on a number of occasions.

By way of example, let me tell you I shifted as many as 72 books last Easter Saturday, courtesy of W H Smith and I shifted a further 68 copies before Christmas last, again courtesy of the same branch of W H Smith. And I can tell you, too, that I will be selling a helluva lot more copies of my books courtesy of W H Smith in the years to come But *through* W H Smith? Alas, no. Not unless they ask me nicely after the way their branches treated me in the past. Now, what exactly does the boy Keeth mean by that, eh?

Well, the W H Smith branch to which I refer is sited within a busy shopping mall (Aren't they all?), and sole traders and charities are permitted to set up shop within that shopping mall from time to time. Which is exactly what I did by arrangement with the management. Which is what I fully intend to continue to do in this and other shopping malls featuring a W H Smith outlet – and outlets for Super Duper Mart, too. As a matter of fact, at the time of writing, I am planning to host the book launch for *Write It Self-Publish It Sell It* in this very same shopping mall and as near as I can get to W H Smith's front door.

If other self-published authors care to pursue a similar sales campaign, they would be well advised to heed the two important provisos I set out below:

- I will never set up shop in a shopping mall which also features a bookshop, such as Borders or Waterstone's or an independent sales outlet with which I already do business; and,

- I will always seek permission to stage such an event from management *in situ*, as opposed to imagining I can talk turkey with some far-flung property management company where the personnel walks about at cloud level in ankle-deep Wilton carpeting, their heads full of magic in respect of inflated property rents.

If you deal with management friendly to the locality, your stall could cost you nowt, if you perhaps chip in to a local charity. (N.B. Never contribute, as an author, to a national charity: local charities truly appreciate contributions received and will reciprocate by helping to sell your books. Yes, I know this isn't the *real* reason you contribute to a charity, but *come on* – it's nice to be nice.) And, at the very worst: e.g. at Manchester's Smithfield Market, say, on a Sunday, a stall at present costs £30 or so – it's a worthwhile punt, though that's not to say an outside market is the place to sell your book. Stay under cover, not only for the sake of attracting the right sort of customer, but so as to keep your books in prime condition.

❑ THE GOLDEN RULE WHEN SELLING YOUR BOOK TO PASSING TRADE

If you were selling your book via a book shop, you would expect to pay commission. So why not give that commission to your customers? What I mean to say is this: whenever I sell my books from a stall in a shopping mall or at a book presentation (yesterday, for instance, I addressed the Newton Heath History Group in a north Manchester meeting hall), I invariably take into account the commission I would be paying to a book shop – perhaps even push it to the absolute limit and aim at doing a BOGOF offer: Buy One, Get One Free. (Or a Buy 2, Get 1 FREE offer.) It's a financial balancing act, I know; but it often works because:

- with your book effectively at half-price, there is bound to be some interest – plus a feeling of goodwill generated by the generous sale price;

- there's a positive pressure to buy because the offer won't be available on the morrow;

- people will stop and talk (they really do); and even if they don't buy, they may buy another day, and in any case they can hand your bookmark (you will, of course, be dishing them out like a good-un) on to someone else.

- There is a distinct chance that the mathematics of the situation will work out as follows:

- Half-price goods PLUS lots of passers-by EQUALS a good few sales . . .

- It's a sales technique I call "piecemeal wholesale", which means . . .

- you are Tesco's Jack Cohen for an hour or two, piling books high and selling 'em cheap.

Remember, too, in such instances as these, those copies of your book which:

- the Printer's Devil has had his wicked way with, or

- are the shop-soiled copies you retrieved from the book shops . . .

Plastic-coated perhaps, courtesy of Brodart, this sub-standard stock may reasonably be brought into play on occasions like these. Obviously, you won't be fobbing your public off with upside down or back-to-front copies. But marginally shop-soiled covers rejuvenated, courtesy of Brodart, are no insult to anybody at half the regular going price.

❑ MAILING LIST . . . Remember to keep tabs on every customer who buys your book or attends your book launch, adding additional names as and when they happen to come to hand. Then, make sure you contact each person so listed in respect of future events and/or your next book is published. It is always handy to have advance sales pre-booked, so much so that it is worth offering free p&p to the people on your list so as to procure those pre-booked sales. When all is said and done, remember, p&p expended is tax deductible.

SEVENTEEN: COMPARING NOTES TWELVE MONTHS ON

DD: Hello-o-o!
BK: Sorry. I don't, er . . .
DD: You wrote that self-publishing book, didn't you?
BK: WISP?
DD: Yeah, *Write It . . .*
BK: *Self-Publish It Sell It?*
DD: Yeah.
BK: You read it, then?
DD: Yeah. I've got a book of my own out since.
BK: Hey, good for you.
DD: *MO* by D Ditherer. Remember, you talked me through all that vanity publishing stuff, to kick off with.
BK: Sorry about that. Didn't recognise you straight off. You've, er, put a bit of weight on unless I'm very much mistaken.

DD: All that turkey and plum duff over Christmas.
BK: Wanna watch that. Slow your writing down.
DD: You serious?
BK: Dead serious.
DD: Bit of body weight slow your writing down?
BK: *Your* writing, not *mine*: your body weight, so yours is the writing, gets slowed down.
DD: You *are* serious, aren't you?
BK: Not as serious as my old feller used to be. He reckoned a dose of TB was a good career move for a writer.
DD: Par-ding?
BK: How many writers you know, had TB once upon a time? Lord Byron, John Keats, Thomas Carlyle, Robert Louis Stevenson, Tobias Smollet, Katherine Mansfield, D H Lawrence, John Braine . . .
DD: Hang about, hang *about*.
BK: What?
DD: You and your writers with TB.
BK: Oh, I'm not recommending it or anything.
DD: Should hope you're not.
BK: No, it's the body weight, isn't it? Something all those writers had in common.
DD: Body weight?
BK: The lack of it. Less you have of it, more you want to do – wash the car, trim the privets, whitewash the hens.
DD: Whitewash the *hens*?
BK: An S J Perelman reference, courtesy of my pal, the Richmal Crompton fan. Think laterally, not literally. That's the thing. I'm simply talking about getting the work done. The less blubber you're carrying around with you, the more you'd sooner be up on your feet, doing a bit.
DD: Up on my feet – *writing, stood up?*
BK: *Standing* up.
DD: Standing up.
BK: That's better.
DD: But writing, standing up? You mean it?
BK: Well, no, it wouldn't suit me, I do admit. But Papa done it that way.

DD: *Did* it that way.

BK: You're learning, aren't you? Anyway, Papa Hemingway sometimes wrote standing up leant on a filing cabinet.

DD: *Leaning* on a filing cabinet.

BK: Just putting you on your mettle.

DD: Yeah, but, listen: what you're saying is I need to lose some weight and write standing up.

BK: No. Just lose the excess weight, then you'll be more likely to stick to your writing regimen.

DD: What? The dawn chorus stint on a daily basis? One thousand words a day or bust?

BK: Yeah. Bit of a chore at times, isn't it?

DD: Too right, it is. But I'm learning in that way, too. You see, when I first kicked off I really needed to do it that way, or I'd've never got it done. But nowadays – well, if I need to pop out to ASDA for a pint of milk first thing, I find I'll still get the writing done later on in the day.

BK: You mean the regular dawn routine is something for a beginner; someone who doesn't believe he'll ever get a book written?

DD: That's about it, I reckon. Once you've written a book, you know you can do it again. Physically, I mean. Whether the words want to come or not, I dunno. That's a different thing entirely.

BK: Easier said than done, though. Least to my way of thinking. You still run the risk you won't get the work done if you don't do it first thing.

DD: Matter of preference.

BK: Not really. Suppose your family turns up at noon and you lose a day's work because you need to entertain them.

DD: What's one day?

BK: One 365th of your next book – a page or so.

DD: Even so, I'm halfway through my next one.

BK: Hey, nice one. So you got the first one out okay? Think I saw something or other in the *Daily Mess* now I come to think on.

DD: Andrew Gutter? '*MO* a Go-Go' was the best he could come up with. For a headline, you know.

BK: Still, it's something.

DD: Took me thirty-six tries to get it in there. One try a week for nine months. Painful as giving birth, it was. Sent a copy off to the books' page, initially. No chance. Crispin Catflap, the in-house book reviewer, poor man's Sergeant Pepper without the sense of humour or the music: Zapata moustache, slouch hat, mutton chops. Reviews nowt but Thai cookery, books about ballet, Lakeland flora and Lepidoptera. Half the page taken up by his smarmy, self-satisfied mug each week, with a view of Dove Cottage and a butterfly-net as a backdrop. Complete and utter waste of time and effort.

BK: Still, thank your lucky stars you sent nowt to the *Obverser* or the *Gruinard*. Be two more copies down the pan. They all end up for sale on Amazon. Worse still, you'll find some shysters advertising those self-same discarded review copies for sale on Amazon as New when, as we very well know, they are no such thing. They do the same thing with my books, too. Last time I looked there were ten of them at it – well, eight maybe. Because Amazon's copy and mine were up there too.

DD: How'd you know who the shysters are?

BK: Well, I'm the sole distributor, see. So how on earth can any of those other copies be new, if I supplied nobody with them except myself and Amazon. They may *look* new, but if a book reviewer like Crispin Catflap has had his sticky hands on them, however temporarily, there's no way they're new books. *Like* New maybe; but second-hand certainly.

DD: How d'you deal with that, then?

BK: Complain to the firm doing the advertising, and if nowt happens – and very often it won't, complain to Amazon.

DD: Amazon sort 'em, will they?

BK: Well, yeah. Take ages to do it and seem none too happy about doing it either.

DD: How d'you mean?

BK: Off-hand response when I alerted them to it. So I won't be doing that again. Because any review copies I send out in future will go out with a great big, cheesy personally addressed and dated autograph from Bill Keeth on the title page. Be no doubt about their being second-hand, then.

DD: Rubber stamp'd do the same trick: "Review Copy" in bright blue ink.

BK: You *are* learning, aren't you?

DD: Can't afford not to? Too many literary timeservers taking everyone for a ride.

BK: Who'd you go with, by the way? You get Limited Edition Press to handle it?

DD: No. They were tied up anyway. Seems Limited Edition Press takes no more than a couple of books on at a time, and they were fully booked up for the foreseeable future.

BK: Well, they're a small outfit and they want to stay that way.

DD: What they want is 'all the business they can reasonably handle', is the way they put it.

BK: Fair enough. So what'd you do, then?

DD: Found a good POD outfit in the end. Hundred quid, all done and dusted: handful of books thrown in; and they act as distributor, too.

BK: They okay, then?

DD: I'm happy enough. ISBN number, Barcode, book in the shops, on Amazon, too. Be happier still when I see a bit of paperwork for the books they've sold, of course.

BK: What about the typesetting?

DD: That was the thing, see? I'm a dab hand with a computer, so it was no problem at all.

BK: Horses for courses, eh?

DD: Something like that. Meanwhile, there's the little matter of the other £550 pounds I didn't have to find.

BK: Eh?

DD: I paid hundred quid, done and dusted.

BK: Done, yeah. But you won't be dusted till you see some paperwork, will you? And a few more books, too: I got 50 books, not a handful, remember.

DD: Oh, it'll sort itself out. You'll see.

BK: Apart from another 38 books or so, maybe. Listen. Apart from Andrew Gutter, you get any other press coverage.

DD: No reviews as such. Well, apart from Carl Spiers in that Oldham mag of his.

BK: *Owt and Abowt*. Does you proud, Carl. No edge on him.

DD: Bit of Owdham Edge maybe.

BK: Oh, very droll. Not to put too fine a point on it, *regionally* droll.

DD: *Primitively* droll, y'ask me?

BK: Hah! What about the *Hebers & Tonge Telegraph*? You get a mention there?

DD: Got quite a few, as a matter of fact. First off, when the book was published; then as a prize in their weekly competition, another time when the local vicar threw a wobbler . . .

BK: Vicars don't throw a wobblers, I think you'll find: they'll maybe take umbrage, my son.

DD: Umbrage, *schumbrage – nil carborundum sacerdos* is what I say.

BK: Don't let the vicar grind you down, eh? What about local radio?

DD: Two tilts at it with Watchtower. DJ U E Jay had us on that Sunday morning slot of his.

BK: *U E Jay's Disco Dig 'n' Delve*?

DD: Yeah. Seems he had this brother-in-law, big on books, though not sequels. So I suppose that's me finished, with my second book being a sequel.

BK: That it, then, publicity-wise.

DD: For the time being, yeah. Got dragged on to this book review programme on Watchtower. Another waste of time! Carlton Stuntist, the presenter . . .

BK: From chat line to Melvyn Bragg-dom in a trice.

DD: That so? Who's *he* know? Well, obviously he hadn't read the copy I sent him before he sold it on, so he slagged the cover picture off for a full fifteen minutes to cover his tracks. No one else could get a word in edgewise.

BK: 'Tis said he can't read beyond Dick and Dora. He can certainly mouth off, though. Still, you get 'em, don't you? Less they know, more they want to tell you about it. Tell you, old biddy wrote me a letter, saying she "couldn't get into" my book – meaning *Manchester Kiss*, the second one?

DD: How d'you mean?
BK: Seems this was her idea of cogent criticism. I mean to say, even Amazon wouldn't accept that as a bog standard customer review, would they?
DD: Not if you registered a complaint, they wouldn't. "Not my kind of book", was what some joker had to say about *MO*. So I got Amazon to delete it as invalid criticism.
BK: I got a dafter one than that. "Don't like the format," says A Reader from Rhodes Village. As you say, you get 'em, don't you?
DD: You soitanly do, Ollie. Hurts though, especially if it's book launch week and you're that little bit apprehensive.
BK: Ignore 'em, mate. No sense of occasion, some folk. They know not what they do. So what's the crack, then – saleswise?
DD: Twelve months on, 500 books shifted, give or take a few.
BK: You happy with that.
DD: Could be happier, but it'll do for now. Other fish to fry with the second book. Got the first one in all the bookshops, though.
BK: *All* the bookshops? Smith's too.
DD: You extracting the Michael, by any chance?
BK: Just thought I'd ask.
DD: Long as you don't abuse the privilege.
BK: Super Duper Mart?
DD: *Super Duper Mart?*
BK: The major supermarkets.
DD: Sarcasm is the lowest form of wit, I'll have you know.
BK: Granted. Okay, what about personal sales, one on one, presentations?
DD: Did the book launch, of course: shifted maybe twenny copies. But I don't get as many presentations as I'd like. Didn't get the vicar's lot, for all their promises.
BK: Their loss.
DD: Mine too in a way. Still, there's no pleasing those who *won't* be pleased. And I shifted 55 copies one Saturday from a stall in a shopping mall.

BK: Friends, family. They'd rally round, naturally?

DD: You tranner be funny?

BK: Notta tall.

DD: Remember saying I'd be surprised?

BK: And were you?

DD: I soitanly was, Ollie. My very first sale was to a guy who wouldn't normally give me the time of day. Would you believe that.

BK: Oi would, begob.

DD: It's happened quite a lot, that. Complete strangers coming up to me, cash in hand. Family was a completely different kettle of fish.

BK: Uh-*oh!*

DD: Extended family of around 44, say, half of them have maybe read the book – courtesy of an overly generous 25%. Wouldn't believe 'em, would you?

BK: Oh, yes, I would, mate. They'll be frightened of making you rich.

DD: Hey, and get this. Just about sums 'em up, this. Very first member of the family, I happened to mention I was having a book published told me she'd love to read it, so to make sure to let her know as soon as it was in the library.

BK: As a good friend of mine has it: 'Only family could do it to you, Bill.'

DD: That the Perelman fan?

BK: Nope, the fire chief.

DD: *He's* come on since you sold that oil painting at Gargrave, hasn't he?

BK: Haven't we all, pal? Incidentally, you'll find family's even worse with your second book. I sometimes think there are more kudos to be had from buying a flash motor on the drip. Still, the neighbours were okay, weren't they? Old school pals?

DD: Primary school, yeah – and people I know from youth club years ago: great. Just one sale to a guy I knew in VIth Form. Up in the Land O'Cakes, as it happens. Net result: he's never spoken to me since.

BK: Be that £15 a throw cover price. You know what they say about the Scots, Jimmy.

DD: Och, they'll nae be saying it to me, though. I mean to say, it was'nae a Scot who invented the continental breakfast.

BK: How d'you handle personal sales, by the way. Discount them?

DD: Well, if I'm in the pub at the time, I'll maybe buy the odd drink. Otherwise, I've been known to throw in a bookmark – or a Brodart cover if it's ready-to-hand. Sales through my newsagent, I wrap in plastic pockets to guard against newsprint – another use for substandard copies, by the way: I mean, leaving one substandard book open for perusal. Oh, yes, just the once, I did a BOGOF offer – for the library where I used to study for my O Levels: I was that keen on getting my book in there and Manchester had already had its full quota.

BK: And your personal overall impression of the experience?

DD: Writing it? Self-publishing it? Or selling it?

BK: Well, all three really. And you've got another one on the way, didn't you say?

DD: *Read 'em and Weep.*

BK: What's that supposed to mean?

DD: Dunno. Like you, I never have been able to figure it out. Just seems like an apposite comment at this stage in the proceedings, and an appropriate second title, too.

BK: *Read 'em and Weep*, eh?

DD: Well, yeah. Provided you're a punter who's divvied up the full purchase price for the books instead of taking advantage of a BOGOF offer when you had the chance.

BK: But hasn't someone used that title before?

DD: Barry Manilow, Meatloaf. Yeah. But copyright doesn't apply to titles.

BK: Ooh, you *are* learning, aren't you?

DD: I soitanly am, Ollie. Have a generic bookmark on me!

BK: er . . .

DD: I've got a copy of *MO* in the car, if you're interested.

BK: Well, er . . .

DD: I'll throw in a Brodart cover, if you like . . .
BK: er . . .
DD: I'll throw in a whisky if the Old David's open.
BK: Now you're talking. Tell you what: make it a double and you're on . . .

APPENDIX 1: THE PORTICO LITERARY PRIZE

The Portico Library, Charlotte Street, Manchester, is home to the Portico Literary Prize which was founded in 1985 and is at present awarded biennially for any book of general interest and literary merit set wholly or mainly in the North-West of England – that is to say, in Lancashire, Greater Manchester, Cheshire, the Peak District, Merseyside or Cumbria.

The Portico Literary Prize is presented at a prestigious dinner in Manchester city centre, the Midland Hotel being selected to host the 2006 presentation dinner at which time the prize amounted to £3,000. Speakers and judges in the past have included Ludovic Kennedy, Dora Bryan, Bill Tidy, Alan Garner, Tony Warren, Martin Bell and Kate Adie. Past sponsors have included Granada, the *Manchester Evening News*, the Royal Bank of Scotland and, in 2006, the Zochonis Charitable Trust which, in 2008, will be joined by the Lane-Smith Schindler, Solicitors – Trust and Estate Practitioners, taking the total value of the award to £8,000 in all.

Past winners have included Bolton's Bill Naughton (the author of *Alfie*), with his autobiographical *On the Pig's Back*, Manchester-born Anthony Burgess, with *Any Old Iron*; and ex-policeman John Stalker, with the eponymous *Stalker*.

In 2006 *Every Street in Manchester* by Bill Keeth was one of only three novels shortlisted for the Portico Literary Prize, the other two being *Kalooki Nights* by Howard Jacobson and *The Grave Tattoo* by Val McDermid.

The joint winners on this occasion were Val MacDermid with *The Grave Tattoo* and Dr Andrew Biswell with *The Real Life of Anthony Burgess*, with Dr Biswell being awarded the £3,000 prize.

Quite coincidentally, a slice-of-life sequence of Bill Keeth's second novel, *Manchester Kiss*, which was published on the same date that the 2006 Portico Literary Prize celebration dinner was held, features an exclusive review of Andrew Biswell's *Real Life of Anthony Burgess*.

Past winners of The Portico Literary Prize are as follows, the four fiction winners being delineated thus *.

1985 Gary Messinger with *Manchester in the Victorian Age*
1986 Don Haworth with *Figures in a Bygone Landscape*
1987 Bill Naughton with *On the Pig's Back*
1988 John Stalker with *Stalker*
1989 Anthony Burgess with *Any Old Iron**
1990 Hugh Owen with *The Lowther Family*
1991 Alan Hankinson with *Coleridge Walks the Fells*
1993 Jenny Uglow with *Elizabeth Gaskell: A Habit of Stories*
1995 Richard Francis with *Taking Apart the Poco Poco**
1997 Paul Wilson with *Do White Whales Sing at the Edge of the World?**
2000 John Parkinson-Bailey with *Manchester: an Architectural History*
2002 Shelley Rhode with *The Lowry Lexicon*
2004 Terry Wyke with *Public Sculpture in Greater Manchester*
2006 Andrew Biswell with *The Real Life of Anthony Burgess*, and Val McDermid with *The Grave Tattoo**

APPENDIX 2: LITERARY AGENTS

Readers may perhaps imagine, as I once did, that membership of the Association of Authors' Agents lends an aura of assured dependability to the business practices of any literary agent belonging thereto in much the same way as there is obviously some assurance to be derived from the thought that Ofgas oversees British Gas on the public's behalf. But it would appear that no such inherent warranty should necessarily be understood to be attached to such membership.

And so, it would seem to be the case that literary agents who are *not* Members of the Association of Authors' Agents should not on this account be adjudged inept, amateur or otherwise inappropriate to their representational task. On the contrary, they may be quite as trustworthy and businesslike as Members of the AAA. In any event, in order to qualify for membership of the Association of Authors' Agents, a literary agent who is so disposed to be will need to have, amongst other things, a guaranteed minimum turnover per annum – and this may be set at a level which is probably rather steep for some smaller but entirely reputable agencies, as for instance, a newly-established agency, eager and capable enough to succeed on its own behalf, but which has not as yet succeeded in recruiting a sufficient number of clients.

Experience would tend to show that the literary agents to be wary of are those which seek a fee from the author. And the reason for this is perfectly simple. The point is that most literary agencies survive on their commission income. Therefore it is reasonable to assume that an agent who cannot do so is not very successful at placing his authors' works with publishers. To delve a little more deeply into the reasoning behind this assertion, publishers are only likely to take notice of books put forward by agents whose judgment they trust – and publishers may well suspect that titles offered by fee-charging literary agents have not been selected on purely critical grounds. In other words you may be doing your work a severe disservice by having it represented by a fee-charging literary agent.

APPENDIX 3: EVERY STREET IN MANCHESTER

Every Street in Manchester by Bill Keeth was first published in the summer of 2005 [ISBN 1859880649] and, after two further print-runs, in a 2nd Edition, complete with readers' comments and a different cover illustration, in early 2006 [ISBN 1859880657]. Here's how the Press Release describes it: "*A latter day Manchester man relates his life story in a Mancunian vernacular with editorial assistance from a friend. The result of their joint endeavour is a tragicomic novel spanning the second half of the twentieth century in a northern suburb of the city from where the Third World is temporarily accessed via the Pennine Way.*"

Every Street in Manchester is a love story from start to finish, though this is not to say it's a Mills and Boon, or even a Catherine Cookson type of love story. Because the main character's certainly no catch. But the storyline running through the book is boy meets girl – hey, boy *stays* with girl. Well, as far as circumstances will permit.

It's a love story about a time and place too: north Manchester in the second half of the twentieth century, and it's about the kind of music people enjoyed in that time and place. It's also a story about the world of work – shop work, navvying, office work, taxi driving, delivery work and so on.

There are loads of local landmarks in *Every Street in Manchester*, with the title itself locating the story immediately to the north of the city. But though the man and wife in the story work at a road transport depot on Every Street, Ancoats, the relevance of the book's theme is more wide-ranging than that, like the old Mancunian joke that alludes to potential access to *every* street in Manchester via that eponymous address in the district of Ancoats.

So in a manner of speaking, it's as if Billy Hopkins (best selling author of *Our Kid*, *High Hopes*, *Kate's Story*, *Going Places*, *Anything Goes* and *Whatever Next!*) decked on a bus at Collyhurst Street, and got off it at Moston Lane corner some twenty-odd years later. But there all similarity ends. Because the hero of *Our Kid* always had a lot more upstairs than Tony Dinch, the main character in *Every Street in Manchester*, ever has. Because Dinchy is a bit of a dumb cluck, you'll find: he's thick as a navvy's butty to the power of two short planks; he's the urban equivalent of a village idiot. He doesn't know too much, that's for sure – he can't even speak properly, let alone do any of the other subjects on the school curriculum. Dinchy is socially inept in so many ways too. He's so stupid he needs his more articulate friend, Byron Marlfield, to help him make sense of his story. Heck! He needs Byron to help him tell his story. (Byron is responsible for a good 25% of the narrative.)

But the fact that Dinchy doesn't know too much doesn't necessarily mean he knows nothing at all. He knows where he comes from for a start (the storyline looks back through his grandmother's eyes to the two World Wars); and he knows when he's well off too – with his wife, Shirlee, that is. Not that Dinchy and Shirlee are well off in any material sense that's important to the people around them. No, in that sense, and certainly by the end of the book, they've got nothing at all. But in a kind of a way they've got everything. Because they've got each other, and this is one aspect of the relevance of the spoof quotation on the front cover: 'A voice from the city, a plea for the world'.

Another aspect of the relevance of this same quotation is concerned with the way in which the two narrators (Dinchy and Byron) access the Pennine Way on a sponsored walk in aid of a Third World charity – a charitable effort which is echoed in the real world by the fact that a specific percentage of the cover price of each copy of *Every Street in Manchester* is donated to famine relief.

Here's what it says on the inside back cover. 'As a token of support for UN Resolution 2626 (1970), signatories to which have promised to allocate 0.7% of their GDP to international development, an obligation the UK has yet to honour, 0.7% of the cover price of each copy of *Every Street in Manchester* will be donated to CAFOD for famine relief'.

Every Street in Manchester is published by Limited Edition Press, the original publishers of *Our Kid*. Subsequently shortlisted for the Portico Literary Prize, 2006, the book is stocked by Borders, Waterstone's and Amazon, and has been featured in the *Manchester Evening News* and the *Lancashire Magazine* as well as on local TV and radio stations. Close on two thousand copies of *Every Street in Manchester* and its contemporaneous sequel, *Manchester Kiss*, have been sold to date in the Greater Manchester area and beyond.

Manchester Kiss

Manchester Kiss [ISBN1859880673] is a continuation of the north Manchester-based saga that begins with *Every Street in Manchester*. Here's how the Press Release describes it: "*Patrons of the same public house, a group of north Manchester people now confront the reader (and each other) with personal reminiscences, observations and opinions by means of which they give voice to many of their grievances, aspirations and fears.*"

Manchester Kiss was published in November, 2006, in the same week that the Portico Prize Presentation Dinner was held at the Midland Hotel, Manchester. Here's an extract from an interview with Bill Keeth conducted by Tavistock Greenlee, of the *Sunday Thames* . . .

TG: When did you write *Manchester Kiss*?
BK: Immediately *Every Street in Manchester* was finished. I'd got up a good head of steam, so to speak, and, like a competitor in a race, I had my sights set on some point beyond the finishing post. And things just went on from there.
TG: How long did it take you to write the book, would you say?
BK: I finished it in no time at all really – a few months maybe, though there was an extensive Pennine Way section in the first draft, which I later removed because it seemed even more of a culture shock than having verse and correspondence alongside the narrative.
TG: What made you turn your hand to writing another novel so quickly?
BK: Well, I knew from the start that no commercial publisher

was going to look at *Every Street in Manchester*. Par for the course really – particularly for a northern writer. But you never know, so I still had to go through the motions of submitting it – and I needed *Manchester Kiss* to keep me going when I might be feeling a bit downcast with the expected rejections which duly materialised, of course. With regard to the way in which *Manchester Kiss* is written I had various objectives in mind.

TG: Yes, it's an unusual format, to say the least, isn't it?

BK: I wanted this second book to be completely different from *Every Street in Manchester* – as a personal showcase, for one thing. But I also felt I needed to get away from first person narration so as to stretch myself as a writer. Also, I've got this personal bee in my bonnet about the sort of baggage we carry round with us from our past which can sometimes have as much bearing on the things we say and do today as something that happened only yesterday – and it seemed to me that this idea might best be suggested via the non-linear structure of *Manchester Kiss*.

TG: I hear what you say, but come on, I mean, you've got bits of correspondence and verse intermingling with the narrative, haven't you? And, as I understand it, the reader's invited to tackle the book in any order, isn't he? What's that all about?

BK: The American writer, John Dos Passos used to intersperse his narrative with factual reports from newspapers; and British writer, B S Johnson, famously wrote a novel entitled *The Unfortunates*, which the reader was invited to read in any order. I'm not comparing myself with these two writers in any way, other than in pointing out that the narrative techniques employed in *Manchester Kiss* together with its non-linear format are by no means unique within the novel form.

TG: Okay, but why did you feel the non-linear format was necessary to the telling of your tale, let's say?

BK: Well, it's necessary only inasmuch as I think that to do it this way tends to replicate real life. Ask yourself, for instance – does your own life really run from A to Z in a linear narrative pattern? Does this interview? Or do you mix and match when you get back to the office? And does the past break in on your real life from time to time? Does the future you so carefully planned for yourself sometimes hinge on something uncontrollable – an event in the past or even an accident of birth?

TG: But what about the correspondence and the verse?

BK: The idea of verse and correspondence – and, indeed, the photographic illustrations intermeshing with a non-chronological narrative is simply an extension of this same non-linear format.

TG: So is *Manchester Kiss* linked with *Every Street in Manchester* in any way?

BK: Well, *Manchester Kiss* centres on the lives of a group of north Manchester people, some of whom first appeared in *Every Street in Manchester*. Each of these people has his own career and life story which quite naturally come under discussion when these same people meet up to shared purpose on high days and holidays in the same public house – the North Parade.

TG: Is that a Manchester pub?

BK: It's a fictional north Manchester pub, supposedly on Victoria Avenue East, which is on the northern perimeter of the city. Mancunians might picture it as being somewhere between the Berkshire and the kiddies' party venue that I call the Sticky Warehouse. The location of the pub is important in that legend has it that Victoria Avenue East at that point is as high above sea level as is the top of the tower of Manchester Town Hall. So readers might usefully visualise the North Parade as a sort of conning tower from which the north Manchester social scene may be surveyed during the second half of the twentieth century.

TG: But can this non-linear, interlinked hotch-potch of a novel – if I may call it that – really be part and parcel of literature as we know it?

BK: Most definitely. The characters in *Manchester Kiss* share an affinity with one another, as do the people on pilgrimage in

Chaucer's *Canterbury Tales*, who are temporarily on pilgrimage, and with those in *The Decameron*, who are simply waiting for the plague to run its course in the city of Florence. Their real lives being temporarily put on hold, they pass the time telling stories to one another until their real lives may be resumed.

TG: So how does that work in the North Parade, for instance?

BK: Teachers talk about teaching, policemen talk about police work, the thrifty discuss their investments, jokers tell jokes, people in a relationship discuss that relationship, and the down-at-heart complain *ad nauseam*.

TG: How do the 37 photographs fit in?

BK: The photographs, courtesy of the Manchester Archive, are intended to illustrate two separate bus journeys as if through the window of a bus. Two buses are involved, each of them numbered 72X, and each is travelling along Rochdale Road, the A664. In the first instance (the first half of the photographic collection) a schoolboy is travelling towards Manchester city centre *c.* 1954, as portrayed in Chapter 2 of *Manchester Kiss*; and in the second a young woman, who is about to be married, is travelling home from work in Manchester city centre c. 1965, as portrayed in Chapter 8 of *Every Street in Manchester*).

TG: Are there any other ways the two novels are connected via their storylines?

BK: Oh, yes. They're not instances of any particular importance except to myself perhaps. But an umbrella bent at a party in *Manchester Kiss*, turns up in *Every Street in Manchester*, and a lost cigarette lighter referred to in *Every Street in Manchester* is found in the street in *Manchester Kiss*.

TG: Why?

BK: Continuity and contiguity are the only answers to that . . .

APPENDIX 4: SEVEN PILLARS OF SELF-PUBLISHING WISDOM

Dan Poynter's Self Publishing Manual ISBN 1568601425
1001 Ways to Market Your Book,
John Kremer ISBN 09121411422
101 Tips on Writing and Selling Your First Novel,
Prudy Taylor Board ISBN 0595293131
The Publishing Game: Publish a Book in 30 Days,
Fern Reiss ISBN 1893290853
The Publishing Game: Bestseller in 30 Days,
Fern Reiss ISBN 1893290884
The Publishing Game: Find an Agent in 30 Days,
Fern Reiss ISBN 1893290832
Beyond the Bookstore: Places to Sell Your Self-Published Book,
Rusty Fischer ISBN 1592810390

APPENDIX 5: IS YOUR NOVEL ANY GOOD?

❑ LOOKING AT WHAT YOU HAVE WRITTEN

Let us review the situation you now find yourself in. Because things certainly look pretty grim, don't they? That typescript of yours has been rejected out-of-hand by more publishers than you can shake a stick at. (And wouldn't you dearly love to do just that, the Philistines? Perhaps hit them with it too, though not before you've hammered a six-inch clout nail into the action end of it.) More to the point, though, you no longer know where you're up to, do you? You feel somewhat slighted, let down – *dirty* perhaps, having exposed part of your inner self to the world, as it were, only to have it adjudged worthless, a thing of no account, by a plethora of self-satisfied publishers/literary agents who don't give a tinker's cuss about your work. So, as to whether your debut novel (as you've got in the habit of calling it) really is as unpromising as it would now appear to be, given the aforementioned universally negative consensus of opinion that it's attracted so far – well, *quien sabe*? Who knows, *amigo*? I mean to say, surely you, literary genius that you are (*hah!*) can't be the only person in this great country of ours who knows the truth of things and will eventually be proved right, having had a positive opinion about the Thing from the start. Such an eventuality would surely seem to be most unlikely, wouldn't it? Improbable certainly, impossible perhaps. Still, stranger things have happened at sea, so they tell us. And, as I have myself been known to opine in my cups: 'Wrongheadedness invariably has a majority vote, it seems to me.' (*Vide*, Nazi Germany; the speed bump crazy councillors of Rochdale, Greater Manchester; Soviet Russia; the Spanish Inquisition; Jonathan Swift's "Confederacy of Dunces", as exemplified by the concerted commercial non-recognition that once upon a time concentrated upon the debut (indeed, *only*) novel of John Kennedy Toole – the same sort of concerted commercial non-recognition which has more recently been vented upon your own debut novel.)

So perhaps it might be a good idea to consider an alternative viewpoint, a less negative viewpoint with regard to rejection . . .

❍ "A rejection need never be taken as final. There is no such thing as an objective opinion. What one [publisher] likes may leave another one unmoved," Stan Barstow, best-selling author of *A Kind of Loving*, in his autobiography, *In My Own Good Time*.

So is there scope perhaps for at least one more submission before you commit yourself to the trouble and expense of self-publishing your debut novel? And, if not, are you, despite repeated, concerted – indeed, unanimous rejection, still doggedly determined to self-publish it?

Back off, take time out, consider, re-consider, re-read, ruminate – be honest with yourself! "Haste" is the only word that should have no part in your vocabulary at this – indeed, at *any* stage. Never hurry, never worry. Meanwhile, consider an alternative point of view with regard to your utter disappointment with what little you would appear to have achieved so far . . .

❍ "In my own pear-shaped moments, I think of George Bernard Shaw, who wrote five novels, each of which was turned down by every publisher. Or Van Gogh who, in his lifetime, sold only one of his 1,700 paintings, even though his brother Theo was an art dealer. Or David Hume, who said about his *A Treatise of Human Nature*, one of the enduring classics of philosophy, that it 'fell stillborn from the press'," Rabbi Sir Jonathan Sachs, Chief Rabbi of the United Hebrew Congregation of the Commonwealth.

So would you perhaps be better advised *not* to self-publish on this occasion? Wouldn't you be better advised instead to file your debut novel away for the present – and begin again with Novel No. 2? (N.B. Never ever throw work away, let alone *destroy* it!) And, if so, does the thought of beginning again appal you? And, if this thought appals you, then ask yourself in all honesty if you really *are* cut out to be a novelist.

Back off, take time out, consider, re-consider, re-read, ruminate – be honest with yourself! "Haste" is the only word that should have no part in your vocabulary at this – indeed, any stage. Never hurry, never worry. Meanwhile, consider the following master class of a statement with regard to the writing of fiction . . .

❍ "Don't go with the crowd, don't do anything for the crowd, don't be of the crowd . . . Place an enormous stress on individuality, don't use novelty phrases that bob around in the atmosphere for a few months, like "no-brainer" or something like that, which are ways of signalling to your peer group that you're just like everyone else. Make it fresh, make it your own, make it individual," Martin Amis, on being appointed Professor of Creative Writing at Manchester School of Arts, History and Culture.

Is your novel of this ilk? Or is it a bit samey perhaps? A reprise of another author's best-selling brainwave – and necessarily an inferior novel because of it?

Back off, take time out, consider, re-consider, re-read, ruminate – be honest with yourself! "Haste" is the only word that should have no part in your vocabulary at this – indeed, any stage. Never hurry, never worry. Meanwhile, consider this with regard to the writing of fiction . . .

❍ "The most important rule of all is that there aren't any rules," John Braine, author of *Room at the Top*, in *Writing a Novel* (more recently entitled *How to Write a Novel).*

Well, yes – and, hopefully, your work is a markedly individual effort. But is it perhaps too individual – individual to the point of being experimental? By which I mean to say, of course – is your debut novel *too* experimental?

Back off, take time out, consider, re-consider, re-read, ruminate – be honest with yourself! "Haste" is the only word that should have no part in your vocabulary at this – indeed, any stage. Never hurry, never worry. Meanwhile, consider this with regard to the writing of fiction . . .

❍ "I don't see the point of writing fiction if your real life is full of events," Alive Mellalieu-Campbell, author of *My Story*. [See Appendix 7.]

This is something I really must remember to tackle Alice about the next time we take time out for elevenses at Manchester's North City Library, bless her. For the time being, though, perhaps I had better explain that Alice has very generously (far too generously, in my opinion) stuck to her guns in her autobiographical *My Story,* which just so happens to be a very close-packed 300,000+ words long. Which, given that Alice is a very sprightly and articulate octogenarian, may suit her right down to the ground. However, I do seriously doubt that Alice's advice in the matter is appropriate for an author of a lesser longevity. And so I ask you, is your debut novel autobiographical to such a degree that, unless you perhaps re-jig it, you will have nothing left to draw from the well when you finally get around to writing your second novel?

Back off, take time out, consider, re-consider, re-read, ruminate – be honest with yourself! "Haste" is the only word that should have no part in your vocabulary at this – indeed, any stage. Never hurry, never worry. Meanwhile, consider this with regard to the novel you have created . . .

❍ "The only real influence I've ever had was myself," Edward Hopper, American painter.

Which is, I can tell you, much as I love and admire the work of Edward Hopper, so much arrant nonsense, the like of which I have never heard before. Because, were he influenced by no one and/or nothing, Edward Hopper would have had nothing to say, neither would he, on a quite different level, have had anywhere to turn when it came to learning his painting technique. So despite what he claims, here, Edward Hopper was most certainly influenced by someone or something, as are all artists – and I intend the term "artists" to include writers such as yourself. Anyone who creates something has, to a greater or lesser degree, been influenced by others and/or other things. Thus, in my humble opinion, Virginia Woolf could not have written *Mrs Dalloway* before James Joyce wrote *Ulysses*, and Virginia Woolf had to come up with *Mrs Dalloway* before John O'Hara could write *Butterfield 8*. The question is, however, with regard to your own work, does the necessary influence to which I refer shine far too recognisably through the weft and warp of your debut novel to such an extent that, when all is said and done, it may be seen to be nothing more than a thinly-disguised, influence-acknowledging debut novel? In other words, and to reiterate somewhat, is your debut novel nothing more than a pale imitation of the work of another (certainly better) author?

Back off, take time out, consider, re-consider, re-read, ruminate – be honest with yourself! "Haste" is the only word that should have no part in your vocabulary at this – stage. Never hurry, never hurry. Meanwhile, consider what must now be done. Because you will be doing yourself a really great favour if you just face up to it. Look your debut novel quite sternly in the face – hey, look the Thing quite *implacably* in the face, as if, like those umpteen publishers you recently approached, you too are *no friend* of your debut novel. Indeed, you must pretend that you, like them, are irredeemably inimical to your debut novel. Then ask yourself . . .

Is this novel of mine patently derivative of another novel that I love and admire? Therefore, is this novel of mine, in truth, an inferior imitation of the novel that I love and admire? Alternatively, is it perhaps the case that what I have got into the habit of calling my debut novel is, in actual fact, a bland autobiography of my own even blander life? Remember, too, something that is not generally acknowledged by *Our Kid's* millions of fans is the fact that, whilst drawing extensively upon the autobiographical details of his own very eventful lifetime and career, the author of *Our Kid, High Hopes et al.* was ever to some considerable extent artistically inclined to re-invent himself and his family and his life experience to narrative purpose. That is to say, the author tailored his actual life experience so as to give form and greater impact to the telling of his tale.

And, finally, if after all due consideration at leisure and at length:

- you are positively convinced you have something of importance to say,
- in addition to remaining doggedly determined to say it, then
- pray heed the quotation that concludes this section.

To speak plainly, the quotation to which I refer is more properly applicable to a far greater yearning than personal creativity as evidenced in the desire to self-publish. Even so, I cannot help but feel it contains within it something that is intrinsically linked to any individual's determination to speak out, to be heard, to have one's words adjudged of equal account. Unbelievable though it may seem, I first heard this rallying cry from the man himself at a church service in downtown Manchester during the summer of 2007, the man in question being none other than the Reverend Jesse Jackson, Civil Rights campaigner, envoy to US presidents, twice US presidential candidate, who, amongst other things of moment, had this to say: 'If my mind can conceive it and my heart can believe it, I *know* I can achieve it.'

Take to heart the conditional clauses contained within this statement inasmuch as they apply to the way you *truly* feel about your debut novel, and act accordingly.

❑ JUDGING YOURSELF AS A WRITER

John Braine, the author of *Room at the Top*, was of the opinion that you can't really call yourself a novelist until you've got three novels under your belt. Therefore, I call you a writer. According to the same criterion, of course, I would need to call Katherine Mansfield, William Saroyan, Harper Lee, Nathanael West, Margaret Mitchell, and J D Salinger writers too.

1. A WRITER IS NECESSARILY A READER. Quite apart from the fact that a writer will want to read a lot, a writer needs to read a lot. Because this is the means by which language, grammar, syntax, spelling, dialogue, narrative technique and so many other facets of the tools of the writer's trade are passed on, learned and assimilated.

So, are you a reader by any chance? And if so, how many books do you read *per annum*? Certainly, I'd expect a writer to be reading upwards of 50 books per annum, my counsel of perfection (not always achievable, of course) being 70+ books per annum – which translates as one book per week minimum and one book per day on the kind of holiday I look forward to taking. True, some prolific writers have admitted to being unable to get around to reading very much. John O'Hara was like that towards the end of his life. But O'Hara had been a voracious reader in the past and, not to put too fine a point on it, if a writer has got to the point where he can't find much time for reading, I would suggest that something has gone very wrong – in much the same way that something has obviously gone out of kilter if, say, the local fish fryer really does prefer to spend eight hours a day serving up fish and chips for fifty-two weeks of the year instead of taking a bit of time out on the Costa like the rest of us.

"A writer is a person who writes," says John Braine – to which I'd add a complementary *sine qua non*: 'A writer is a person who reads.'

2. DO YOU READ WITH THE CROWD? What I mean to say here is – well, okay, nobody in his right mind would have wanted to miss out on Frederick Forsyth's *Day of the Jackal* or *The*

Odessa File – or *The Godfather* by Mario Puzo, or, more recently, *Red Dragon* and *The Silence of the Lambs* by Thomas Harris. But can you recognise a good book even if you've never seen it reviewed in the *Gruinard*? A good self-published book, say, because the *Gruinard*, amongst others, is too proud to review self-published books. Would you be able to pick out a good book that has never won the MAN Booker Prize, say, or been shortlisted for it, or nominated even. Take *True Grit* by Charles Portis, for instance. In her introduction to the most recent Bloomsbury paperback edition [ISBN 0747572631] novelist Donna Tartt says her mother was "so crazy about [*True Grit*] that when she had finished it, she turned back to the first page and read it all over again." Only once in a bibliophiliac lifetime was I similarly affected by a book, and that, too, was a western: *Hombre* by Elmore Leonard. And I love *True Grit* almost as much. But the well-thumbed copy I have to hand is a child-oriented Puffin edition – which tells me without a shadow of a doubt that, *circa* 1969, someone at Penguin (*hah, hah*) messed up big style.

3. IS *THE SILENCE OF THE LAMBS* A GOOD BOOK? I think it is: a true exemplar (like Eric Ambler's *A Passage of Arms*) of how a thriller should be written. Is its sequel, *Hannibal*, better or worse? It's certainly thicker. So does this count for anything in establishing its credentials? (Incidentally, I mean *Hannibal* by Thomas Harris, not Ross Leckie's *Hannibal*, which will certainly pass muster until I find a better book, though that better book will not be *Scipio* by Ross Leckie, still less *Carthage*, the two titles by means of which Ross Leckie completed his Carthaginian trilogy and, quite possibly fulfilled a three-book deal with Canongate.)

Is James Ellroy's *Clandestine* (arguably the best of his noir thrillers) a good book or half a good book? By the same token, what about *Paper Moon* by Joe David Brown? Or, *The Collector* by John Fowles? (All these books have superb first parts, and second parts, I find, I can take or leave.) And, whilst Robert Tressell's classic novel, *The Ragged-Trousered Philanthropists* quite deservedly has a following of millions of fans worldwide, ranging from George Galloway MP to actor Ricky Tomlinson, is it a good book or a bad book? Or is it instead one of that very peculiar breed, a good bad book?

4. DO YOU BRING A DISTINCTIVE NARRATIVE VOICE INTO PLAY IN YOUR DEBUT NOVEL? Do you know what I mean by a distinctive narrative voice? It is a very particular and individual way of telling your story that has the potential of grabbing the reader's attention immediately he opens your book, thereby making it a possibility that the reader will voluntarily surrender his interest (and his valuable time) to you, enabling you, having buttonholed him at the start, to drag him, kicking and screaming (in enjoyment, rather than in protest) into your story and out the other end of it. By way of example, consider twenty very different examples of the narrative voice within the book titles that follow, each one of which is wonderful in its own way in addition to its being immediately discernible from the very first sentence of each respective Page One: *Treasure Island by* Robert Louis Stevenson, *Room at the Top* by John Braine, *Appointment in Samarra* by John O'Hara, *The Big Laugh* by John O'Hara, *The Great Gatsby* by F Scott Fitzgerald, *The Pat Hobby Stories by F Scott Fitzgerald*, *The Long Firm* by Jake Arnott, *A Clockwork Orange* by Anthony Burgess, *Paper Moon* by Joe David Brown, *The Curious Incident of the Dog in the Night-Time* by Mark Haddon, *Jack's Return Home* (aka *Get Carter*) by Ted Lewis, *I, Claudius* by Robert Graves, *A Passage of Arms* by Eric Ambler, *True Grit* by Charles Portis, *Hombre* by Elmore Leonard, *There is a Happy Land* by Keith Waterhouse, *You Know Me Al* by Ring Lardner, *The Catcher in the Rye* by J D Salinger, *A Kind of Loving* by Stan Barstow, *Kate's Story* by Billy Hopkins.

Hopefully, in some of the above instances you'll be drawn in to read a truly distinctive narrative voice you've never heard before – or to re-read others you are more familiar with.

Incidentally, notice how I instinctively say "a narrative voice . . . you've never *heard* before". How can you *hear* when reading is something we do with our eyes? Or do we, in fact, use more than our eyes when reading? Not always, of course. But, certainly, wherever a good piece of writing is concerned. Because, with a good piece of writing, it is as if the author specifically encourages the reader to write the book with him, relying (as it were) upon the reader's own life experience to enable him to expedite the matter. To illustrate this phenomenon in simple terms, if the writer says: 'It was raining,' then the reader need not necessarily be told about the wetness abounding since he will have had his fair share of wet weather in his time. True, an inhabitant of sub-Saharan Mali will not have had "his fair share of wet weather", as I put it, but this will perhaps serve to make his response all the keener.

Enough prattle. Please read and enjoy the distinctive narrative voices listed above – in addition to ensuring that the narrative voice in your debut novel draws attention to itself in similar (albeit not identical) fashion.

5. WHERE DO YOU STAND WITH REGARD TO LITERARY PRIZES? Do you nod sagely in agreement with each yearly shortlist handed down by the MAN Booker/Whitbread Prize judges, immediately rushing out to buy or borrow the titles so shortlisted according to your wont in such matters? Or, are you of the other camp? The multifarious misery-guts amongst us who perennially fret and fume, not to say splutter and expostulate on noticing the same half-dozen names plus a token Commonwealth citizen being trotted out yet again, protesting to no avail (in 2007, for example) that at least one book shortlisted for the MAN Booker Prize was a novella, not a novel and, as such, was ineligible for entry, never mind inclusion on the shortlist. [BK: Sincere apologies. On checking John Braine's *Writing a Novel* again I see he allows that, with regard to the Novel: "The minimum length in this country is 40,000 words, and 150,000 the generally accepted maximum." Ergo, I stand corrected – and so the MAN Booker shortlist, 2007 consisted marginally (that is to say, in respect of that lower qualifying number of words) of novels in its entirety.]

Incidentally, have you ever read even one MAN Booker or Whitbread Prize winner that was any good? Because I have, I'll have you know, lest you adjudge me a misery-guts by choice. As previously indicated, the book in question was Whitbread Prize winner, *The Curious Incident of the Dog in the Night-Time* by Mark Haddon. And what puzzles me is how the heck an undoubted masterpiece like *The Curious Incident of the Dog in the Night-Time* managed to squeeze through the perennial Net book agreement, so to speak?

6. DO YOU FIND YOURSELF WANTING TO WRITE YET NOT WANTING TO WRITE? In other words, do you find yourself inventing all sorts of jobs you need to be doing (e.g. shopping, paying through the nose at the Post Office, banking, worming your pet pooch etc.) before you will be able to settle down to doing a bit of writing, as you really and truly intended to do all along?

A recent television programme featured a former Booker shortlisted, James Tait Black Award winner, not to say two-time Whitbread prize winning novelist, supposedly settling down to doing a bit of work – then contriving to do anything and everything but. Some of the woman's diversionary tactics took her as far as Scotland by rail. Luckily for me, I have never felt inclined to go to so much trouble and expense, work avoidance schemes invariably suggesting themselves to me at a very commendable bargain basement economy rate.

Time wasting is an occupational hazard for writers, you'll find. Only regular hours (of physically writing) will counteract the temptation – or, if you favour Bernard MacLaverty's regimen (see his website), *half*-hours, having contrived to fettle which you must *then* be on your guard against making any of your characters go (as Christ foretold of Simon Peter) where they would rather not go in order to do what, in real life, they would never dream of doing in a month of Sundays to the tune of a Preston Guild.

Yet despite all that, when the writing's right, do you love it?

I can remember an English text book when I was at primary school (*First Aid in English* or some such) featuring a list of – well, "blessings" or "virtues", I suppose you'd call them, which, so we were assured, a whole list of people would claim to be: "The Best Thing In Life". So, for instance, the litany ran 'Health,' said the Doctor, 'Courage,' said the Soldier; and so on. Whereupon, the Writer, alphabetically last in the list, as I recall, chose as his benison 'The End'. (So why didn't the Doctor say 'Decomposition'? The Soldier say 'Peace'?) Because the real truth of the matter is that, though, of course, it's a great feeling to finish a specific written project, the Best Thing in Life for the Writer lies in "loving the work he is at present embarked upon, and knowing without a shadow of a doubt at the start of the writing day that there is nothing in the whole wide world he would rather be doing instead." (Sum that up in one word if you can. If you can, you're an Analyst; if not, you're a Writer, being inclined to the prolix.)

It isn't always like that, of course. First drafts can be tough going, with mistakes being made and diversions along the wrong track, too. But re-writing is very often a pleasure that I compare to tying your shoelaces nice and tight, then bounding, ready for action, on to the field of play, having painstakingly threaded those shoelaces through the eyelets during a previous writing session as if with the hands of a child. It isn't always like that, as I say. But if it never, ever feels like that, that you're simply enjoying writing well, that there's nothing else in the whole wide world you would rather be doing at that moment in time, then, I'm sorry (and I really *am* sorry), but what you are writing will never be good enough to publish. Well, anyway, not for the present.

7. HAVING WRITTEN IT, DO YOU RE-WRITE IT – THEN RE-WRITE AGAIN? Unless you're a journalist on a daily newspaper, and are perfectly well-acquainted on a daily basis with transmitting information (or its opposite) at the drop of a hat, re-writing is probably the only way to do it. In a kind of a way, once you've got going, the real problem lies in knowing when to stop. Ernest Hemingway is said to have re-written the ending of one of his novels a zillion times or so. Whereupon he glumly observed: 'I suppose they'll now say it's hurried.'

8. DOES YOUR WORK "TAKE OFF" AT ANY POINT? When you were writing your debut novel, was there ever a time when, having written something, you perhaps stopped on a whim, looked back on what you'd just written, and thought: 'Hey! Get you!' Or

some such? Not in admiration, I hasten to add. (Imagine loving your own work as much as that!) But certainly in wonder – as if someone else (or something) had, however momentarily, taken over from you.

Certainly, I can recall at least one such instance from when I was writing *Every Street in Manchester*, though I hesitate to say where and when it was, so as to deter disgruntled MAN Booker inbreeds from pouring scorn upon it. And, in any case, it wasn't *much* of a moment, I don't suppose (double negatively) in the greater scheme of things. But, for all that, it's *there* – and I revisit it from time to time. As I say, it's nothing at all really, a bit of business (as you'd say about an actor strutting his stuff), a flick of the wrist ("that's what the showman said"). But it's *my* bit of business, *my* flick of the wrist. Most probably I learned the technique involved as a reader, though I honestly don't know where or when. But, at that particular point in the narrative, I felt for a moment as if the novel were writing itself.

Was there ever a time, however fleetingly, you felt that way when you were writing your debut novel? Be fair to yourself. Yes, above all else, be fair to *yourself*. And be honest.

9. DO YOU AGREE WITH YOUR MP? According to recent newspaper reports, some MPs (yours too perhaps) are of the opinion that the legal drinking age in the UK should be raised to 21 years of age as a means of dealing with excessive boozing that is said to be currently endemic amongst young adults.

Do you agree with them? Or do your hackles immediately rise on hearing an assertion like this, no matter how many *anno domini* have grizzled those hackled hairs on the back of your neck. Because you, personally, find it distasteful, to say the least, that the legal drinking age should be so cavalierly adjudged a more suitable item for postponement amongst the adult citizenry of this country than their taxable status, say, or the very great privilege they may continue to enjoy of dying in uniform in Afghanistan or Iraq?

No answers on a postcard, please. No letters to the press. The point at issue here is neither boozing, nor tax paying – nor even duplicated military sump holes wherever our politicians may continually contrive to unearth them for us. (You may be surprised to learn, incidentally, that with the sole exception of 1967* the British Army has been on active service somewhere in the world in every year since the end of WWII.) No, my intention at this point is to underscore the apparently ornery, instinctively anti-establishment, invariably awkward – nay, *philosophical* frame of mind that tends to inform the mindset of many (most?) writers of fiction. Are you one such? Or are you the exact opposite to a philosophising writer of fiction: an admirer of knee-jerk legislation like Disgusted of Tunbridge Wells and (allegedly) your MP? (* Ref. James Ferguson, *F.T.*)

10. WHAT WOULD YOU DO IN THIS SITUATION? I write a monthly book review for magazines in my locality which share a readership 7,000 strong, and it's a job I really enjoy. Now, imagine yourself doing something similar. You write a regular book review for a magazine, and two years down the line, say, a book written by a sworn rival arrives on your desk, at which point you discover it is a wonderful book, a book that's really needed, a work of genius, no less. Not to put too fine a point on it, it is a book you only wish you had had the foresight, the inclination, the nerve, the determination – and, yes (admit it!), the *talent* to have written yourself.

What do you *do*?

Do you perhaps take a well-earned break at Lake Como, hoping some other mug cops for the review whilst you are cruising twixt Lecco and Como aboard the *Alessandro Manzoni*? Do you ignore the book completely in the manner of a *Gruinard* reviewer on the grounds that the author in question isn't Oxbridge? Salieri-like, do you perhaps write a damning review. Or do you write a balanced review as always, the kind of review you know you really ought to write? Well, yes, of course, you do. Enthusiastic? Mm, that too. A review replete with adjectives tripping the light fantastic, not to say superlatives socking it to your readership by the score? Most certainly, you do, you tell me – or, rather, I hope you do, if you're the writer I take you to be.

Of course, there is room for all shades of opinion and approach – and no doubt someone of the calibre of Auberon Waugh or Joe Orton, say, might, even in the circumstances described above, have taken issue with this wonderful book in the catty, even bitchy manner that was their hilarious wont. Meanwhile, John O'Hara might have dealt with the same situation half-jokingly, as for instance his biographer, Frank MacShane, sees him doing on learning John Steinbeck had been awarded the Nobel Prize for Literature: "Congratulations!" O'Hara wired Steinbeck, "Can think of only one other author I'd rather see get it."

But you're a reviewer, remember. You're not John O'Hara (more's the pity), and you're not Auberon Waugh or Joe Orton (thank, God: because you've got plans for your retirement years). So you've got to deal with the situation *as* a reviewer. And when you get right down to it, what is important to you if you are a real writer is, not your personal self aggrandisement, however much you may think it is, but rather the Word itself. That is to say, your *true* word as a writer – by which I mean to say, of course, your very personal word of truth as you honestly and truly perceive it, which (within reason) you *must* utter, *must* publish, *must* shout from the rooftops, as it were, no matter what the apparent cost to yourself personally. Because anything short of this is a lie or propaganda and, as such, is unworthy of a real writer. And, whilst uttering an untruth will not detract one whit from your sworn rival's worth in the greater scheme of things, it will (over a period of time, certainly) savage and leave lying in shreds your very *raison d'etre* as a writer. This is not a new idea. The way I see it, it's an idea that's been around for 2,000 years and more. Originally, it was more simply stated thus: *In principio erat Verbum* which, translated, I'm sure I hardly need say, means "In the beginning was the Word". Or to put it more succinctly – having been quick off the mark to apply rigorous standards to your MP's (alleged) action, I must not, as a writer, fail to apply them to my own.

Ooh, er . . . Now, let's not get too serious about things. Because if, no matter what you do, the rejection slips just keep on coming –

well, wouldn't it make a refreshing change if once in a while a rib-tickler like the following turned up, this being said to have gone out to a Chinese writer from a Chinese publisher?

❍ "We have read your manuscript with boundless delight. If we were to publish your paper, it would be impossible for us to publish any work of lower standard. And as it is unthinkable that in the next thousand years we shall see its equal, we are, to our regret, compelled to return your divine composition, and to beg you a thousand times to overlook our short sight and timidity."

APPENDIX 6: 33 POD COMPANIES & ACCESS TO LOCAL PRINTERS

❑ PRINT-ON-DEMAND COMPANIES

*Lulu: www.lulu.com/uk
Parchment: www.printuk.com
* # Amolibros: www.amolibros.com
* Proprint: www.proprintpublishers.co.uk
Trafford Publishing: www.trafford.com
Publish and Be Damned: www.pabd.com
Think Ink: www.think-ink.co.uk
iuniverse: www.iuniverse.com
* Antony Rowe: www.antonyrowe.co.uk
Book Printing UK: www.BookPrintingUK.com
Writers World: www.writersworld.co.uk
Spire Publishing: www.spirepublishing.com
Arima Publishing: www.arimapublishing.co.uk
The Book Printing Company: www.bookprinting.org.uk
The Lavenham Press: www.tlg.uk.com/lplweb
* The Better Book Company: www.thebetterbookcompany.com
Choir Press: www.thechoirpress.co.uk
* Upfront Publishing: www.upfrontpublishing.com
Diggory Press/Exposure Publishing: www.diggorypress.com

Print on Demand Worldwide: www.printondemand-worldwide.com
Yorkshire Publishing Services Ltd: www.yps-publishing.co.uk
The London Press: www.thelondonpress.co.uk
Grosvenor House: www.selfpublishing.co.uk
Matador: www.troubador.co.uk/matador
Author House: www.authorhouse.co.uk
Authors On Line: www.authorsonline.co.uk
Print on Demand: www.printondemand.co.uk
Lightning Source: www.lightningsource.co.uk
Book Force: www.bookforce.co.uk
Blue Ocean: www.blueoceanpublishing.biz
Tucann books: www.tucann.co.uk
Into Print: www.intoprint.net
Fast Print: www.fastprint.net

Other than Limited Edition Press, the author has had no personal experience of any of the companies listed above, other than to say that he has seen recent specimens of the work of just two of them, and of all the self-published book titles which are listed in Appendix 7.

* Marked by an asterisk are POD companies about which a Society of Authors' information sheet has this to say: "Here are some companies . . . about which we have heard good things from members". Whether prices quoted for self-publishing by these POD companies and/or the quality of their publications are both good is not known. But, given the provenance of this comment, it would be reasonable to assume that the cost *and* quality of work produced by the POD companies so recommended are both worthy of mention.

The hash mark sits alongside POD companies of which Johnathon Clifford, perennial bane of "vanity publishers" down the years, describes as "recommended" [see page 306 of *The Writers' & Artists' Yearbook*, 2008]. Now, Johnathon Clifford is the very man who claims to have invented the phrase "vanity publisher" back in 1959/60 [see Appendix 9, specifically, www. vanitypublishing.info], so he's certainly a fuss-pot on stilts. (Quite

right too!) But exactly what he recommends about these POD companies (the cost and/or the quality of their publications) is not known. However, it should perhaps be borne in mind that the man entertains very exacting standards in respect of quality and expense.

❍ It should perhaps be noted, too, that just one POD company is listed with an asterisk and a hash mark, both. That is to say, the Society of Authors *and* Johnathon Clifford are in agreement about its exemplary character. Readers must decide for themselves whether this is sheer happenstance or, indeed, something they need to take especial notice of since this author has no personal knowledge of the POD company which is so impressively recommended.

Always compare prices before committing yourself to a self-publishing contract. Remember that the old adage "you get what you pay for" does not necessarily apply on every occasion. For instance, it may be possible to obtain a perfectly serviceable and economically-priced house re-wire without contracting one of the major utility companies which will possibly nail your hat on price-wise simply because they are in a position to do so. Similarly, you must be wary of any POD company's being tempted to do likewise on the strength of favourable opinion expressed by literary pundits. This is not to say this will necessarily happen – just that it most definitely will *not* happen if you remain vigilant in the matter of comparison of like with like.

❑ ACCESS TO LOCAL PRINTERS

Alternatively, with regard to finding a local printer to publish your book, the Society of Authors offers this advice: "Seek out local companies through the telephone directories and web searches, checking that their expertise is in books." The website of The British Printing Industries Federation is: www.britishprint.com – and a list of local printers of the type you need to contact may be obtained therefrom.

How will you know which local printer is for you? Well, like any other good tradesman he will not suck his teeth or shake his head when he hears what you want him to do; neither will he eat his lunch whilst talking to you, nurse his grandchild, hurry you up, or pull his face in distaste at the project you envisage. Rather will he prove to be friendly, efficient, imaginative, businesslike and full of ideas. Do not put up with anything less: there are good tradesmen out there, ready to do business. Why ride shotgun with a cowboy?

APPENDIX 7: SELF-PUBLISHED BOOKS TO ACCESS & STUDY

The Idle Hill of Summer by Tony Bowers (pub. Diggory Press/ Exposure Publishing) ISBN 1846854784 *Fiction: rites of passage tale set in Nottinghamshire during WWII*

***This Truckin' Life* by Laurie Driver (pub. Diggory Press/ Exposure Publishing) ISBN 1846852366 *Reminiscences of a Manchester-based lorry driver*

Cop Out by Dennis Foy (pub. Publish and Be Damned/PABD) ISBN 0954334019 *Fiction: a Manchester-based policeman goes bad*

Ten sporting biographies by Brian Hughes MBE:
**Jackie Brown – the Man, the Myth, the Legend* ISBN none
Starmaker, the Jimmy Murphy Story ISBN 1901746267
For King and Country (the Johnny King story) ISBN 1901746232
Jock Macavoy – Portrait of a Fighting Legend ISBN 196746178
Willie Pep – the Will o' the Wisp ISBN 1901746
The Tommy Taylor Story – the Smiling Executioner
ISBN1901746216
Violett (with Roy Cavanagh) ISBN 1901746399
The King – Denis Law, Hero of the Stretford End
ISBN 1901746356
Reaching for the Stars: the Howard Winstone Phenomenon
ASIN: B000PVTQV8

Peerless – the Sugar Ray Robinson Story (with Damian Hughes) ISBN 0955184819

Every Street in Manchester & Manchester Kiss by Bill Keeth (pub. Limited Edition Press) ISBN 1859880657 & ISBN 1859880673 *Fiction: Manchester-based in the second half of 20th Century and beyond*

Our Kid by Tim Lally (pub. Limited Edition Press) ISBN 1859880134 *Fiction: Manchester-based, creative reminiscence, 1920s – 1940s*

My Story by Alice Mellalieu-Campbell (pub. Parchment) ISBN 0955398509 *Reminicences of life in Canada and the UK*

****Doing Our Bit** by Martin Purdy & Ian Dawson (pub. Moonraker) ISBN 0955447204 *Local History: the letters and diaries of servicemen reveal the part played in WWI by the people of Middleton, Greater Manchester*

***The Moston Story* by Fr Brian Seale (pub. the author: Tel. 0161 681-6844) ISBN 095525650X *Local History: the north Manchester suburb of Moston*

**In the Town Where I Was Born* & **100+ Oldham Characters* by Carl H. Spiers (pub. Chas Promotions: Tel. 07716 845511 & 0161 626-6329) ISBN none *Local History: Oldham from the 1950s onwards*

* Titles itemised by a single asterisk, lack an ISBN number and so cannot be registered with Nielsen BookData. Consequently, they are not listed on Amazon and must be accessed direct from the author.

** Titles itemised by a double asterisk are reviewed on Amazon by Bill Keeth.

❑ NOTE WITH REGARD TO BOOK TITLES BY BRIAN HUGHES, MBE,

Readers may choose to ignore the last four titles listed, should they so choose, and on the grounds that:

- these four books are hardbacks and, due to the extra expense involved, there is no way I would advise any reader to self-publish a hardback book;
- a sports biography is a sports biography is a sports biography – and, popular as these titles may be, your personal interests may well be focused elsewhere.

However:

- *Starmaker – the Jimmy Murphy Story* is a hardback book, but the rest of it is well-worth considering by anyone looking to self-publish fiction in a suitable format.
- *Jackie Brown – the Man, the Myth, the Legend* may prove elusive due to its possessing no ISBN number, so concentrate on other books by Brian Hughes, MBE, as listed.

In conclusion, I would just remind readers, if I may, that there is absolutely no reason to buy any of the book titles mentioned elsewhere and above. What I do recommend is that you should have *sight* of them, should *handle* them, and should *study* the format of each of them over a period of time. To do so, there is no necessity for you to buy a single copy; you may order every book possessing an ISBN number through your local library service.

APPENDIX 8: ESSENTIAL TEXTS ABOUT WRITING FICTION

There are countless books in the bookshops and the public library system purporting to advise and lend other assistance to readers seeking to write publishable fiction. As a general rule, though, it is perhaps best to shy away from books by any author promising such help despite the major disadvantage of his never having published fiction himself. Please note, however, that this is a general rule only. Because just as a successful association football manager may not have made a particularly distinctive contribution to Premier League soccer in his days as a player, there are helpful experts in every form of human activity, who can perhaps talk or plan a better campaign than was ever delivered by themselves personally on the actual field of play. You will recall, by way of example, that there were two gods of war in Ancient Rome: Janus, the strategist; and Mars, the man of action. Both types are necessary to military success.

This said, then, listed below you'll find a seven-deep list of books about fiction writing which I personally have found to be the most helpful by far. I've read every one of these books, of course, and I've *re-read* all but one – and I know even as I write these words that there are some I am going to want to read again. Briefly, how many book titles can you say *that* about? Briefly, too – far too briefly to do these top-class books true justice – I intend to mention some aspects of them I think are good (meaning *excellent*) and, indeed, some I feel are not so good. But make no mistake about this: there are positively oodles, if not lashings, of good ideas in each of these books, and I hereby recommend them to you unreservedly. So please do not regard any negative judgment on my part as being ultimately definitive. Because in certain of the instances in which I describe the books as being "not so good", what I am really saying is nothing more adversely critical than this: 'This particular idea does not quite fit in with my own *modus operandi*, and/or chime strongly in unison with my personal opinion and experience in the matter.'

- *Writing a Novel*, John Braine, ISBN 0413315401, Eyre Methuen, 1974 (More recent editions are entitled *How to Write a Novel*.)

GOOD a) "A writer is a person who writes," says John Braine – which is sterling advice of the *sine qua non* variety. So set yourself a regimen, and stick to it. b) The author also supplies several examples of good writing, explaining why it *is* good writing. And c) As ever, John Braine is eminently readable, presenting you almost unawares with a first rate example of exactly what I mean when I refer you to the need for a good narrative voice in your debut novel.

NOT SO GOOD Initially, you may welcome (as did I as a novice) the way in which John Braine suggests you should structure your debut novel. And he really does have some excellent, eloquently argued ideas. On the other hand, you may come to find some of his ideas stultifying over time, in that they don't quite suit the way you need to work and/or present your own work.

For example, John Braine says a novel should have at least 20 chapters, but it ain't necessarily so. (Check out Alan Sillitoe's *Saturday Night and Sunday Morning* and *Borstal Boy* by Brendan Behan – which is not to say, of course, that these other authors are right in having no chapters at all in these books – well, no *numbered* chapters at any rate.) Also, you may come to find that John Braine's insistence on physically writing, writing, *writing* is not what your novel requires at any particular juncture. At some point you may need, for example (as did I with *Every Street in Manchester* at one stage), to link together two seemingly disparate strands of your story, a problem I succeeded in tackling by means of a dreamy weekend in Paris with no notebook (or fiction book) to hand, but just the determination to think things through and get it all down on paper immediately I got back home again. This was, of course, at a time in my life when I already had thousands of words of fiction under my belt; but way back when I had very few words written, the regimen and structure suggested by John Braine were a godsend.

❑ *On Writing*, George V Higgins, ISBN 0805016872, Henry Holt, 1990

GOOD "Don't read fiction while you're writing fiction," says George V Higgins, author of *The Friends of Eddie Coyle* and other exemplary models of present-day idiom and speech patterns. Higgins says the danger is that you will inadvertently copy another writer's style: "involuntary plagiarism", he calls it. But, to my mind (and certainly for an unpublished beginner, I'd say), it is much more likely to be the case that reading your favourite writers whilst you're writing your own stuff will just make you feel inadequate to the task.

So how should you handle this problem? And it is certainly a problem, believe me. Because a writer will want – heck, a writer will *need* to read even when he's writing. Well, the answer would appear to be to read something in another genre. So, according to Elmore Leonard, he reads non-fiction when he's writing his thrillers, as does Michael Connelly when writing his police procedural/LA *noir* series of books featuring Hieronymus Bosch – and, Jane Davis, Michael Connelly's webmaster, also tells me: "Michael often reads novels by foreign authors, because the rhythm, language, and culture feel sufficiently different that they don't interfere with his own work."

I'm with Michael Connelly on reading fiction of a different genre. Because, though I *do* read non-fiction whilst writing (if I may paraphrase a lyric from the Billy Fury number, 'Halfway to Paradise': lyrics: Goffin/King), non-fiction 'can do just so *mu-u-uch*!' So, like playwright Jim Allen (*The Spongers, Hidden Agenda*, *Raining Stones*), who once upon a time revealed to me that he'd turn to thrillers whilst working on one of his heavy political themes, I read thrillers, too, when writing – and mystery stories and police procedurals too.

This is not to disparage these literary forms in any way. Because I really do believe reading thrillers assists me with my work. Quite apart from any other consideration, if there is anything that writers like Michael Connelly and Ed McBain and Elmore Leonard and George V Higgins know how to do, it's how to move their characters around convincingly in time and space – and get 'em shooting off at the lip too, as opposed to relying too exclusively on the pistol-packing hip.

NOT SO GOOD No book ever improved anybody, says George V Higgins. He means: 'Don't preach: it's counter productive!' And that's true: preaching has no place in fiction. It is the novelist's job to hold a mirror up to what he sees about him – and to tell his readers what he sees about him in his time and place. But can it really be true that books like the *New Testament* and/or *The Koran*, never improved anybody? And, irregardless of any tendency to preach, should a writer, therefore, only depict the vain, venal and villainous in society when, should he care to notice them, there may be examples of sheer goodness to be seen all around him?

Another way in which George V Higgins is perhaps not quite as successful as he might have been in transmitting handy writing techniques is in his espousal of the reportage of *New York Times* journalist, Guy Talese. Higgins' recommendation, good as Talese's prose is, backfires on him for two reasons: a) he lets it run on for some 7,500 words, so it's too wordy by far; and, b) the subject matter of Guy Talese's piece is the American folk hero, Joe DiMaggio, a former baseball player and one-time consort (as, indeed, were countless other men) of the film star Marilyn Monroe. Yet, Talese (and by implication, Higgins) would appear to be in awe of DiMaggio on account of this tainted matrimony as if of someone (or something) of real worth – Balboa, the first European to see the Pacific Ocean; Alexander Fleming, unearthing the cure-all that is penicillin; Stafford Cripps, pointing the way towards the Welfare State; Laurel and Hardy, causing us to laugh in the face of our troubles.

❑ *How Not to Write a Novel*, David Armstrong,
ISBN 0749006803, Allison & Busby, 2003

GOOD Do you *really* want to vilify your nearest and dearest for the sake of a story? Don't do it, says David Armstrong. This is a book to come back to time and time again: a book that repeatedly says “Don’t Do It” in another sense – that is to say, “Don’t Write”. Yet the author just as often allows that writing *must* be done by those who feel they must do it. A self-effacing book, a very warm and welcoming book written by a novelist for whom it was, as I understand it, the first of his books properly to pay off.

NOT SO GOOD Pick your book titles from Shakespeare or the Bible, says David Armstrong. Not for me, I’m afraid. How ever much I’d love to emulate Hemingway’s resonant titling of his works, it would feel pretentious. Instead, I say, give your book a “working title”, then forget it until you’ve finished. Thereafter, don’t worry about it. If what you’ve written is any good, the “right” title will invariably suggest itself to you whilst you’re writing it.

❑ *Becoming a Writer*, Dorothea Brandt, ISBN 0333346734 & 0333653777, Macmillan, 1983

GOOD The exception that proves the rule. I have never heard of any fiction title penned by Dorothea Brandt, but she certainly provides a sure fire way of getting the words down on paper by setting you a stiff regimen.

NOT SO GOOD I didn’t come across this book until I’d finished my debut novel. *Thank God!* says he. Because you can work up a sweat just *reading* this book! (Joke.)

❑ *On Writing*, Stephen King, ISBN 0340820462, New English Library, 2001

GOOD Whether you like Stephen King’s books or you don’t, the man is consistently cerebral about his work. (As also, incidentally, is Dean Koontz.) The best advice I can recall from this volume is to read through your stuff when you’ve finished it, then revise, striking out maybe a 10% surplus. And, for writers struggling to find the time to read, Stephen King recommends that you ditch the CDs and listen to audiotapes in your car. Don’t tell me you won’t reach your 70 books per annum quota if you follow Stephen King’s advice in this respect.

NOT SO GOOD As I understand it, Stephen King writes with heavy metal music playing in the background. *Yikes!* Pray fan my fevered brow!

❑ *An Artist is His Own Fault*, John O'Hara, ISBN 0809307960, Southern Illinois University Press, 1977

GOOD The voice of authority. A top class writer talks about writing.

NOT SO GOOD An optional read. O'Hara can be a bit off-putting – but don't let him be. O'Hara wasn't just good, he was very likely the best there is. The trouble is he *knew* it. And it was the fact that he never could keep his big gob shut about how good he was that ensured he never did receive (unlike his contemporaries Faulkner, Hemingway and Steinbeck) the Nobel prize for Literature. A singular injustice! Because, in my humble opinion, John O'Hara deserved the Nobel more than anyone else who ever won it in the last half-century and more.

'Who reads O'Hara nowadays?' I recall Anthony Burgess once asking in that unfortunate sneering tone he would too often adopt in respect of his fellow authors. (See *Homage to Qwertyuiop*.)

'Oh, I do,' I'd have loved to have had the opportunity to retort in respect of John O'Hara – '*Re-read* him too.'

Why?

Well, the epitaph on O'Hara's headstone says it all, I suppose: 'Better than anyone else he told the truth about his time. He was a professional. He wrote honestly and well.'

These are sentiments we writers might all take to heart – always provided, of course, that we succeed in suppressing any tendency to titter at the thought of the epitaph on O'Hara's headstone being penned by the great man himself.

❑ *501 Writers' Questions Answered*, Nancy Smith, ISBN 0749914971, Piatkus

GOOD Though this book is not in the same league as the other books on this list, it is somehow reassuring to have a book you can turn to in a world where all around you are talking about *Coronation Street*, the score at half-time, the weather, the price of kippers, the latest wizard wheeze the Government has got away with that should, if justice anywhere prevailed within these shores, have seen every last one of them hanged – and nobody ever wants to talk about writing.

NOT SO GOOD A Comprehensive Guide to Writing and Getting Published' proclaims the front cover. Sadly, the book won't get you writing and it won't get you published.

And now . . . Cue: *ragman's trumpet*: *dah-dah-dah-dah-dah-ah . . .*

❑ BILL KEETH'S PERSONAL FOUR-PENNORTH ABOUT WRITING FICTION, WHICH READERS MAY TAKE OR LEAVE AS THEY CHOOSE

1) Lose weight if you're overweight, go hungry from choice, then you'll feel more inclined to activity, and therefore more inclined to write.

2) If your aim is to "play for your country" by being published nationally, follow the advice of English cricketer Ian Botham's father, who is said to have advised him, when he was looking to be selected for the First XI, to be a batsman and a bowler, both. In other words, tell whatever story you have to tell (be a novelist) and make sure you season it liberally with the appurtenances of the time and place in which your narrative is set (be a diarist, too).

3) Write about what you know, 'tis said. And I agree. But sometimes you cannot really *see* what you know. So, go *away* from what you know (James Joyce, Henry James, The Beatles) and, if you cannot go away from what you know, immerse yourself exclusively in the literature of another time and place for a few years.

4) If someone tells you your work is rubbish, ignore the complaint unless a more detailed critique is forthcoming – and

ignore *the critique*, if it is delivered by a know-nothing. That is to say, how dare anyone who never opens a book from one year's end to the next presume to judge a book? Furthermore, ignore all criticism of your novel that emanates from a non-novelist on the grounds that what you have written is certainly better than your critic's non-existent novel.

5) The last great sports novel, to my way of thinking, was David Storey's *This Sporting Life* back in the early 1960s. Take note, ye storytellers, that the great association football (Soccer) novel has *yet* to be written – and it will not be written by me. So, over to you on the volley.

6) If you cannot please a publisher, please yourself. Write what's in your heart. You may be surprised to find you're a nicer person than you think you are. If you were not, you'd be out there creating mayhem, not writing . . . Oh, you don't *care* about being a nicer person? You just want to be a writer?

Now, hear *this* (as Jeff Chandler used to call over the tannoy, togged out in his US Navy whites) . . . I am making a very serious point about writing, here, and about affective writing in particular. Because perhaps, like me, you happen to have turned to writing (that is to say, to writing with serious intent) in anger and frustration at things that were going pear-shaped in your professional and personal life which you were unable, otherwise, to do anything about. (And why ever not? I ask. Leave the daffodils to William Wordsworth – and leave him, too, to tell the lie about the view from Westminster Bridge: for pain is a vital creative force, whereas contentment probably is not.) Do not, though, if such be the case, make the mistake of imagining that your impotent bellows of rage, however well-justified they may be (effluently-arraigned with coarse invective, as they perhaps are, too), will serve as your passport to being read and enjoyed by a wider public. Because swear words, if they are used at all, must be used sparingly, or they lose their power to shock.

This is by no means a prissy point. Rather is it a question of whether your writing "works" or not. Because if your writing doesn't "work" (and to my way of thinking, a superabundance of swear words does not work in literary terms), that is to say, if your writing does *not* do the job you set out to do, then it is writing that does not "work". True, swearing may well be wrong according to:

- ❍ current legislation (e.g. racist epithets), or
- ❍ a set of religious beliefs, or
- ❍ a personal code of ethics, but
- ❍ this isn't what concerns us, here.

No. Rather is what concerns us in this present instance intrinsically linked with the problem of a writer's doing his level best to arrive at the truth of things as he sees them, and then set that truth down for his readers to see. So our problem, here, in respect of any potential superabundance of invective within your narrative is concerned with the basic utility of words. Or, to put it in a nutshell, repetitive swearing simply does not [BLEEP! – Ed.] work.

APPENDIX 9: BASIC REFERENCE BOOKS & USEFUL WEBSITES

❑ BOOKS DEALING WITH THE ENGLISH LANGUAGE AND PRESENTATIONAL STYLE

Chambers Dictionary ISBN 0550101853
English Made Simple pub. W H Allen ISBN 04911019203
pub. Broadway ISBN 0385174837
The Elements of Style by William Strunk & E.B. White
ISBN 7609200544
The Chicago Manual of Style pub. University of Chicago Press
ISBN 0224103897
Eats Shoots and Leaves Lynne Truss ISBN1846680352
MHRA Style Book Modern Humanities Research Association
ISBN 0947623612

F Scott Fitzgerald was a writer of great distinction yet he was notoriously poor when it came to spelling. So his editor, Maxwell Perkins, invariably had to tidy up his typescripts once they'd been submitted. Similarly, Perkins would find himself called upon to knock some sort of shape into Thomas Wolfe's rambling and repetitive manuscripts before they were sent off to the printer. So there are certainly precedents for sloppy work being made acceptable. Unfortunately, if and when *you* finally get around to self-publishing, you are going to be on your own, with nary an editor in sight. So you had just better get it right.

You may get lucky, of course. My publisher was prepared to proof-read *Every Street in Manchester,* but due to much of the book's being written in a Mancunian vernacular, I had to pass on his kind offer of assistance. This is an extreme case, so perhaps you may be able to use your publisher's offer of assistance, if such should materialise (as I subsequently did to good effect with *Manchester Kiss*) – or you may have someone closer to home who's a dab hand at spelling, punctuation and the rest of it – and can be trusted to do the job for you. For instance, I am given to understand that Mrs Clara Hopkins, retired teacher that she is, undertook responsibility for casting a cool corrective eye upon the respective typescripts that would eventually be published as *Our Kid*, *High Hopes*, *Kate's Story*, *Going Places*, *Anything Goes* and *Whatever Next!* And a pretty keen eye she brought to the process, too, it seems to me.

But personal assistance notwithstanding, there are bound to be certain rules applying to writing a book which never come into play in the realm of normal correspondence – the use of italics, say; the precise use of brackets or parentheses; how properly to represent a numeral, large or small; the use of the ellipsis . . . And you, self-publisher that you now are, are just going to have to get these things right.

Dither ye not, dear reader. Because the last book listed above, the *MHRA Style Book*, is a veritable mine of such information and will surely enable you to iron out all those points you will need to be aware of if you are intent on self-publishing your work. For example:

- In what sequential order will your book need to be organised? (e.g. title page, dedication, contents list, Foreword etc.)
- When do foreign words need to retain their accents? And when should foreign words be represented in italic print?
- Which words require a hyphen?
- How should you represent place names, personal names, Slavonic names?
- How about the abbreviation of titles and the names of American states?
- What about parentheses and brackets?
- When and where should you use capital letters?
- Should you use Italic print for the titles of books, films, song titles, works of art?
- How would you represent numbers, Roman numerals, currency, dates, weights?
- How ought you to represent short and long quotations from other peoples work?
- What about footnotes?

The answers to these and much more besides will be found in the *MHRA Style Book*. It is a fascinating book, not only for the writer, but for anyone who is interested in the English Language. And though at first the process will be a slow one, you will (honestly and truly) get much more adept at it as you go along – even going so far as to retain much of the information so gleaned. After all, you are a writer now, and the *MHRA Style Book* is simply another tool of your trade. Two points I would emphasise, though, are these:

- Rather than attempting to read the *MHRA Style Book* from cover to cover (or, indeed, any other handbook connected with your new trade) you should only open it in order to focus upon a specific topic: e.g. How should I represent in print the book title *Room at the Top*? In italics or no? It should be written in italics, by the way; just as what follows is the way the title of a song should be represented: 'There's a Guy Works Down the Chip Shop Swears He's Elvis'.

- Should you want to read the MHRA Style Book from cover to cover (or, any other handbook), do so on a daily (or rather, a nightly) basis by utilising it as bedside reading, taking in just a small section at a time.

❑ ON WRITING

Ernest Hemingway On Writing ISBN0684854295
Is There a Book in You? by Alison Baverstock ISBN 0713679328

❑ ON MARKETING

Marketing Your Book – An Author's Guide by Alison Baverstock ISBN 0713659693
Marketing Your Book – How to Target Agents, Publishers and Readers by Alison Baverstock ISBN 0713673834
How to Market Books by Alison Baverstock ISBN 074950207

❑ USEFUL WEBSITES

As is sometimes the way in such matters, certain of the websites listed below may, need more extensive rooting out than indicated due to re-arrangement by their respective webmasters of subject matter, titling and/or indexing. So, just occasionally, it may be as well to search for the required piece by means of its title rather than relying on the website details alone. Also, though every one of the pieces listed here lies ready-to-hand at the time of writing, I tender my sincere apologies lest any one of them does not remain so by the time you need to access it. All I can suggest by way of making reparation is:

- that some of the sources mentioned will remain utterly reliable – the Society of Authors, for instance, and (I should think) Johnathon Clifford, whose interest in his subject goes back to the early 1960s;

- that very little goes unnoticed and unread on the internet. So, by the time you need to access the kind of information that I've listed below, there may be any number of new websites dealing with self-publishing and ancillary issues available to you, and there is a very good chance that any of these will be better informed than the websites I recommend to you for the present. *Vide*:

❍ ON WRITING

www.writersservices.com
www.howtotellagreatstory.com

❍ ON VANITY PUBLISHING

'Free Publishing Advice', Johnathon Clifford:
www.vanitypublishing.info

❍ ON SELF-PUBLISHING

'The Very Best of British', Mike Etherington:
www.publish-yourself.com/index.shtml
'How to Publish Yourself', Peter Finch:
www.peterfinch.co.uk/howpub.htm
www.spacejock.com.au/SelfPublishing.html:
'How to Self-Publish a Book and Who Should Be Doing It'.

❍ ON PRINT-ON-DEMAND

'The POD Quandary', Brenda Rollins:
www.writing-world.com/publish/POD.shtml

❍ ON MARKETING YOUR BOOK

www.alisonbaverstock.com is a really helpful website for writers who aim to be published. If Alison Baverstock were a publisher or a literary agent, she would be the publisher or literary agent we all deserve to have. Check out Alison Baverstock's diary of events, and make sure you book yourself a place at the venue nearest to your home address.
www.justaboutwrite.com/BookMarketing/27809.php:
'Ready, Set, Go – Sell Your Book in the Real World':
1001 Ways to Market Your Books by John Kremer:
www.bookmarket.com
Marketing Your Self-Published Book:
www.aetbookbindery.com/MarketingComplete.htm
Press and Other Media Matters:
www.naturenet.net/education/press.html

and,

The Society of Authors also offers a series of Quick Guide publications dealing with Vanity Publishing; Self-Publishing and

Print-On-Demand; Marketing Your Book; Author Appearances at Schools, Colleges, Festivals, Libraries; Authors' Agents; Publishing Contracts; Electronic Publishing Contracts; Permissions; VAT; Libel. A full list of Quick Guide publications is available from www.societyofauthors.org [See Appendix 10 below.]

APPENDIX 10: THE SOCIETY OF AUTHORS

The Quick Guide Publications mentioned above are free for the asking to members of the Society of Authors, being downloadable from the Society's website. Non-members may obtain these quick guides at a small charge by writing to: The Society of Authors, 84 Drayton Gardens, London SW10 9SB

Membership of the Society of Authors is restricted to published authors, either commercially or self-published, and readers really should give serious thought to applying for membership immediately they are published. The annual fee may seem a bit off-putting for those who have only recently paid to be self-published. But there are concessions made for younger authors and for membership fees paid by annual direct debit – and the membership fee is tax deductible, remember. The benefits of joining the Society of Authors are manifold, some of which are listed as follows: 10% discount on books purchased at all branches of Waterstone's and Blackwell's on production of a membership card; 25% off the entire range of books from Oxford University Press; free advice to members on almost every aspect affecting authors, including contract advice; free membership of the Authors' Licensing and Collecting Society (ALCS); members only web pages for downloadable Quick Guides; a quarterly magazine, *The Author*, mailed to your home address; discounts on car and van rental from National Car Rental.

My personal experience of the Society of Authors, gleaned over the past two and a half years or so is that:

- its officers will respond helpfully and informatively to e-mail queries within three working days;

- there seems to be a pleasing willingness to assist with members' queries;

- interesting seminars and lectures are on offer from time to time, the majority of which are London-based, though there is evidence of a new intent to field some events in the north of England. But the London-based seminars would themselves prove much more attractive to provincial members were just a month's notice or so given in order to facilitate access to Apex train fares at a bargain rate.

Here's what the late and the great have had to say about the Society of Authors:

'We all, eminent and obscure alike, need the Author's Society' George Bernard Shaw

'The advice and help that the Society's staff dispense, and the weight of experience that they can bring to bear, are immensely valuable' Philip Pullman

I could not agree more, though to all appearances the "eminent" are perhaps fending for themselves nowadays, or, at least, pretending to do so. That is to say, you are never going to bump into Ian Rankin, P D James, Bernard Cornwell or any other writer you've ever heard of at a Society of Authors' seminar (except as a guest lecturer perhaps). However, you will (as I did at Harrogate on one occasion) meet fascinating characters such as a self-published lady of mature years, who (Hannah Hauxwell-like) was enjoying a day away from the herd of Friesians which demand her attention for the other 364 days in the farming year. And you may occasionally come across the contiguously famous – as I also did recently at a "Self-Publishing" seminar at the Royal OverSeas Club in London, namely, Caro Fraser, daughter of the late, great George MacDonald Fraser, author of the Flashman series of books.

Of Caro Fraser I make especial mention at this point because you'll find the Blog on her website – www.caro-fraser.com (which includes a contribution from her friend, Mary Cavanagh) and contains some interesting snippets about self-publishing, and also about fielding a book launch, the sort of event you yourself will need to cater for in the near future. More about which anon; but see also David Armstrong's *How NOT to Write a Novel* for advice about organising a successful book launch.

APPENDIX 11: THE COMPONENT PARTS OF YOUR NOVEL

MO by D. DITHERER,
pub. A. POD Publisher,
complete with an
apposite DEDICATION and EPIGRAPH

NOTE Rather than use a dozen or so separate A4 pages for the following task, which would be a waste of paper and a bit of a cop out, too (or so it seems to me), each of the pages in Appendix 11 is marked by lined spaces representing pages. Details of the book, *MO* by D. Ditherer are in bold font. Please refer to the list of self-published books in Appendix 7 in order to see: a) where bold font will be required; and b) how the various wordings should be arranged on the page. Please check with the format of other books in your library if in any doubt about the format as follows . . .

❑ The front cover, page 1, with illustration but no number, right-hand page

MO
by
D. DITHERER

❑ The inside front cover, page 2, not numbered, blank, left-hand page

---

❑ page 3, blank flyleaf, not numbered, right-hand page

❑ page 4, blank flyleaf, not numbered, left-hand page

❑ page 5, title page, not numbered, right-hand page – featuring book title, author's name, publisher's name

MO
by
D. DITHERER

A. POD Publisher

❑ page 6, bibliographical details, not numbered, left-hand page – publisher's name and address; copyright statement; ISBN number (page may be left blank for the publisher to complete)

A. POD Publisher
Underthearmville
Dumplington
UK

etc. (see biographical details of *Every Street in Manchester*)

❑ page 7, DEDICATION, not numbered, right-hand page

To my dad, Dolittle Ditherer

❑ page 8, blank, not numbered, left-hand page

❑ page 9, epigraph, not numbered, right-hand page

Look before you leap for as you sow, ye are like to reap.
Samuel Butler

❑ page 10, blank, not numbered, left-hand page

❑ page 11, the narrative commences, numbered right-hand page

It was a dark, dark night . . .

11

❑ page (numbered page: whatever the number is*),
the narrative concludes,

. . . and they all lived happily ever after.

?

---

* It is, of course, quite impossible to know at this stage, whether your narrative will conclude on a right-hand page or a left-hand page. Does this matter? Well, only in the sense that:

❍ if your narrative concludes on a left-hand page, you must remember to specify the inclusion of a blank flyleaf to follow before the inside back cover/back cover, so that the ending of your narrative is properly obscured from readers' eyes, but,

❍ if your narrative concludes on a right-hand page, that right-hand page will be backed by a blank page to the obverse side, so there will be no need to specify the inclusion of a blank flysheet before the inside back/back cover.

APPENDIX 12: PUBLISHING WITH LIMITED EDITION PRESS

IMPRINT OF THE SMALL PRINT

Limited Edition Press: www.limited-edition-press.co.uk

I submitted the 50 questions which previously featured in Chapter Seven: Choosing the Right Publisher for You to my publisher, Limited Edition Press. What follows is a personal message from him and his response to the 50 questions I pose therein.

❑ A PERSONAL MESSAGE FROM LIMITED EDITION PRESS: "This book publishing business is registered as, and is called, The Small Print. Under the aegis of The Small Print books are produced under the imprints: The Small Print, Limited Edition Press and Leopard Press. Also, I thought it might be helpful for you to provide your readers with some of the details a publisher needs to know before a quotation may be supplied. By way of example, when an author requiring details of my publishing services approaches me, I always ask them to provide answers to the following questions:

- In which format will you be submitting the book?
- How many words are there in your book?
- How many illustrations are there in your book, if any?
- What size would you like your book to be? (A4, A5 or some other size)
- What colour cover would you like?
- Would you prefer hardback or paperback?
- Would you like a laminated cover – gloss or matt?
- Do you have an illustration or a photo you'd like to appear on the cover?
- How many copies would you like to order? (The recommended minimum is 50.)
- Finally, where do you want the finished books delivered?

Then further discussion via telephone is usually necessary."

❑ 50 QUESTIONS TO ASK YOUR LOCAL PRINTER AND/OR POD COMPANIES

1. May I submit my book to you as the A4 Word document via e-mail attachment to be typeset by yourselves? Limited Edition Press: *Your document may be submitted to me in any word processor format, though Microsoft Word is preferable and it may be forwarded via email or posted on CD/DVD/floppy disk.*

2. I still use a typewriter, I'm afraid. May I submit my book to you, typewritten in A4 hard format, leaving the typesetting to you? LEP: *Yes, your work may be submitted to me in typewritten format for scanning (at extra cost) as long as the typewritten document is clear. Faded print due to faulty or dry typewriter ribbons is impossible to scan satisfactorily, so a dark photocopy of the entire manuscript would need to be provided.*

3. Or do you specify that my book must be submitted to you as a typeset pdf document? LEP: *No, but if no other word processor format is available to you, I can work from pdf documents. However, if you have already typeset the book and only require a printing service, this can be provided instead of what I personally tend to regard as a full publication service whereby I, rather than the customer, would typeset the book.*

4. What is the minimum number of copies I must order from you as a first print run? LEP: *The minimum run we can provide is 25 copies but this would be costly. I, therefore, recommend a minimum of 50 copies which, whilst still costly, would work out proportionately less costly than 25 copies.*

5. Should I decide to place an order with you, how long will it be before the books are delivered to my door? LEP: *Every book is different. The time spent typesetting depends very much upon the author. But if the work submitted to be typeset is finished with no re-writes, then usually about 3 weeks to typeset + 3-5 weeks for printing, including customer approval of final print run proofs.*

6. Are you willing to publish the size of book I prefer – e.g. A5-sized, A6, Royale (B5), A4? LEP: *Yes and more besides. If you*

require a book to be published to your size specifications, this can be worked out after discussion.

7. May I choose the paper I prefer, white bond or bookwove? LEP: *Yes.*

8. If I were to opt for bookwove, what quality would it be? LEP: *Author's choice.*

9. I know the text of the book will be justified. But, should the narrative occasionally require the text to be centred – or perhaps aligned differently to right or left, would you be able to accommodate these variations? LEP: *Yes.*

10. Do you have a selection of cover artwork from which I may make a selection? LEP: *No.*

11. Would you be prepared to accept a photograph of my own for cover artwork? LEP: *Yes.*

12. Do extra charges apply if I opt for a full colour cover? LEP: *Yes, but if a colour cover was first specified in details about the book, the colour cover will have been taken into consideration when working out the price.*

13. May I use an imprint of my own? LEP: *Yes, by arrangement.*

14. If I use your company imprint, do I still retain my copyright and international rights in every respect? LEP: *Yes.*

15. What written assurance, warranty or guarantee will I have about copyright retention? LEP: *Discussion with the author would be required, but any form of warranty can be accommodated.*

16. How much will it cost me for the first print run? *LEP: Every book is different – size, number of pages, paper, etc. So a price can only be given when all facts are known.*

17. How long will it be before the books will be delivered to my door? LEP: *See Answer 5.*

18. If I were to order a few thousand copies, say, would the cost per copy be more advantageous to me? LEP: *Yes, but don't order more books than you know you can sell.*

19. Do the quoted costs include the cost of delivery? LEP: *No.*

20. Do you then retain the digital file of my book in the event of my requiring further print runs? LEP: *Yes.*

21. Will I be committed to a long-term tie-in of some kind? LEP: *No.*

22. Should I be dissatisfied for any reason, may I go elsewhere for future print-runs? LEP: *Yes, but I'd hope the customer would want to discuss the situation with me in the first instance.*

23. Will the cost of a second print run be any cheaper? LEP: *As the initial typesetting work has been done, future print runs will be charged at a discounted cost minus the original cost of the typesetting.*

24. If I order a second (third, fourth) print run, how long will it be before it is delivered to my door? LEP: *3 weeks maximum.*

25. Will you let me have a recent sample of your work free-of-charge? LEP: *Yes.*

26. May I arrange to purchase a recent sample of your work? LEP: *Yes, but why would you want to do so since I'll supply you with a copy free-of-charge?*

27. May I telephone you to discuss things from time to time? LEP: *Yes. In fact, I prefer it.*

28. May I pop into the office or meet up with you to iron out any problems that may arise? LEP: *Yes, by appointment.*

29. Will my requirements be attended to throughout by a named member of staff? LEP: *Yes.*

30. Will I at any time see a proof copy of the book you propose to publish so that I may proof-read it, amending or correcting it where required? LEP: *Yes – only one print-out but as many pdf documents as may be required until YOU (the customer) are satisfied. It is YOUR book, so I work at your pace.*

31. On how many occasions will I be sent a proof copy for inspection? LEP: *See answer 30.*

32. Will you be prepared to advise me about a suitable retail price for the book? LEP: *No. I am not in the marketing business and so I would be the wrong person to ask.*

33. Do you provide the necessary ISBN number? LEP: *Yes.*

34. May I provide my own ISBN number? LEP: *Yes.*

35. Do you provide a Barcode with the book? LEP: *Yes, if required. The cost is determined by an outside generating company.*

36. Do you attend to all requirements under the Legal Deposit Scheme? LEP: *Yes, if published under LEP imprint.*

37. Will you provide me with a certain number of author copies of the book? LEP: *No, as you are already buying all of them.*

38. Will you register the book with Nielsen BookData? LEP: *Yes, if published under LEP imprint.*

39. Will you list a) the book; b) details about the content of the book; and an image of the front cover of the book on Amazon? LEP: *Amazon lists the book on its own behalf immediately the title is registered with Nielsen BookData. Thereafter, assistance in registering further details is available upon request.*

40. Once the book is published, do you then distribute it on my behalf? LEP: *No.*

41. Do you distribute the book via Gardners, Bertrams and Askews? LEP: *No.*

42. Do you make the book available to all the major bookshops and the independents? LEP: *No.*

43. So, is it the case that you will sell the book on and pay me royalties? LEP: *No.*

44. How much do the royalties amount to? LEP: *Not applicable.*

45. How and when will royalties be paid to me? LEP: *Not applicable.*

46. Does the fact that you distribute the book prevent my contacting the various bookshops and public libraries and asking them to stock my book? LEP: *Not applicable.*

47. Would the various bookshops and public libraries then send their book orders to you directly? LEP: *They do, but I then forward them onto the author.*

48. Does the fact that you distribute the book prevent my selling the book at a book launch, presentations and to friends and acquaintances? LEP: *Not applicable.*

49. How and when may I pay you when I commission the first print run? *LEP: Payments can be made by cheque or by PayPal. A deposit of at least half the quoted price is payable in advance of work starting, the balance being payable in advance of final delivery.*

50. How much will it cost to commission a print run of 5,000 copies, say? LEP: *See answer 18. I repeat, don't order more books than you know you can sell.*

BK: Readers will be quick to note that Bombardier Billy Wells and his gong are conspicuous by their absence. In other words, there is no way LEP is a fast-buck operator. I would just remind you, though, that LEP does NOT undertake to market customers' books – which may well be a facility you require.

APPENDIX 13: BOOK PRESENTATIONS BY BILL KEETH

Bill Keeth is available for bookings from social/leisure groups that meet on a regular basis and may occasionally require the services of a guest speaker – e.g. Over-50s, Over-60s, OAPs, women's groups, Ladybirds, readers'/writers' groups, schools, colleges – or other parties who may be interested in hosting a one-off book presentation. If your social/leisure group is interested in hosting a book presentation tailor-made to your requirements, Bill Keeth will gladly:

- ❍ deliver a book presentation as your guest;
- ❍ provide you with A4 advertising materials;
- ❍ bring along some deeply discounted copies of his books for sale.

  N.B. Guests will be under no obligation to purchase a copy of the books.

❑ Contact Bill Keeth by e-mail in the first instance to discuss your requirements:

- ❍ e-mail: billkeeth@novelnovella.com
Tel: 0161 643-4786
Bill Keeth,
3 Naunton Road,
Middleton,
Manchester
M24 1FX

APPENDIX 14: THE ORIGINAL PRESS ADVERTISEMENT FOR *OUR KID*

the funniest kid you'll meet this year!

THE HILARIOUS STORY OF A WORKING-CLASS BOYHOOD

- "Reading 'Our Kid' was a very moving experience. I was born in Salford and so you can understand my deep emotion at reading your wonderfully written, deeply touching, extremely heart-warming memoirs. Congratulations!" *John Sherlock, University of Dublin*
- "This rags to riches tale, set in my own lifetime, recalls wartime boyhood, is packed with nostalgia, filled with laughter and often tinged with pain. As a tale it is compelling and difficult to put down. A good Christmas book." *Robin Hull, M.B., FRCGP, Professor of Medicine*
- "'**Our Kid**' awoke in me so many memories: school life, bullies, pastimes, family rows, pals, escapades, day-dreams, ambitions - and the war." *Dan Murphy, retired teacher.*
- "I nestled into '**Our Kid**' like an old easy chair. I found it entertaining, endearing, charming." *Shirley Kent. Singer & Composer.*
- "I read 'Our Kid' quickly within two days of receiving it, and then took it with me to Turkey, to read more slowly and to savour. I think it is every bit as good as Roddy Doyle's 'Paddy Clarke, ha ha ha' which won the Booker Prize. Your book deserves to be widely acclaimed." *Joan Kennedy, Manchester 19*
- "Congratulations on an excellent book. I laughed & cried, it was so delightfully warm and funny" *Mrs Anne Greenhalgh, Sorrento, W. Australia*
- "I read ***Our Kid*** in 2 days. Hardly paused for breath." *William Mowbray, Retired Headmaster, Lot et Garonne, France.*

The story recalls an upbringing and an environment now vanished. It is an evocation of a working-class boyhood in the 1930s and 1940s taking us through the pre-war period, the war, evacuation, the blitz, and VE and VJ days.

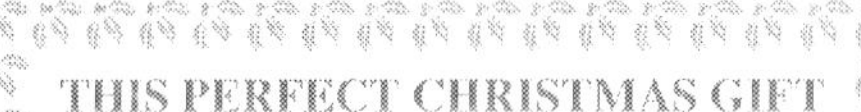

As advertised in *The Oldie*, the *Catholic Pictorial*, and *Practical Gardening*.